MW00917028

IMPACT!

HOW TO MAKE A
POSITIVE DIFFERENCE

May You
have a
Positive
Impact
on
Everyone
You
meet!

Blessings

Geo

BY

GEO ROBERTS

xulon PRESS

IMPACT!
How to Make a Positive Difference
by Geo Roberts

Printed in the United States of America

ISBN 9781615793112

www.xulonpress.com

This book is dedicated to my fantastic wife, Heidi, our sons, Nathan, Tim and their wives, Lucy and Helen, and our precious grandchildren, Bethany, Christopher, George, Hannah and David who inspire me to live as God intended me to live.

Acknowledgements

For those of you who have written books or painstakingly created anything, you know of the hard work from a variety of people and resources you need to depend upon to bring this about. IMPACT! is no different. First of all may I acknowledge Heidi, my wife of 41 years, who has stood beside me and co-produced this book. Because of her, it finally got finished. She edited, changed, organized the graphics, and in a thousand chats and mealtime discussions helped to create this book. Thanks, Babe. You have been terrific! Esther Birtwistle, thank you for helping us put things in the proper phraseology and sentence structure. Your painstaking efforts are really appreciated.

There are many people mentioned in the book who have made contributions, and I thank each and every one of them. Some I have mentioned by name; others I have used pseudonyms to ensure their privacy. Thanks also to the authors of many books I have read, and seminars or conferences I have attended over the years. All of these have played their part, and left their indelible mark on me. I have made every attempt to acknowledge your work in the book and references. Apologies for any oversights. To my colleagues in work, church and family life, I also offer my heartfelt appreciation for the contribution you have made. Nathan and Timothy, there has been a marked change in our relationships as you have grown to manhood. You are now, together with your wives, Lucy and Helen, our first line of advisers and confidants. What a blessing you are to us.

May I also acknowledge my lifetime business partner and friend, Simon Wilsher. He has from the first day I met him nearly 30 years ago been my biggest encourager and fan. Thanks, Simon and Sue, for letting me tell a portion of our story in helping people make life-long IMPACTs in their worlds.

And of course, to my Friend, Lord and Savior, I thank You, Jesus, for not giving up on me, nor letting me lay this down, which I wanted to many times. Thanks, Lord for Your Grace and Mercy.

Preface

The idea and attraction of developing foundational skills and attitudes has been around since time immemorial. The Greeks would stand around in the town square and debate the nature of 'man' and how he should live. In many ways this book is a descendant of those and other generations who have sought the wisdom of the ages to throw light on how we can be most effective.

What I believe makes this book different is that it comes out of the practical experience of hundreds of thousands of hours of working face to face with people in today's society as they work out those ways of being even more effective in their daily lives. So this book is not about a latest theory but principles and practices that work. We know they work because they have been tried, tested and found to work well so many times.

So to get the most out of this book take a principle at a time and put it into practice the same or very next day. You will be amazed at the results. These results can help you be even more effective at work, in your sporting life and hobbies, with your family and with your friends. That is one of the beauties of this book. It works for everyone whether you are a president of your organization, just starting out in your career, at leisure or still at school. And it will work with people from every background, culture and creed. It just works. So what about the author?

Geo has dedicated his life to people who want to improve their lives. Not only is his focus been that complete but he is a genius in this area too. That genius is a product of his passion, his generosity to share what he has and his talent in this field. (If there is anyone who is better I'd like to meet them). There are many books on self improvement written by people who know the theory but I doubt you will find any with more substance or one that is written by someone who is as good a practitioner.

That is what gives this book integrity and substance. That's what we find people want nowadays and it is what you get all in one book. You probably won't need another on self help. It's that good.

Simon Wilsher
Chairman of The Wilsher Group

Table of Contents

Introduction to IMPACT!

W ho is this book written for? Anyone who believes that it is important for us as human beings to make a positive impact in the world in which we live. As Simon said in the Preface, it could be to help the young person getting ready to leave the educational institution and join the world of making ones mark on it. It could be the person returning to work from a time out of work raising a family. Perhaps it is a person who has developed some technical competence and wants to or has been placed in a position where getting results through people is as important or more important than the work done by him or her. I believe it can be of help to anyone who can read, from our grandchildren to our grandparents. If the person can't read, perhaps you could read it to them! One day, it might be in an audio book, so it could be listened to while travelling, working or walking your pet.

It is a big ask that the target audience in marketing terms is so broad, so do excuse the moments in the book when the examples might not relate to your situation. Yet I believe if not your situation, it just might be someone whom you do know, so hopefully will connect. As it is a "journey book", you will have time to reflect upon what you are reading, and can contemplate the principles and ideas shared so that their relevance and application will become powerfully evident to you.

You may want to seriously consider a journal, or "thought catcher" as you begin reading this book. Many have found this a wonderful practice, to get their fleeting thoughts on paper to reflect upon and review later. It does not matter whether it is a physical notebook, your PC or pocket PC. Just keep it with you and when you come to some sections of the book which provoke a response from you, write it down in your journal. It may prove to be the best part about the book. Have a marvelous time reading this book - may you be inspired as I have been in writing it.

One

Cleared For Take-Off

"Redstick 34, you are cleared for takeoff." My 23-year-old heart was in my throat. Breathing very deeply, I could hear the fluttering of the oxygen mask valve as I replied, "Roger, Redstick 34 cleared for takeoff." I slowly advanced the two throttles connected to the jet engines that sat behind my supersonic jet, the T-38 Talon, and released the brakes. My legs began to shake uncontrollably, and I wondered, "Can I really hold the brakes while I run up the engines, or will I be slipping down the runway looking absolutely stupid?" Then I pointed the nose of the sleek, pristine 'white rocket with jet engines' down the center of the runway. As it came to a halt, I ran up the engines to full military power. I quickly checked the engine tachometers and other gauges to ensure everything was normal and pointing at 9 or 3 O'clock, then released the brakes, and advanced the throttles into full afterburner. BANG! went the engines as the full power hurled me back into my seat... 5 seconds, 10 seconds, everything was okay, then at 130 knots groundspeed, I pulled the joystick back between my knees to control the pitch of the airplane. The nose rose slowly to 10 degrees above the horizon, as the airspeed reached 150 knots - I was airborne! Quickly raising the gear handle I felt the landing gear retract into the belly of the aircraft, and zoomed out and up to 30,000 feet within a couple of minutes. I was piloting a supersonic aircraft solo!

With the coolest voice I could muster, I radioed the tower, "Redstick 34 airborne, switching to Departure." "Roger, Redstick, have a good flight." This was instantly more than a good flight as I was solo, in my own three-dimensional world, flying at 30 to 50 thousand feet, dancing amongst the clouds, and totally in control of that airplane. I was not simply flying the T-38; it was an extension of me, my personality, my will – whatever I wanted it to do within reason, it would respond, so long as I respected its boundaries and followed some basic deeply ingrained flying principles. On many subsequent flights I would take even more risks and climb to the edge of space until curvature of the earth was dramatically contoured – the sky appeared an eerie dark blue beyond the earth's luminous curve. Mystically, the airplane slips through the sound barrier into mach 1 – I am flying faster than the speed of sound!

Breaking Through Mental Barriers

Allow me to explain the correlation between my flying solo in a supersonic aircraft and making an impact in life. As a youngster from a rural farming background in mid-America, to break the monotony of farming and ranching the 2,250 acres heavily mortgaged by my father, I would sit on the tractor and dream of flying one day. This dream had become a reality! Even for me! As I think of how my life changed as I followed my dreams, it has been fascinating to see how the invisible barriers, like the sound barrier for an aircraft, can be overcome.

If you cannot relate to the flying experience, consider driving. If you have a driver's license, can you remember what it was like before you had unlimited access to a car or the legal right to drive it? You depended upon others for transportation, waited for the bus or train or you were being confined to a bicycle for rapid mobility. Then remember the liberating joy of being able to go wherever you wanted to go, when you wanted to go, and not having to ask for permission? New dimensions of your world previously unavailable to you now became possible! With this new freedom, of course, came basic principles and procedures to follow, and you had to develop a whole new perspective, set of skills and behavior in order for you to earn the right to have the freedom. You had to learn a new language and set of words to accompany your new freedom in order to effectively function within the new world of motor vehicle driving.

Words Have Power

Just as I needed to grasp the full implications of what "Cleared for takeoff" meant, so we also need to grasp the essence of words before we can begin to think of positively impacting our worlds. My hope is that you are beginning to read the words in this book because you want to make a positive impact in a specific area of your life – it may be whilst you are at school, or in your home and social life. Perhaps your journey has led you to a working situation in an organization where more is being demanded of you, and you are under increasing pressure to perform. Conversely, perhaps you are in an un-fulfilling job that is not that rewarding, you are not able to make an impact, and are therefore looking for ways of changing things. What ever the reason, may I start off by saying, if you embrace both the words and the spirit behind the words I will communicate to you over the next few chapters, you will find yourself making some profound life and career changes in your attitudes and behavior that will make your world and your work environment better places to be. Here is what some precious words did to me early in my life!

"Geo, are you aware of the damage you are doing by behaving that way?" Strong words spoken to a 14-year-old in a small rural town high school! Those life-changing words were administered by Wayne Wallace, my junior high football and basketball coach and geometry teacher as he peered straight into my eyes and through to my soul. Understandably. I was late for practice one day because I had been kept after school by the science teacher for cutting up in class, disrupting what he was teaching, and allowing my boredom to become vocal. When I finally arrived at basketball practice, I was an hour or so late. Mr. Wallace, as we called teachers in those days, made me sit out the rest of the practice, watching the others, and then approached me. He asked, "Why are you late for practice, Geo?" I laughingly and sheepishly replied, "Mr. Matheson kept me behind because I was disruptive in class." Sure, it was fun making the rest of the students laugh, and having a ball in class. Mr. Wallace continued his sermon; 'But are you aware that because you find school unchallenging, because you have been given a good quick mind, excel at sports, and make friends easily, you have a responsibility to the school, your classmates and the teachers to consider the way you behave? People are watching you, and if they see you doing these things, they will feel it is acceptable for you to joke about, not participate fully and act the clown. Whereas you may be able to get away without concentrating in class, and being the life of the party, some of those kids with less potential cannot afford it. You could be responsible for their lack of achievement, and for holding back our team!" He paused, and then said, "Geo, people look to you for leadership, and right now, the type of leadership you are providing is disruptive and irresponsible. It is about time you shaped up, took your responsibilities seriously, and made a positive impact instead of a negative one!"

I would have felt better right then if Mr. Wallace had whipped me with a belt, the way Dad occasionally did, to reinforce the point. Instead, he simply and calmly instructed me to run a lap for every minute of practice I had missed, and to reflect upon what he had said. As I was running, I did some soul-searching, and something inside of me changed. Being the 3rd son of 4 in our family, I had never thought of myself as being a leader. I spent most of my family life following what everyone else wanted – my Dad, Mother, my two older brothers – but here Mr. Wallace was saying I was a leader - wow! People were watching me, and interested in the way I performed and behaved - wow!

These words dramatically changed the view I had of myself, and since that event, with increasing regularity, I changed my attitudes and behavior. I graduated top in the class. I was nominated for a number of scholastic honors, including a Regents Scholarship, fully sponsored collegiate fees at a local university and most importantly a nomination to be the first ever applicant to the United States Air Force Academy from our community. *Words change things*, especially timely words delivered from a respected source with our best interests at heart.

Self-Prescribed Limitations and Possibilities

One of the limitations, the boundaries, if you will, that needed to change for me was the "3rd Son Syndrome." To truly overcome this for me took years, but that day as a fourteen-year-old misbehaving youth the entrapment began to loose its grip. Whether by nature or nurture, we all have limiting boundaries and constrictions that shape the way we think and behave most of the time. These boundaries are sometimes the windows, the lenses, that color or form our perceptions. Stephen R. Covey, renowned psychologist and behavior development author, describes these perceptions and boundaries as *paradigms.*

> *"Each of us tends to think we see things as they are, that we are objective. But this is not the case. We see the world, not as it is, but as we are—or as we are conditioned to see it. When we open our mouths to describe what we see, we in effect describe ourselves, our perceptions, our paradigms."[1]*

If we consciously determine our own view of the world, this leads to exciting possibilities and with it an awesome set of responsibilities. Our perceptions, the lenses through which we view things, are a figment of our own imaginings, our own thoughts of "how things are." If we want to change our world, we can begin by changing how we think, first of all about ourselves. Houdini, one of the world's finest magicians, some decades ago in Great Britain was challenged to escape from a prison cell. He boasted about his ability to get out of any locked and confined space. Accepting the challenge, he was placed in a cell, and worked tirelessly to try to escape. Despite using all of his cunning, his training, his knowledge and experience of how to break locks and remove barriers, he was not succeeding. He therefore tried even harder. The harder he tried, the more frustrated he became, because the world-famous escape artist could not break out. Finally, he gave up, exhausted and defeated, and admitted failure. The dignitaries approached the cell door, and without inserting a key they effortlessly swung the door open. Houdini had imprisoned himself – the door had never been locked in the first place! His prison was in his mind! Before we criticize Mr. Houdini too quickly, how many of us are prisoners in our own self-made cells, because of the thoughts we allow to penetrate and take up residence in our belief systems about ourselves?

My writing is based on some assumptions and perceptions. As I said earlier, one of my assumptions and hopes is that you are reading this book because you truly want to make a more positive impact in your life, or you have a responsibility to help others to develop their skills, habits and lifestyles as their mentor, coach or counselor. Perhaps you are their parent, boss or leader, and feel the responsibility of speaking the right words, creating the right environment for others to grow and change their behavior. Whatever the case, if my assumption is correct, you are challenging me to provide some "How-To's", techniques and processes that you can use to help change to take place in yourself or others.

Something on the cover or in the preface must have whet your appetite and filled you with enough intrigue to want to pick this book up and browse through it for some wisdom, knowledge or expertise that *may help making an impact become a reality*. I trust you will not be disappointed. I am writing this book with the paradigm in mind that you are *"ready" to learn*. Unless that is the case, there are no "silver bullets" or magic formulae that will really make a difference.

Getting Ready to Learn and Change

In my view and experience, change can only occur when we have the right "perceptual readiness" - in other words, the right mindset to embark upon the journey of shifting our paradigms.

"When the student is ready, the teacher appears."

How do we go about ensuring we are perceptually ready to change? I conclude that in my role as coach and trainer for over thirty years with people from every continent, background and role imaginable, 'perceptual readiness' distils to four crucial attitudes which must come from deep within. We start the change process:

- · Want – when we *want* the change
- · Need – when we sincerely perceive the *need* to change.
- · Believe – when we *believe we can* change
- · Will – when we make a choice that *we will change*

As far as I have observed, change cannot be conferred upon us through hypnotism, drugs, repeating mantras to ourselves, or 'wishing it were so'. We must truly desire the change in our heart and have enough reasons for wanting to change. These reasons *justify that the need for making the change outweighs the consequences for staying as we are.* Then we must have enough belief in ourselves to at least say, "I believe it is possible for the change to happen to me, and this is good. Therefore I am willing to have a go." No amount of knowledge, procedures or information will help until those four attitudes are present. In fact, the people who really need to change the most will not pick up a book like this, so already I can believe that you are reading this because you have the *readiness to change*. So let's get started!

I do not pretend to be a psychologist. However, having worked in the area of behavioral development many years, I have recognized a number of things about the way the mind works. One of the books that impacted my thinking and therefore my behavior so effectively over 25 years ago was "As a Man Thinketh" by James Allen[2]. He quotes a Proverb from the Bible (which, by the way, I see as the best source of Wisdom Literature around) that states,

"As a man thinketh in his heart, so he becomes."

A modern paraphrase could be, "People say one thing with their mouth, but what is in their hearts is what they really mean." The text was referring to someone who invites you to dinner, and says, "Have a good meal," when inside they might be saying, "I hope you choke on it"! As we delve deeper into Mr. Allen's interpretation of this phrase, he is postulating that we become what we truly think inwardly about ourselves, not what we portray to the world. Charles Reade, (1814 - 1884) English novelist, is purported to have said:

> *Sow a thought, reap an action,*
> *Sow an action, reap a habit,*
> *Sow a habit, reap a character,*
> *Sow a character, reap a destiny*

When I first reflected upon these truths, they made so much sense, yet challenged me to my very core. If we believe that the thoughts we plant into the soil of our minds in the end will reap the fruits of those thoughts in how our lives turn out, it places a significant burden of responsibility upon what we allow ourselves to think. Thoughts, even unspoken ones, trigger a series of activities, events, emotions, etc. that affect the way we behave. The seeds of thoughts that shape the way we behave produce certain behavior and habits that inevitably produce a propensity to respond to certain outside events naturally, without our being conscious that this is happening.

Let's test this with a little exercise. In a moment, I will ask you to say out loud or at least record your first thought as I ask you to finish a sentence for me. Don't think about it first, just naturally respond with the first word or thought that my sentence provokes. Ready? Ok, please complete the sentence,

"The moon is made of _____."

What did you say or think? Was it cheese? Was it green cheese? Was it Swiss cheese? Almost 100% of the people I get to do this answer by saying "cheese" of some sort. Perhaps you didn't because your teaching when small was woefully deprived. For those of us who did answer, "Cheese" in some way - how do you feel? A little silly? Of course the moon is not made of cheese. Yet long ago, when you were younger, someone implanted the thought, "the moon is made of cheese," and it stuck. We look into why this happened later when we explore the Laws of Learning. What it tells us is that our thoughts once powerfully formed affect the "within-the-heart" response Mr. Allen relates is his profound book. It matters what we think, and the start of change is to recognize that we can change who we are and what we are by changing what we allow to get imbedded in our brains!

Applied Knowledge

Unlike Sir Francis Bacon who quoted, "Knowledge is power," I believe knowledge is not power, and the retention of knowledge is not wisdom or success. In order for us to really develop the power within, and to transfer the knowledge into something useful and practical that truly makes an impact, we need something extra. We need to process the information, ideas, thoughts and feelings into useful and useable action, through our minds and hearts. W. Clement Stone, an author, philanthropist, businessman and builder of one of the most successful financial service organizations of his time, described it best for me in a book entitled, "The Success System That Never Fails"[3]. He sifted through many of his experiences in life and condensed his discoveries about success into a system of thinking and behaving that transformed him, and no doubt many others. It certainly served as a framework for me to dramatically change my life.

My summation of what he said is this: Whenever we have a thought, read a book or piece of information, or have an experience, we could do ourselves a great service if we:

1. Recognize this idea, thought or experience as significant, and worth learning from.
Then we could benefit greatly if we:
2. Relate to the piece of information, principle, or thought and ask ourselves:

·   "How does this relate to me and my experience?"
·   "Is this a confirmation of something I have already heard or learned?"
·   "Is this a new thought I have never had, but still feel it has relevance and significance for me?"

· "Are these feelings and thoughts I am having about my thoughts and experiences profound in some way?"
· "Where have I heard of them before?"
· "How do these 'fit in' with other thoughts, knowledge, and sayings, experiences I believe or do not believe?"

Once we have settled within our thinking that this is, in fact, something worth holding on to for ourselves, and then we take the next step:

3. Assimilate this idea, thought, saying, knowledge, or piece of information into who and what we are. We take on the language of the knowledge as if it were our own. We use it in conversations, share it with other people, and test our theories and ideas about this piece of new-found wisdom on other people who will sympathetically respond. This step helps us confirm and affirm what we are learning, so we can confidently begin to apply its lessons to our own lives in the future, starting today! Next comes the most important step of all. That is to really start to understand our new found wisdom through taking a dramatic step:

4. Apply the information into our daily lives – for instance, let's say the new piece of wisdom we have recognized, related to and assimilated is a way of setting goals. Rather than waiting until we fully understand all there is to know about setting goals, and all its pros and cons, the Success System says to apply *massive action*. Embrace the idea fully as your own, as if you had thought the thought first yourself, and somehow within the next two to three weeks, apply the idea, thought or knowledge at least 13 times to 21 times according to behaviorists. These conscious repetitions done enough times form new synapses in the brain that turns the new way of thinking and behaving into a habit.

Demonstrate for Yourself

Let's demonstrate through the use of the topic, "*memory*." How many of us would readily admit that our memory lets us down at times? Probably most of us. Neurologists would have us believe that their evidence of studying the brain indicates that we all have "perfect memories." Skip Ross, in his book, Say Yes to Your Potential, relates that our brain records every thought, experience and input, and stores it somewhere in one of the thousands of millions of synapses we have. So why the discrepancy when in practice, we forget names of people, how to get somewhere we have been before, leave our keys in strange places, etc.? It seems that at times when we desperately need our subconscious mind to deliver to our conscious mind the words, actions, or thoughts to rescue us from a situation (like what to say when confronting an awkward or new encounter with someone we want to impress) nothing happens!

Is there hope for us? Behaviorists say yes. So does my personal experience. There are a number of powerful methods, and techniques that help us retrieve vital information when we initially store it effectively. It goes beyond simple repetition and rehearsal. One of the methods is called "*stacking.*" Stacking involves using the most powerful part of the brain, our creative right cortex which stores thoughts and comments as images. These images, like computer menu files, are linked to many other images that are related in some way. Therefore, if, when we meet someone that we wish to remember later, we can open a file that contains the "visual store" filled with relevant information about the person, for example: name, where they live, what they do for a living, etc.. By taking extra care when we store the information, and creating conscious visual links, we will find the retrieval much easier later on. Here is a 'conversation' or 'social' stack, for instance, to try. Please photocopy or scan this if you do not want to write in the book. However, I believe the best way to use the book is to make it your own by making notes, underlining or highlighting parts of it, writing in the margins, etc.

Conversation / Social 'Stack'

Sketch your own pictures here

'Word picture'

Brass name plate

House

Portrait

Business card

Tennis racquet

Goal net

First of all, memorize the words on the left, then sketch your own 'picture' and link them together in a "video or media clip" in your mind. Don't concern yourself with what they mean at first, just firmly implant the images of the pictures in a stack or linked set of images.

For instance, "The brass name plate is attached to a house with a red door. You proceed through the red door into the house, and on the right is a room with a fireplace. Above the fireplace is a family portrait. Tucked in the lower right hand corner of the portrait is a business card. Hanging from the business card is a tennis racquet. The strings of the racquet stretch amazingly into a football/soccer net used in a goal." Once this video is firmly implanted in your brain, then you can use the pictures to remind yourself of things to ask someone you are meeting to establish links with the person, and remember things about the person for later use or retrieval.

Conversation / Social 'Stack' Reminders

'Word picture' — What it represents

Brass name plate — Person's name

House — Where the person lives

Portrait — Family information

Business card — Job or occupation

Tennis racquet — Hobbies or interests

Goal net — Goals and ambitions

The Conversation Stack has proven immensely popular when we are in social situations where we are looking to 'connect' to people. Time and again former delegates of our IMPACT! Program, a personal development course, have expressed how more confident they felt having memorized a set of questions to ask that help establish common interests.

Head Knowledge Is Not Enough

Let's return to the postulation that having "head knowledge" alone is not enough, although it serves as a foundation for learning and developing essential skills and habits.

Suppose I were to say to you, "I'll teach you to fly jets!" Despite the fact that some people are terrified of flying, many of us would jump at the chance to experience High Flight and "...slip the surly bounds of earth, and dance on laughter-silvered wings..." (Gillespie Magee). If you are one of those people, then your heart may start racing at the very thought. Just think, freedom to fly amongst the clouds, and thrill at the views of the mountains, lakes and streams from above. To get where you want to be at a lightning pace, and be totally in control of the speed, direction and distance! Wow! Yet wanting to fly, being eager and excited by the prospect, and having the will to do so wouldn't be enough. You would need lots of information and knowledge, wouldn't you? So let's say I do that – I place you on a strict regimen of learning all that is needed to develop the language of flying. This involves Theories of Aerodynamic Flight, what makes a jet engine propulsion system work, Federal and Civil regulations regarding control of airspace, getting clearances, maintaining separation from other aircraft and other "traffic rules" of flying. After a period of intense, concentrated tuition, you would be able to pass every exam we could give you on how to fly, rules to follow, emergency procedures and the like.

At last, your moment has 'arrived', we metaphorically pass you "fit for flight," and hand you the keys to your very own supersonic jet aircraft. How tough do you think it might be to find a passenger to go with you on your first flight? No doubt it would be impossible! But why? You have all of the knowledge don't you? You've passed the tests – so what is stopping you from performing at a high standard on your first flight? "Well, you idiot", you might exclaim, "It's because I have the head knowledge, I know *how* to fly but I am not *trained* in the use of that knowledge so I can *apply* what I have learned." Precisely. If we take this analogy further, why is it not as absurd to think that by reading a book, searching the web or attending a lecture on a topic gives us true learning and skill on the topic?

Rather than reading this book, your learning would be far greater if you could enroll on our IMPACT! Program, where you could discover and experience first-hand the process we call the Cycle of Experiential Development. So what is this Cycle, and why do we need it?

We all have a Comfort Zone (CZ). This zone can be defined as the physical, mental and spiritual space where we feel we fit. It is like a good fitting pair of slippers, or a soft easy chair we settle into, and can occupy without pressure. In life, we need our areas of comfort. We need time to chill and not be stressed. The dilemma is we cannot stay here all day every day. If we do not venture out of our Comfort Zones, we will find it difficult to grow, change or develop. By their very nature our Comfort Zones hold us back, keep us safe and secure. Kids have very large Comfort Zones, by and large. We all can no doubt recount telling a two year old, "Don't!, Stop!, No!" as they ventured outside of the realms of safety to hit something, run somewhere or put some foreign object in their mouth. Yet for the most of us by the time we are in our teens or early 20's, our Comfort Zones have well-established boundaries, if not walls. We have found that venturing too far outside of our CZ most often will produce failure. Why? Because by the very act of doing something we are not skilled at or are not familiar with, we are most likely going to fail the first few times. Usually, when this happens, we do not get positive reinforcement or support. In fact as we grow older, most of the time the failure experience makes us cry "Ouch!" at least inside, and we quickly rush back inside our CZ and say to ourselves, "I'm not going to do that again."

Figure 1.1 Going Outside of Our Comfort Zone

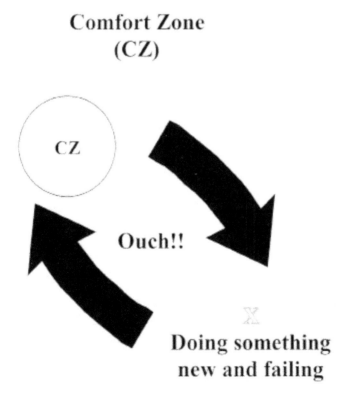

Comfort Zone
(CZ)

CZ

Ouch!!

Doing something
new and failing

Sometimes this is a good thing, as we learn what hurts and what doesn't. But much of the time, it conditions us to not attempt to grow, but to play it safe. Our Comfort Zone can become a *Comfort Trap*.

Figure 1.2 Building Our Comfort Trap

Comfort Zone (CZ)

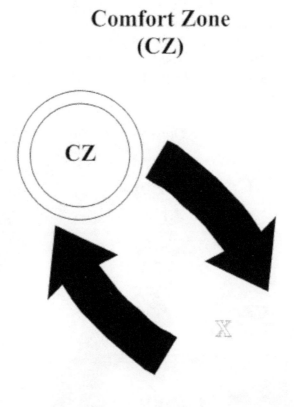

Comfort Trap!

We rationalize all kinds of reasons for not trying to do better, be better or get better. How do we then motivate ourselves to change, to grow, when doing so may cause pain and ridicule, if not abject failure? Here is where the model of the Cycle of Experiential Development can serve to help us activate W. Clement Stone's "Success System

That Never Fails". The Cycle is a way to expand our CZs in a systematic, small step, bite-sized way. In order for us to get perceptually ready, as we have discussed earlier in this chapter, it means we need to establish the right attitude. We have already said the right attitude to change involves having the *want, need, belief* and *will* to change. In our Cycle of Experiential Development Model, this represents the first quadrant.

Figure 1.3 Cycle of Experiential Development Quadrant 1

ATTITUDE

As we understand from our discussions of the Success System That Never Fails, the right attitude is not enough. We also need to have the 'How To'. If we cannot recognize a good idea, or relate to it, it is useless. Therefore the second phase or quadrant is developing the knowledge to help us expand our Comfort Zone.

Figure 1.4 Cycle of Experiential Development Quadrant 2

- Bite-sized
- Self-selected / acquired
- Adapted to circumstances
- Commitment to apply

KNOWLEDGE

It helps tremendously if the knowledge is provided bite-sized. This means in digestible chunks that make it easy to grasp, cogitate over, debate, etc. No doubt we can all relate to experiences where we were bombarded with too much information all at once, and as a result became confused, overwhelmed and lost. Good teachers fully appreciate the need to give just the right amount of information to allow someone to use or practice using the new piece of knowledge so it becomes familiar to them. This aids the learner tremendously in becoming confident with the new thought, idea or concept. A third element of knowledge acquisition is self-selection. We accept without too much argument the ideas we like the most are our own. So if in gaining knowledge of how to do something we do so through self-selected discovery, we are doubly likely to remember and be willing to have a go putting it into practice. Read Timothy Gallwey's "Inner Game of Tennis" if you want more on this theory. Adapting the information to our circumstances is crucial. If we find it hard to relate to, we are not going to be confident to use it in real life.

All of these ways of dispensing and acquiring knowledge are meant to lead to the learner developing a keen commitment to apply, as Stone indicates in his Success System. It is so easy for some of us to think we *have it* if we have the head knowledge before we even attempt to apply it. The application is the hard bit that really stretches our Comfort Zone. So let's move on to the most powerful part of the Cycle.

Figure 1.5 Cycle of Experiential Development Quadrant 3

. Immediate
. Coached
. Feedback
. Repeated

CZ

PRACTICE, PRACTICE, PRACTICE

Practice, we know, makes perfect... or so we have been told. Actually practice does not make perfect but only more permanent. Therefore to improve performance, we need to focus on practicing in such a way as it helps us grow and develop. The best type of practice is therefore most effective when it is coached practice. So what is coached practice? It is practice that is undertaken with some oversight and encouragement in a friendly environment where it is safe to get it wrong. Coached practice by a skilled observer who can give immediate feedback that helpfully points out what went well and what can be improved. Learners can repeat this application of the new technique, method, concept or idea in a controlled environment. Then the learner has the confidence and skill to go try it for real in their own world. Once this new application is tried outside the controlled environment, they are more likely to have a successful experience which further expands their Comfort Zone. The final quadrant articulates this new found skill or habit.

Figure 1.6 Cycle of Experiential Development Quadrant 4

SKILLS AND HABITS

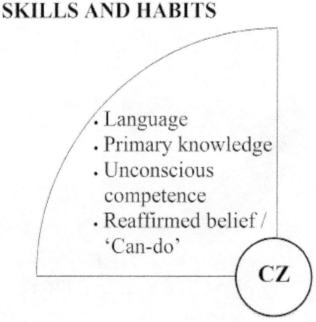

We now have learned the language of success. The knowledge is not second-hand knowledge, but the learner's own primary knowledge. The skill or habit is so ingrained it becomes unconsciously competent. We do it without even being conscious we are doing it, so effortlessly can we perform it. This of course reaffirms the learner's belief that the skill or habit is possible and they have reinforced their own 'can do' attitude. It is not surprising the learner is then more likely to want to learn something new, and thereby once again go around the cycle.

Figure 1.7 Cycle of Experiential Development

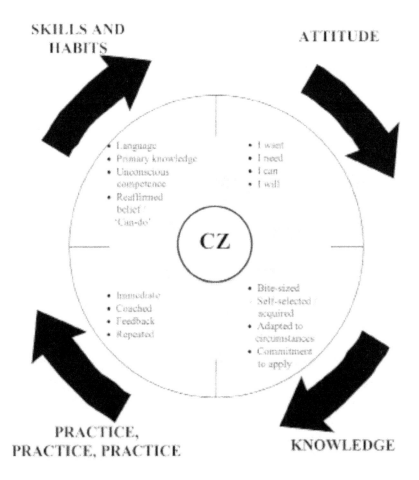

It is also why, in order for you to get the most from what you are reading, I have included a series of questions to help guide you in your application and learning from what you are reading. I commend this process to you to enhance your learning from 10% to

65% at least. Therefore we conclude we must practice, practice, and practice using our knowledge rapidly, at the *speed of life*, as I heard someone describe it, if we are to truly develop and make an impact.

Let's Explore the Cycle in Life Situations

What kind of practice works best? Can we accelerate our learning by ensuring we have the best practice?

I adored my high school English teacher. For some reason, she also took a liking to me and I could tell she really wanted me to do well. Mrs. Johnson, as I'll call her, loved to talk, and as long as we listened to her, laughed at her jokes, and the essays and précis were submitted on time, I got top grades. She was so helpful, that even when I was asked to give the Valedictorian address at our class graduation because I was the student with the highest Grade Point Average, she even wrote my speech. Consequently, I never learned how to express myself well in a written form. In fact, when I went to the United States Air Force Academy (USAFA), I had the misconception I was a good communicator and writer, only to find out that I was not! This rude awakening of thinking I was better than I actually was has resulted in a life-long setback, and a contributor to the length of time it has taken to write this book. Mrs. J., for all of her desire to want to see me succeed, actually hindered my growth! On the other hand, we no doubt all can think of teachers, parents, authority figures and significant others who have unknowingly hindered our growth because they did not believe in us or even care if we succeeded long-term.

As we said earlier, we need the right type of support, encouragement, challenge and help in order to develop skill through best practice. Experience has shown skill is developed through:

- practicing while being coached
- receiving immediate feedback
- coaching which stretches Comfort Zones
- receiving tons of encouragement and belief-reinforcement

Applying the Cycle

Christina was in a state. She had worked for a large organization most of her working life. She had a secure home life with two wonderful kids, and this was part of her dilemma. She was referred to me by her boss, who stated, "Please help Christina to move on. Although good at what she does, she is not satisfied, over-protects her team, and as we intend to make changes to how her functional area operates, we want her to be happy and supportive of the process. If not, we risk losing her and the vast knowledge, skill and attributes she brings to the organization."

Christina and I already had an excellent working relationship based upon previous workshops and meetings with the team she was a part of, so we were quickly able to get right to work. She was perceptually ready to change, and it was not long before we had established she had the right attitude for change. Through use of some coaching tools and techniques, she was able to tap into some how to's needed for moving forward. Each time we met or discussed where she was in her thinking and where she wanted to go, we were able to identify specific practical steps that Christina needed to take to reach her goal.

There were setbacks, of course, and each one was a terrific learning situation that helped her to reach inside herself and resolve to overcome the obstacles. Some obstacles and barriers were *internal*, within herself. Others were *external*, and caused by other people. We had introduced early on the Cycle of Experiential Development, so each time we encountered events or perceptions that might be holding her back, she was able to grasp the essence of what needed to change and move forward.

Two years on, Christina is a different person. She is now in a new challenging and fulfilling role, with better family and work life balance, and is much more positive and confident in her own ability to make an impact.

Our effectiveness as a learner is accelerated if, during our practice sessions, we have a heightened awareness of what it is we are doing, and how well we are doing it, when we understand what is and what is not working, and we can accept our own sense of responsibility to get better at what we are trying to learn. As a reminder, I believe you are reading this book because you see yourself as a leader – as someone who wants to make a positive difference and sort things out in your own life, work or career. Therefore, we will return to the role and duties as a coach of other's learning and development when we look at our impact as a leader.

Who Wants To Be Constantly Out Of Their Comfort Zone?

Some of us might be saying to ourselves, "This is all well and good, but you don't know the struggles I have had, and if only you knew how hard I've tried to expand my boundaries and improve myself. I deserve a break from all this stretching, reaching out, helping others. I just want to rest." I do understand that at times in our lives we need some time to stop and smell the roses. Psychologists will admit that we as *human beings* are also *human doings*. This means we were meant to learn, to develop, to explore, to grow. Let me illustrate:

One of the things we pilots hated was to be assigned to a jet that had not been used for awhile. This happened quite often after a long period of bad weather which kept us from flying, or an aircraft had had an engine change or radical overhaul. This airplane that had not been in the air for a long time had a high rate of failure or "abort" as we call it. Why? Not because the ground crew had not serviced it properly, or had not fixed the airplane's problem, but because an airplane is meant to fly, not sit on the ground! When confined to the ground, it developed leaks, mechanical and electronic problems, you name it. So the best way to ensure we had a good airplane to fly was to fly it frequently!

It is the same with us, I believe. Leave us "rusting" on the ground, or meditating for hours and days on end, we will become lazy, low on energy, doubting of ourselves and become great pro-crastinators. We will develop every excuse we can to keep us from thinking "outside the box." An imbedded *"rigor mortis of the soul"* will keep us in our Comfort Zone, causing it to shrink and become a *comfort trap*.

The Comfort Zone Can Trap Us

Our *comfort trap* can be thought of as a psychological wall, gap or even an abyss that provides a buffer to keep us from danger – from getting hurt, taking risks, being embarrassed, getting lost, feeling angry, lonely or any other adverse emotion. Hypnotherapists call it our 'subconscious persona' - some call it our 'saboteur' or 'gremlin'. Whereas this comfortable safety zone can be good for us from time to time, like the airplane, if we stay within this Comfort Zone too long, our confidence, our world view, our beliefs about what we are capable of learning and doing diminishes to such an extent that we could for practical purposes be declared "dead."

Figure 1.8 Comfort Trap

Recently a woman (we will call her Jane) who was highly respected in her field as a dynamic corporate mover and shaker lamented to me, "Geo, I don't know what has gotten into me. Just a few years ago before I stopped to have our child and develop the home, I was very effective at meeting even very senior corporate people on their own turf and challenge them to make changes in their information systems and convincing them to invest huge sums of money. Now that I am returning to the world of business and commerce, and know what I need to do, my confidence has been eroded. What can I do to get it back?"

She found herself in a *comfort trap*. During the next two years Jane completed a series of development activities, events and coaching which rebuilt her confidence and competence beyond its former strength. Soon after she accepted a government job in Wales, and to my knowledge she continues to make a significant impact in her new role.

Summarizing Why We Take the IMPACT! Journey

Let's do a quick recap of the journey you are going to take as a result of reading and acting upon the contents of this book, and why it is a worthwhile experience. First of all, as the famous hair dressing and cosmetics company would declare, "It's *because you are worth it.*" There will never ever again, even if they perfect the cloning process, be anyone just like you. No one will ever have the talents, experiences, background or education that match yours. So unless you use what you've got, and develop what you can of yourself, then not only do you lose, but so does the rest of the world! It is said the best fruit is found on the ends of the branches, not safely tucked up near the trunk. Being 'on the edge' is perhaps nature's way of getting us out of our Comfort Zones and motivated to enjoy the better things of life. Unless we are tingling with excitement, nervousness, joy, even sorrow or sense of loss, we are eroding our life and dying a little each day. Skip Ross, one of the most motivational and inspirational leaders and speakers in the world, calls this approach "Dynamic Living":

> *"Living a life filled with joy and happiness all the time.*
> *Completely free of fear and worry, and totally devoted to*
> *accomplishing worthwhile goals in all areas of our lives![4]"*

How would you like that as your Impact Journey? Diligently use your IMPACT Creative Action Steps for Making a Difference at the end of this and every chapter. To aid your learning and help you increase significantly the likelihood of application, I suggest you take the time to complete *each part* of the IMPACT Creative Action Debrief to improve your Impact Journey prior to reading further chapters.

In the next chapter we'll explore why the world needs you to become a person with Impact

IMPACT Creative Action Debrief Chapter ONE

Complete these before continuing to Chapter Two!

1. Using Figure 1.9, draw Your Own Comfort Trap – what are some of the reasons you use to keep you safely inside?

Figure 1.9 Your Comfort Trap

2. Contemplate your Comfort Zone, then describe below how you would like to expand it. What areas of growth come to mind?

[handwritten] Acceptance in who I am and the security in myself that I can and will be successful

3. Describe the Four Parts of W. Clement Stone's "Success System That Never Fails" from earlier in the chapter. How could you begin to apply this process before carrying on to Chapter Two?

[handwritten] Believe in the road to success take action in getting to college aquire knowledge and put it into practice.

4. Complete your Cycle of Experiential Development. Label all parts. Fill in the gaps based upon what you read in this chapter

Figure 1.10 Your Cycle of Experiential Development

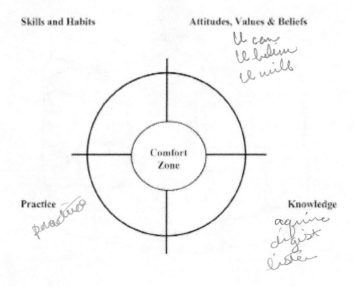

Two

How Constructive is Your Impact?

W here were you on the 11th September, 2001 when the World Trade Center in New York was demolished by those airliners? When most people are asked that question, they can remember precisely where they were. Someone or some group had decided to make an impact to change the world, and it has changed the world, undoubtedly. We are now more fearful of people that look different to us, we think twice before we travel to certain parts of the world. Prolonged waiting at airports for security checks is now a way of life. Businesses were dramatically affected. Some airlines have not survived, others have been amalgamated, and although other businesses have recovered, for some while after 9/11 the whole world was gripped by terror. We certainly live in a 'post- 9/11-era'.

Journalists, psychologists and philosophers who have tried to delve into the heads of those who see suicidal bombings as the highest purpose for their lives, could conclude that these people are not crazy, they simply have convinced themselves that this is the right thing to do, to kill as many people as they can for their cause. In the world-turned-upside-down we live in, to say to anyone, "you're wrong" and hold a view there is a right and a wrong about people, events and activities seems to be the only "wrong" there is! In this type of world, terrorists have a field day.

Before we consider your impact and how we can ensure it is constructive and not destructive, let's explore the world we live in, and see what is "naturally" produced if we don't do something about it. We will look at a number of scenarios that most of us can easily identify and relate to.

Disaffected Young Adults

In recent years' news, violence and gang approach to resolution permeates our school rooms. Young children get hooked on computer games that promote violence, then re-enact this for real with other kids they dislike or simply take a whim to abusing.

Columbine High School is a poignant example where two students, Eric Harris and Dylan Klebold, embarked on a shooting rampage, killing 12 students and a teacher, as well as wounding 23 others, before committing suicide.[5] Almost monthly, teenagers are killed because they will not deny their faith in God or try to stop some misguided youths from randomly shooting or stabbing whomever they pointed the gun or knife at. From a few more years back in the United Kingdom the world was shocked at the random murder of Jamie Bulger apparently as a re-enactment of a computer game two young lads decided to carry out.[6]

Fear seems to rule – politicians and parents speak of trying to legislate for ways to control hooligans and hoodies, binge parties, use of weapons and even fox hunting. Children are told not to speak to strangers, not to go out by themselves and to always stay in well lit areas. All of these well-meaning "Don'ts and Not's" have an impact, but the effect is one that reinforces the evil in the world, and traps us into a way of thinking about ourselves and our world that amplifies our inability to make a difference and take a risk to break free from this negative, downward pull.

Honor Killing

Recent news stories are dominated by parents from different cultures who exact their revenge over a daughter who chooses to break from the past by conducting an "honor killing" that even gets the support of their local spiritual leader and community. It seems the parents and relatives of this daughter who has "betrayed" them is better off dead rather the family being forced to cope with the change! What a way to reason and deal with our world!

Disgruntled Employees

A few years ago Simon Wilsher, co –founder of The Wilsher Group, and I were on a business trip in Atlanta staying in the center of the city. Within a few hundred yards of where we were, a fairly typical tragedy unfolded in the news that has left a strong impression on me. A disaffected stockbroker or analyst had gotten into financial difficulties, and decided to take his revenge on his ex-employer. The revenge resulted in death for himself as well as other innocent people. We were caught up in it, as the perpetrator was still on the loose, and because no one at the time was aware of the motives, we all thought, "Could we be the next victim"? This incident demonstrates the futility many people feel with events in their lives, and their inability to change their circumstances.

As part of our business philosophy to reinvest in the community, The Wilsher Group supports a number of efforts helping the long-term unemployed to regain their self-respect and re-enter the job market. On one particular session, we asked the delegates to describe on a flip chart their hopes and strengths, and what they wanted for their futures. Hearing these broken men trying to verbalize how they wanted to pick up the pieces of their shattered lives brought me to tears. Grown men expressing simple aims and desires for respect that one would have expected to have heard from a primary school attendee – what had happened to these men to destroy their view of themselves as capable, functional contributors to their families and communities? Did they ever possess a perspective of themselves as people who were worth it, potentially valuable contributors to society? Surely society owes a debt because of the part it plays to erode and marginalize people's self- belief.

Erosion of Moral Leadership

The people I meet in the business world and personal life almost all agree that our value systems and education systems and even many of our businesses and government do not reflect what is good about our world. Every business is not an Enron, nor are all corrupt insurance magnates. When we ask people to express their individual values and hopes for the future, there is a common clarity that relates to what is good about people and cultures, not focusing upon what is bad.

During my days at the Air Force Academy in Colorado, I was struck by the beauty and applicability of the "Honor Code" we subscribed to. In order to stay at the Academy, we all subscribed to a code of conduct that included our "Honor Code":

> *"We will not lie, cheat or steal, nor tolerate among us those who do."*

The transformational affect this had upon our lives was phenomenal – regardless of background, race, religion or culture, four thousand of us chose to live by this code. It meant we did not have to lock the doors or storage places when we weren't present. We could treat what each person said as the truth, and not have to check up on them. When we turned in our work, it was taken for granted that it was our own, and not someone else's. The freedom of having a consistent set of values and living by them was truly remarkable. Although we had a few incidences when 10% of the people decided to "buck the system", in the main, most of us were very happy to align our beliefs and values to this code.

Forty years on, there has been an incessant attack upon the values of the Academy. Recent years have been dominated by claims of sexual assaults, honor violations, whether or not the "honor code" should continue, as it no longer represents society. On a visit there a few years ago, one of the officers in charge of the rehabilitation and re-establishment of discipline amongst the cadets related that, "The moral values represented by the Honor Code were so far removed from the way even the cream of American youth were raised meant it was almost impossible to enforce the Honor Code from the start of a cadet's enrolment. We have to slowly introduce this concept, because it is so foreign to them." No doubt we could have this conversation in almost every culture, certainly in the West.

Bunker Mentality

It seems every generation since man has populated the earth has had its Hitler, Ayatollah Khomeini, al-Qaeda and Attila the Hun characters who attempt to express themselves through spreading a dogma of hate, racism, nationalism or whatever cause they think is worth killing others for. Does that mean we are doomed to live helplessly, taking on a bunker mentality? Let's hope not.

Lack of Role Models

Many of us could say, "I grew up in an environment where I had no heroes, or role models to look up to." The role models of the current generation are usually celebrities who have very little to celebrate. They find fame, fortune and success, only to find it is very fickle, invasive and hollow. Magazines and tabloids are full of the fallen-from-grace, who seem unable to handle the fame. If these become our role models and heroes, what will become of us?

We Can Make a Positive Difference

Someone I was training on a communications and interpersonal skills course over 20 years ago gave me a book from a used book shop written by Samuel Smiles, an 1850's British author. Peter said, "Geo, you ought to have this book. He is saying some of the same things you are about how to live a better life, written last century!" Mr. Smiles recognized this deterioration in society even back then. In his book, "Self Help," he said,

> *"The government of a nation itself is usually found*
> *to be but the reflex of the individuals composing it ….*
> *National progress is the sum of individual industry, energy,*
> *uprightness, as national decay is of individual idleness,*
> *selfishness and vice."* [7]

A very simple truth deeply impressed me; we *can* impact our world in a positive way. Each and every one of us has the power

IMPACT!

within to really make a difference. Two of my friends and class-mates from the USAF Academy have done their part in helping us live in a safer world. They have taken the bad other people have created and have seen it is an opportunity for them to devote their lives to making a positive difference. One such person is Charles Holland and the other is Ed Eberhart. Chuck and Ed are my heroes.

General Charles R. Holland (Ret) served his country for 35 years and as Commander, Special Operations Forces for all services had overseen the establishment of units throughout the world fighting terrorist units over there before they get to our villages, towns and cities. During our 35th Class of 1968 reunion he inspired us all by his tales of bravery and service men and women of the Special Operations do on our behalf, quietly, yet professionally, so all of us can sleep just a little bit better. He has more medals and awards than you could imagine, yet the truth is Charles is an ordinary guy powered by an extraordinary passion to serve his country and make this a better world. He's a very accomplished speaker, yet not flash, no big ego that needs massaging. Just a truly dedicated professional. That's what I call a life making an impact.

General Ralph E. (Ed) Eberhart (Ret) up until 1st January 2005 was Commander of North American Aerospace Defense Command and U.S. Northern Command, Peterson Air Force Base, Colorado. This was the last of 22 active duty postings Ed had during his illustrious career. He also served as Vice Chief of Staff of the U.S. Air Force, Commander, Air Combat Command, Commander, Air Force Space Command, and as Commander in Chief, U.S. Space Command. Yet I knew him as our Cadet Wing Commander when I had the chance to be a Cadet Squadron Commander of 7th Squadron our senior year. Ed is an outstanding leader who found his purpose in life to serve his nation during three wars, force reduction programs and eight US Presidents. Ed, like the rest of us, had rather ordinary beginnings. Nothing regal or flash, simply a genuinely nice guy who disciplined himself to learn to serve others in an honorable way.

We may not be able to stop all the terrorist attacks, but we are much more prepared and able to protect our borders not only in the United States but across the world as well because of these two men and thousands like them. To be an Ed Eberhart or Charles Holland or Samuel Smiles. This world needs a new breed of heroes and heroines who base their lives on character as well as competence. People who measure their success on helping people live, not who see how many can be blown to pieces.

After The Elephant

Simon Wilsher, Chairman of The Wilsher Group, has increasingly found people he knows in significant roles appreciate the opportunity to talk about their future. This, of course, is natural and good but it is increasing. It also seems that people in large organizations and cities can feel 'stuck' in their place of work. Conversations that help people work out what is best for their future and how to get there he calls, "After the Elephant". The Elephant represents the large, hard to shift part of their working lives. Apparently, according to research by a well known university in London, 70% of senior executives interviewed in 2004 said they would "prefer to be somewhere else" — some indictment of the way large organizations engage their people[8].

"Geo, when you grow up, why not become a lawyer?" My Mother's great idea, I thought. Consequently, I took a course in Law at the Air Force Academy. *Big mistake!* I thought law was about doing the right things, enforcing a moral code of behavior that helped people and governments to operate effectively - wrong! The professor assured us that, "Law is not about what's right and wrong, it is focused on what is legal and not legal." As a result, we have legal systems that our common sense tells us are inappropriate, but it's the best we can do.

My cousin, Charles E. King, is a practicing lawyer who became disenchanted with litigious legal work helping families and businesses split apart and treat each other with contempt. Instead, he and his son, Chad, have set up a legal practice where they can operate both morally and legally. They are not chasing the buck or running after ambulances so they can file suits for people. They can advise their clients in a wholesome, constructive way that makes a significant difference! What if we had thousands of solicitors, lawyers and barristers who had a belief in doing the right thing as well as keeping it legal? How many disputes and cases could we see settled without involving the overcrowded and expensive court systems? As a matter of fact, Chuck did an "After the Elephant". He has become the Dean of the Business School at Colorado Christian University and is thoroughly living life as he always wanted it. He's left Chad to take on the reshaping of the legal system.

What Can We Do With the Media?

Can you imagine a media culture where journalists are truly interested in what is **right**, what is **good** and what is **excellent**? Not simply fault-finders, but committed to finding alternatives for improvement. No more intrusive journalists who make celebrities' lives miserable, and devote time to making news rather than reporting the news. Could we dream of responsible journalists, editors and publishers who recognize what a fantastic role it is in a free society to look for truth, and congratulate those people, places and organizations who help bring about what's best in any society? Media people who really make a positive impact. What a difference from our current view of media – of their predicted fifty-six recessions only two have actually happened. This lack of consistency and truthfulness would not be allowed to exist in other fields of endeavor, but in the media, we tolerate innuendoes, mistruths and outrageous claims without a fuss. Conversely, we buy their news stories and read their juicy gossip columns.

Let's see what someone in the music world did with his celebrity to make a constructive impact.

The Cry

I like a good song and decent movie as much as anyone. We love to visit places like Barcelona, Rome and Athens to see the contributions painters, sculptors and musicians have made to the world we live in. Yet we also see so many people, in the name of art, who devote their lives to producing pop songs and creations that add no value whatsoever, from my point of view. Unlike Adrian Snell.

Adrian, who lives in Bath, England, is an accomplished composer and musician who makes a difference. While on a European concert tour a number of years ago he visited Auschwitz. So moved by the horrendous atmosphere, with the thought that man could commit such atrocities on man, Adrian sensed he could hear the walls cry out! Never again! This awareness prompted him to compose and deliver an album dedicated to those who perished and whose lives were affected by the holocaust. Adrian also presents programs at school assemblies in which he exposes the horrors of the holocaust to young people who may never have the opportunity to visit and who otherwise would remain unaware of what evil men and societies gone haywire can do. These events change lives. If you ever get the chance to attend "The Cry" or any of Adrian's concerts, I promise you a treat! It will leave you with something more than a good feeling. It may make you say, "Let's do something differently about the way we live and view things."

Adrian has not stopped there. He also believes we can help other sufferers, for instance, with those with mental disabilities. He has designed a program to help mentally disturbed people find their way to wholeness and healing through use of music. He devotes some of his time every week to working with an organization that connects with people who are seeking better mental health, sitting with them, teaching them to sing, play, and compose their own music as a therapy for improving their lives. That is making a *positive impact*! We need more 'Adrian's' amongst our entertainers and artists, wouldn't you agree?[9]

So What Is The Point?

As you can tell I believe there is something we can do, regardless of who we are and what we are currently doing, to put hope back into our societies, businesses and nations. We can, as Samuel Smiles said, *change our world by changing how we think and behave towards one another.* We can all make a *positive impact*.

Although I don't specifically know your circumstances, I do know this: We can either live *under our circumstances*, and suffer with the weight of how awful and fearful the world is to live in, or we can make a choice to make a difference and *rise above our circumstances.*

Taking Control

Here is a paraphrase of what Dr Covey says:

> *We all have concerns, we all have the ability to influence to some degree, and we all have control of certain things and ideas. Highly effective people have the ability to focus on the things where we have control, and not focus upon our concerns.*[10]

Consider this: if we focus upon our concerns - like terrorism, inflation, violence in society, tsunamis, earthquakes, rising taxes, poor schooling for our children - psychologically, these issues and concerns tend to "grow" in our thinking and proliferate until they dominate our lives, causing us to complain, mutter and do nothing but live fearfully, expecting the worst to happen. One experience in the Bible gives an excellent example of this.

The Israelites, under Moses' leadership, picked a dozen of the strongest and most capable leaders to go explore the land God had said was given to them and come back with their report as to what they had found in preparation for taking possession. Like a house-hunt many of us have done prior to moving to a new area, the dynamic dozen did just that. They spent a few days walking around the place, tasting the food, seeing the inhabitants and came back with their reports.

Two very differing views were expressed – one group, consisting of ten of the twelve, *focused upon their concerns.* "Those people are like giants, they're fierce and too many for us. We will all be killed!" The minority report, from two of the fellows named Joshua and Caleb *focused upon things they could control.* "The land is full of good food, there's plenty of luscious ground to plant and grow our crops, and to roam and take possession of. There are big people there to conquer, and lots of them, too, but if God says he'll be with us, we cannot fail!" Same circumstances, different focuses.

The story in the short term was not a happy one. The people believed the majority report, focused upon their fears and concerns, rebelled against the leadership, and were forced to live another 40 years in a desert until everyone who complained had died. Only Joshua, Caleb and Moses were allowed to live until it came time to then take control of what was actually theirs.

We Have Choices

Clearly, we have choices as to where we focus. If we choose to concentrate upon what we can control and influence, the psychological affect is that we spread our sphere of control and influence. If our focal point is our concerns over which we have little or no influence or control, then these concerns begin to dominate our thoughts and control how we behave. If you want to make a difference, then you can, by choosing to *focus upon what you can control and influence, not on things you cannot.*

One person who illustrated this approach with his life was Christopher Reeve. Christopher, as you may recall, starred in a series of Superman movies. Chris died rather suddenly in October 2004. Tall, dark, handsome, intelligent, strong, rich, Christopher had it all until he fell from his horse and was left paralyzed from the neck down. Boy, did he have concerns! He needed a machine just to breathe, let alone eat and drink! He could have ended things there, just passed away, or wasted away his life as another paraplegic, full of bitterness and pity about the way life had treated him. Miraculously, he lived a vibrant nine more years.

A couple of years ago on the Larry King Live! talk show, both Christopher and Dana, his wife, were being interviewed by King. They explained what life had been like before the riding accident, and then what it was like afterwards. I was amazed at the Reeve's positive spirit! Despite the circumstances, the hardships, the struggles in doing things most of us who are able-bodied take for granted. Christopher and Dana made a positive choice to control what they could. So they set up a foundation for scientific research into stem cell development that might find a way to grow damaged spines that would give those who cannot use their limbs an opportunity to live full lives again.[11] He continued to make appearances and do physical rehabilitation so that just before he died he could wiggle his fingers and sense feeling in parts of his body that since the accident had been lifeless.

Christopher and Dana hoped for a better future, not just for themselves, but others in the same or similar situations. Because they chose to look at their circumstances differently, many others in the future will be able to live richer and fuller lives. That is having a positive impact.

"I am very sad at Christopher's death because he set such an extraordinary example over the last nine years, showing courage and tenacity in finding a new way of life. His focus on stem cell research, on getting himself better as an example for other people, was very inspirational. I think we have lost a very brave and courageous and dedicated individual. Christopher and I saw a lot of each other on the Superman set, and we'd have lunch together and saw each other socially. He was very like how he comes across on film - very strong, very brave, very forthright and very generous-spirited. He was earnest and dedicated to making Superman so that he would not disappoint children or adults who had grown up with the Superman comics. Christopher really wanted to personify and become the character of Superman and I think he did that wonderfully." - Susannah York, who played Lara (Superman's Kryptonian mother) in the Superman films.[12]

We have come full circle when reflecting on people who have made an impact across the globe, reflecting first on the destructive and then the constructive. Over to you - are you now ready to move on to the positive impact?

Zig Ziglar tells us in "See You At The Top" about Satan having a meeting with his demons – how can we keep people from making heaven on earth. "I have one suggestion, let's get everyone to believe they can change things, really make a difference, and do something worthwhile with their lives". Satan said, "How will that help? It is exactly what we don't want to happen". "I know," said the demon, "but we'll plant the thought that all they have to do is believe they can, and they can always wait until tomorrow to do so." "That's perfect," says Satan. "They will think that by having good intentions, that will be enough! They will then leave it to others who will take action, but of course no one will!" [13]

Before you launch on the next part of your Impact Journey, let's pause and reflect upon what Chapter Two helped to highlight. Then you can begin your journey in earnest

IMPACT Creative Action Debrief Chapter TWO

Please stop and do these steps before continuing to Chapter Three!

1. What are three reasons why you think the world needs to be changed for the better?

2. What role could you play?

3. What one thing could you do, if you really thought it were possible?

Three

Think and Act Now!

W hat did you write down in the Debrief for Chapter Two about where you could make an impact? Did you skip over that part, thinking, "I'll just give it some thought while I continue to read the book?" May I suggest you return to the Chapter Two Debrief, and actually answer the third question:

> *"What one thing could you do, if you really*
> *thought it were possible?"*

Write it down here, or in your note taking journal you keep for such sessions.

I fully understand your reluctance to commit yourself, and that you may have moments of anxiety thinking that maybe, just maybe, your world needs you, as it did some of the people mentioned in the last chapter. You may not be an Adrian Snell, but you could be a *fantastic you*, if you dared to believe in yourself. In the next chapter, we will explore the facts about yourself that will amaze you, or, if you have "heard it all before," perhaps this time you will embrace it even more fully, and start to act on what you learn.

Strongholds Are Like Comfort Traps

Dave Halls, a pastor and good friend of mine, uses the powerful word "strongholds" to describe inappropriate moments of anxiety, disbelief in our ability, and restrictions that prevent us from believing it is possible to be a great contributor to make this world a better place."

> *"Strongholds," David states, "are those mindsets, attitudes and beliefs that trap and constrict us. They are the vice-grips that keep us from living the way God wants us to live."*

The good news is we do not have to be trapped by these mindsets. We can overcome debilitating strongholds by changing the way we think. Contrary to some theories that state we are who and what we are because of what we were born with, in my view we are not born with these strongholds; they must have been acquired. If we can acquire them from parents, teachers, traumas and developing destructive habits, then we can change these strongholds if we *alter the way we think*. American psychologist, William James, once said,

> *"The greatest discovery of my generation is that a human being can alter his life by altering his attitudes.."*[14]

I, for one, think he was spot-on. What if, by changing your mind, you could become a truly great person with magnificent impact?

May I gently challenge you to consider all of the creative power you already possess which could be unleashed for the good of so many people?

Determining Our Worth

Where does your sense of worth come from? Let's start by exploring how special you are. In the 1980's, Jim Janz, a highly successful entrepreneur from Canada, spoke to a group of us who were aspiring to build our businesses about our uniqueness. Here is a paraphrase:

> *"There are two things that those of us interested in the arts look for that give us a measure on how great and expensive a painting is. The first aspect of the work of art is, 'Who created it?' The second thing we look for is, 'How many of them were made?'"*

The painter, if established as a Master Artist, can almost sneeze on his canvas and the result is a desirable masterpiece which merits our admiration, "Van Gogh painted that," or, "Look at that landscape by Gainsborough." Master creators demand high fees. As a believer in God, you might be able to tell yourself the same about yourself; if God is my Creator, and He was a Master Creator, then that makes me quite special. I am made in His image. If He took the time to make you, then you certainly aren't junk! Even if you are not a believer in God, but think we are all here by accident, can't you see the logic of thinking, 'I am somebody made special for this world, this time, this place by some power,' rather than think of yourself as some "accident"?

The second aspect of a work of art that gives it value is how many reproductions are in circulation. If we have the one-and-only original, we have something of unique value. Who wants something everyone else has as well? The uniqueness of the work of art therefore carries with it some intrinsic value, especially if it is created by a Master Artist. The same is true for you and me. We are created as a *one-off*. Even the "Dolly the Sheep" cloning process revealed that there were differences. Identical twins also corroborate this evidence. So far as we know, there are no parallel universes that duplicate each person and moment in time. Even if there are, we will be highly unlikely to ever experience it in our lifetime. Therefore, we might as well look at ourselves as unique, special, one-of-a-kind human beings and consequently of immense value. There we have it – created by a Master as a one-off. How more special and priceless could we possibly hope to be?

You Are a Miracle

You know this already, yet it bears repeating – your conception was a miracle of huge proportions! The fact you exist because of a miraculous event called childbirth should inspire you to make the most of your life. Just think of it; prior to your conception, millions of tiny sperm were swimming their way fast as they could to unite with your mother's egg – only the fastest and fittest made it! The ones who lost didn't survive. Each of those sperm was different, as was each egg your mother produced before and after your conception. So the fact is, the DNA and chromosomes that led to you being you were truly amazing and unique. So you are one in six billion. Even with the cloning that scientists are now doing, the clones are showing differences despite being supposedly exactly the same. Just as identical twins are different despite the same DNA, so are clones.[15]

Are you aware that you have multi-billions of brain cells? As we have declared earlier, these cells each interconnect with up to 10,000 other stem cells, and therefore form spaces to store neurochemical "memories" that make the world's best and fastest computers pale into insignificance! We are walking, talking interactive miraculous minds that also have a heart and a body to propel us.

Skip Ross, author and creator of the "Dynamic Living" concept, declares in his book, "Say Yes to Your Potential," we all have God-given equipment that gives us seeds of greatness. He sites, for instance, how when put under stress and need for survival, petite people can lift huge weights like a car or a log off of a loved one in a crisis situation. Our rate of thinking can work so quickly that between the instant of meeting someone and introducing ourselves the mind can suggest up to twenty-five different responses that would be appropriate for the situation. Then between the inner dialogue of the conscious and subconscious, in a millionth of a second the brain determines which response to make. It has had to sift through over eight hundred impressions from the environment, the look of the other person, the way they smiled or not smiled, what they did with their eyes and handshake, what they were wearing, the smell of the person, etc.! Now that is astounding! No one but a genius could do that, and it is true we do this time and time again, every day, every phone call, all of our lives! Zig Ziglar, one of the best known motivational speakers and authors states:

> *"Man was designed for accomplishment, engineered for success and endowed with the seeds of greatness."*[16]

As I stated earlier, just as an airplane is meant to fly, and will suffer leaks and cracks if left disused on the ground for too long, so will we suffer if we are not seeking to grow and improve. Greatness, in some form, is within the grasp of any living human being. The seeds are there, and this book will help you to make you become the great person you were designed to be!

Use it or Lose it

What happens to unused potential? *You lose it*! Remember my story about Jane, the working mother? Here's another example:

A friend of mine, Rosie Hoy, is a physiotherapist for the National Health Service in England. She recalls time and again the number of people who need physiotherapy to cope with aches, pains and dysfunctioning body parts. What is the cause in the majority of cases? Is it the over use of their muscles, bones and other tissue? Rosie says overuse can cause us to lose the proper functioning of our limbs, but in the majority of cases it is to the contrary. The *lack* of use is the major reason for the ailment. If these people had exercised their bodies effectively and watched their diets, they would not be in need of any physiotherapy because their aches and pains would disappear. The same is true of our minds and our skills. As we discussed in the

Comfort Zone analogy, not only will failure outside of the Comfort Zone cause our Comfort Zone to become a trap, but so will misuse.

As we have said, the tragedy of not using one's potential spreads beyond the individual to the family, the community and world. Everyone loses. Perhaps you could be the one to discover the cure for AIDs or the common cold. Maybe it is you who will help unite the Islam and the Jew. Who knows if you do not endeavor to use your full potential?

Our Choices Change Us

Heidi, my wife has a brother and sister who are twins – obviously born in the same family, raised in the same part of the country, went to the same school, yet so amazingly different! If you did not know they were twins, you'd think they are from different planets! In habits, in work, in lifestyles, in beliefs, in almost every way imaginable Don and Dianne are different.

The point is this; our experiences, thoughts and responses to our environments all make us unique. Because of this uniqueness, the good news is that we are not stuck with who we are now. We can change. This change is possible because we can choose to respond to the events and circumstances that life presents us, and *make positive choices* about what we allow to influence us. Allow me to illustrate.

You are going to catch a train to attend a business meeting somewhere across the country or state. You arrive in plenty of time, and you are looking forward to spending the time working on the journey, instead of driving all the way yourself. You are staying for a few days, so you have your bags with you. As you pull into the parking lot, you notice that there are not many spaces left. After driving around for a few times, you finally notice a space that is a tight squeeze, but if you are careful, your car will just about fit. After you have pulled in, parked, and tried to open your door, you notice you cannot get out. So you back up and park again, being mindful of leaving room for the people to get in and out of the cars on either side. Finally, all is well, and you set off to get a ticket to attach to the windscreen showing you are parked legally.

Trouble is, the ticket machine is on the other side of the car park. A few more minutes pass by, but you left in plenty of time, so no need to panic! Now you have parked, paid for the space, left the ticket visible in the windscreen, got your bags, locked the car, and head off for the station.

Next, there is a line longer than expected waiting to buy a train ticket – never mind, you have plenty of time, so you queue (as any person living for a long period in Great Britain would do) and wait your turn. It's your turn, but for some reason, the credit card machine will not authorize payment for the ticket – never mind, you have other cards, though not company cards, so it means you will have the hassle of making a claim against expenses unnecessarily. Now it is time to climb up the steps dragging your bags, and into the waiting area for your train.

As you had plenty of time, there is no panic, so you stand in line once again to get through the turnstiles that prevent unpaid passengers from entering. Now you start to get a bit worried – what was the time for that train? You look quickly at your watch, and realize it is due within a minute! So you rush down the corridor, and sure enough, your train is at the platform! You still have 30 or more steps to trundle down, and there is no elevator. So you hurry down, and half way down the steps hear the platform manager blow his whistle. At last, you make it, but you cannot get on! The manager informs you that although the train has not departed, you cannot get on, because he has blown his whistle! So the train leaves without you, and you have no idea when the next one is leaving for your destination.

What is your reaction? How are you feeling right now? What would you like to say to that platform manager? You would probably do as I did! I ranted and raved at the platform manager, told him how unreasonable he was, explained to him how important it was for me to be on that train, and yet, the train left without me! The Platform Manager did his job. He did his best to explain how for safety reasons it was necessary to close the doors on the train thirty seconds before departure, so that no one would get hurt as the train pulled away. Now I had a choice – was I going to let this event affect my attitude, and therefore my day, and how I treated others, or was

I going to choose a different course of action. After a few minutes of feeling righteous indignation for having been treated so unfairly, especially when I left in plenty of time, and really planned my journey well, I made a choice to apologize to the Platform Manager. I asked for the time for the next train going to my destination, and got out a book I was reading. I enjoyed the rest of the day!

This silly incident hopefully illustrates the role our choices make in how we live our lives. We all have these choices to make each and every day, and each one shapes who and what we are. Like a mosaic on a wall, or a thread in a tapestry, *each experience and choice we make* adds to the picture of our life, forms our patterns, and determines our character. It is one of the reasons we are so unique.

My father was a farmer and agrarian, so I grew up in the country, with lots of green, growing plants, trees and flowers all around me. We had a vegetable garden where my parents and brothers and I would plant our tomatoes, squash and beans that would feed us in the summer growing season and in the winter as well. Although when we planted the seeds, we were never sure whether or not they would grow, one thing was certain – when the conditions were right, we knew we were going to have to handle the weeds. Weeds did not need to be planted – they grew naturally! *Weeds* represent for me the "bad things" we don't like about our current condition. They represent the beliefs and habits that constrain us and squeeze the life out of our best intentions to change. If we are to use our potential, we can be sure that "bad things" will arise to block or destroy our efforts to get better. We cannot just rely on our *desire* to want to improve to be enough. Neither can we just allow ourselves to develop "naturally." Whether we like it or not, deny it or not, we live in a world that has a negative, downward pull. Just as gravity holds us to the earth and keeps us from flying off into space (thank God for gravity!), there is a downward pull to life that keeps us from being all we can be (maybe it is a good thing as well?).

Very few people who have an addiction to nicotine would admit that one day they decided they wanted to be addicted to smoking, so set a goal to become a chain smoker! From those I know who smoke, most of them did it because it looked "cool." It was something our parents didn't want us to do, and we wanted to explore the forbidden, so we did it! The first one almost made us ill. We gagged and choked and coughed, and what an awful taste it left in our mouth. Our nose burned and eyes watered, yet because it was the "thing to do," we persisted. And before we knew it, the smoking of one or two cigarettes became a very expensive habit that controlled us! If we are therefore going to change, it is going to take effort, and we cannot expect to change for the better by simply doing what comes naturally. What comes naturally will shorten our lifespan, destroy our self image, and lead to broken dreams, relationships and lives.

We Need to Have Plans

In a workshop I recently conducted, we were discussing the need to have a plan for our lives. One particular fellow, about 23, let's call him Gary, said; "I don't want to plan! I want to be free! I want to wake up in the morning, and just go with the flow. This planning is not for me." We can all understand this sentiment. Would it not be a joy if we could be free by not planning? However, the opposite is true. By not planning, we are surrendering our future, and our future happiness to someone or some organization, and because they do not have our best interests in mind, we may not like what they have in store for us! *Plans are there for those who want to chart their own course and produce the impact they want to make in life.*

As Gary found out, because he had no plan, his girlfriend was not committed wholly to him. Because he had no plan, his job role continued to change, and not always for the better. Because he had no plan, he could not look back with satisfaction at the things he had accomplished on a daily, weekly or yearly basis. So, convinced to give it a try, Gary wrote a 'Vision' for what he wanted to become, to do, and to have. He started with what he wanted to *become. Being comes before doing or having. Doing* is the acting and behaving part of life. It is measured in activity and results others can see. Very often, *doing* is the *fruit of our being. Having* is generally described by what we possess. For most people 'having' involves *external* things – houses, cars, jobs, status, position, family, holidays, etc. Whereas it is ok to have things, having, like doing, works better for us as the *fruitfulness of being.* Otherwise *what we have has us!*

It's early days, but already Gary has found his life more enriched. His written 'Vision' included being married, devoting more personal time to fishing, and other joint pursuits with his significant other. He wanted more control of the time he spent at work and in travel. Gary wanted some say in which projects he took on, how he motivated and built his team. His plan for how to reach his Vision was one of the best I had seen. He was so motivated by it his whole demeanor and respect for himself grew.

Subsequently, so did the view others had of Gary. His boss went to work on helping Gary improve the way he was viewed higher up the organization. He and his girlfriend (now wife) are planning to buy their first home. He has structured his job, and is focusing his efforts on the places that will yield the better returns. He is more respected not only as a person, but as the enthusiastic leader he was meant to be. All because of the power of a well defined plan. What is yours? We will take a hard look at planning and how to develop a life-changing, purposeful focus for you in Chapters Eight and Nine. If you can't wait, then skip to those chapters now and begin!

You Just Don't Know Whose Life You May Influence

Annie was locked away in a mental institution just outside Boston, Massachusetts many years ago. She had built up a grudge against the world for leaving her so handicapped. This left her bitter, twisted and incorrigible. The authorities had given up on her, as had society, until one day, an elderly nurse came into her life. The nurse found within herself a love for this poor, unsociable young lady whom the world had written off as no better than an animal. Patiently and con- sistently, the unnamed nurse nurtured, cared for and developed her relationship with Annie.

Slowly but surely, Annie began to eat regularly, and with the encouragement and support of others began to change, to laugh, to interact, and to live again. She found new purpose and belief that maybe she could be a somebody, and did not have to live her life tucked away from the world in some institution and rot away her existence. When told she was free to go home, she decided to stay, as the "home" she had found had left her with a desire to help others just like her. One of her students went on to be given the highest award to a foreigner by Queen Victoria of England. She was a blind and deaf young woman named Helen Keller. Helen had been nurtured and disciplined by Anne Sullivan, the "Annie" who was locked in a dungeon of a mental institution before someone cared for her. She went on to give this "breath of life" to a woman who in turn became an outstanding author and promoter of women's rights and socialism. Yet she may not have been able to do what she did, had not Anne Sullivan made an impact on her, and therefore passed on the torch of purpose.

Who is it you know that you might help be the next Helen Keller, Gandhi, Martin Luther King or Mother Theresa? You may hold the keys to releasing so much good in the world! Be a role model for those with whom you live and work. You can be a hero for someone that may just light a fire that revolutionizes our world!

Defining Beliefs

What might hold us back? For most of us, our biggest limiting factor is our *own self-limiting beliefs*. These "defining beliefs" keep us from being able to jump that abyss or stronghold you read about earlier when we discussed the Comfort Zone.

What about us? How many of us live in our own cells of wishful thinking, held captive by imaginary walls of fear, doubt, and self deprecation? What boundary could we and should we be pushing now to find our new sense of freedom?

"In the beginning, God created ..."

These are some of the most famous words ever written. They convey a belief many people around the world hold as true that we are made in the image of God. Therefore, we, too, have creative power, given to us by God. Even for those of us who are non-believers, we probably deep in our hearts through our own soul-searching or experiences can admit that people have creative and imaginative powers that separate us from all other living things. Of course we can use this power for creating destructive as well as constructive thoughts, beliefs and actions. Let's concentrate on creating something that would make the world and our lives better.

How does this happen? Stephen R. Covey says everything has two creations[17].

> *"One creation is when we think it, the second when we*
> *bring it about through ours and other's thoughts,*
> *words and deeds."*

I suggest there is another preceding creation, if we are truly going to produce something that is worthwhile, sustainable, and world-enhancing. This first creation is God has the idea, and plants the seed in us to bring to germination when we take the time to listen, think and verbalize. When we finally think it, that is in fact the second creation! This leads to *three* creations, not just two:

1. God's thought
2. Our thought
3. Actual implementation through an action, spoken word or physical creation

Now does this mean we are incapable of creating our own thoughts and ideas? Absolutely not! Through our God-given power of choice, we can think all kinds of thoughts and create all kinds of ideas. The problem is, if the thoughts and ideas are not aligned with what God wants us to be thinking and doing, we can create something that may damage us and the world, rather than construct and build the lasting quality of life we truly desire.

An extreme example may be to look at the suicide bombers amongst the terrorists who create havoc through fulfilling what they believe is their "Life Purpose." It is possible for any of us to pick a dream, an idea, etc., and claim 'this is it'. The tragic result may be that it is not aligned with our higher calling or best use of our lives; and both we and the rest of the world have to live with the consequences.

I'm not saying it is easy for us to determine the difference between our ideas and the God-implanted ones. Nor we can sit around and wait for these impregnated ideas to surface. Sometimes it is better to do something and get moving, rather than to wait. On the other hand, God may force us to wait to discover how the idea will germinate and produce fruit – as did Abraham in the Bible. How do we determine what approach is appropriate?

Your Idea

Here are some thoughts:

- Does the idea excite and enthuse you?
- Do you feel inspired when you think of it?
- Would you take the idea and advance it towards the 3rd creation for no reward?
- Does the idea continue to resurface time and again, even when you have laid it down for a time? (We will explore this further when we delve into making the dream a reality.)
- Is it a big idea that seems beyond your ability right now to pull off? Will you need the help of God and other people to make it a reality?
- Will the accomplishment of the idea produce something truly worthwhile? Not simply appeasing people's epicurean appetites, but making the world a better place to live?
- Are the fruits of the endeavor love, joy, peace, patience, kindness, goodness, faithfulness, gentleness and promotion of people's self-control?
- When people use your idea will it lead them to think and behave in a manner that promotes cleanliness, purity, wholeness, excellence, God-honoring, inspirational, uplifting, morally acceptable behavior in others? If everyone in the world was using the idea, product or service you are thinking of, would the world be better off?

If you can answer "Yes" to most of these, then you can develop the confidence to act upon it.

Collecting Your Thoughts

Let's have a go right now at collecting some of your big ideas, things you'd like to accomplish or pull off – remember, some of them may be simply your creation; some may be God's creation for you. But let's believe that for the moment God has already given you some of His thoughts as you now read this. Turn to the IMPACT Creative Action Debrief at the end of this chapter and write down some of your thoughts. Better yet, you may have a journal that you use to record your thoughts, in either your own longhand or as a computer document. In whatever way that is simplest and easiest for you to capture, take at least fifteen minutes now, before you proceed, to collect these initial thoughts by answering Question 1. Before you do, you may want to put on your favourite music, something that inspires, yet relaxes you. Breathe deeply, close your eyes, and allow yourself to get into some meditative or prayerful state. Then ask yourself the question, and write down whatever thoughts come to mind.

As we have read about the talents and abilities of others during earlier chapters, what do you have in common with them? What strengths and competencies have you developed that have helped you get where you are to date? How can these help as you attempt to explore how you can impact the world? As you did for your dreams and initial thoughts, now list your talents, gifts and abilities in your journal or wherever you have decided is appropriate. Then go to Question 2 in the IMPACT Creative Action Debrief for this chapter. Come back to this section once you have finished and we will explore what to do next.

Remember our discussions on self-defining beliefs? I heard someone say, *"one cannot consistently perform at a higher level than the view we have of ourselves"*. This means that unless we know what it is we value and hold most dear, especially about ourselves, we will automatically limit or filter our thoughts and reduce our ability to recognize and use "God thoughts" when we get them.

So let's have a go at defining some of the things we value most, care about, and hold most dear. These will be the building blocks for the new future we are going to construct.

Each "Value" as we will call them, will be one of the foundational building blocks upon which we can layer the world we want to create. Now I ask you to record your values. Return here for continued guidance once this has been completed. It should only take you fifteen to thirty minutes. Stop reading now and go to the end of this chapter and Question 3.

Done it? How did that feel? Can you see a connection or alignment of your ideas, abilities and your values? Are there conflicting ones? Don't be too concerned if there are, this is normal. We will sift through this later on. At least you have now captured your initial thoughts, your abilities and your values. The engine that will drive your Purpose for Life is beginning to gather the energy it will need to help you fly!

One of the useful tools many of our colleagues and friends use, and no doubt you may have heard of is a "Wheel of Life." I have used this to balance my life and develop my lifelong, yearly, monthly and weekly goals for thirty or more years. It has kept me from pursuing wrong actions, feeling guilty about pursuing others, and given my family, friends and work colleagues a "reality check" of accountability. I introduce it here to help you find significant balance that will positively impact your journey.

In 'airplane speak,' the center of gravity is a theoretical spot calculated from the laws of aerodynamics to determine where to place the various objects in the airplane. Another calculated point is known as the center of lift, used as the point around which all the lift produced by the air flowing over the wings so we can control both the stability and the maneuverability of the airplane as it takes off, maneuvers, and propels itself in flight. These two points, the center of gravity and the center of lift and the theoretical distance apart they are located on the airplane determine how stable and how maneuverable it is. If we, for instance, have a center of gravity located too far towards the rear of the aircraft behind the center of lift, it becomes highly unstable during flight, and could if not controlled properly, mean that when we attempt to take off, the aircraft will climb straight up, on to its back, and crash rather dramatically back onto the runway! If, on the other hand, the center of gravity is too far forward of the center of lift, we are likely to run out of runway and ideas long before the aircraft has generated enough speed and lift to ever take off! In summary, then, positioning the weight and wings within the frame of the aircraft is highly important if we want our aircraft to fly high and far. So "balance" in an aircraft is vital. Something to ponder on your next vacation or business flight!

A more simple analogy might be how important it is to have "balanced wheels" on a car. We have all experienced what an unbalanced tire will do when we are traveling, or even more drastically, if you have ever been in a car as you had a "blowout" or puncture, you'll appreciate how travel is inhibited (to say the least!) if our tires are out of round or unbalanced.

How to Detect Your Own "Balance of Life"

Most people have a number of areas in their life they consider to be important to them if they are to be successful, and feel life is worthwhile. These areas, for most of us center around our health, our happiness, our peace of mind, our sense of worth and well being. Stephen R. Covey describes just four –to live, to love, to learn and to leave a legacy. Abraham Maslow described them as "needs" – Survival, Security, Social, Self-Esteem and Self- Fulfillment. Whatever they are, for the purpose of description and to get you started on your balanced Wheel of Life, let's go with the eight:

- Spiritual Health
- Mental Health
- Physical Heath
- Career
- Financial
- Family
- Social
- Community

If we were to plot these on a wheel, it might look like this:

Figure 3.1 Wheel of Life

If we were successful in each of these areas, we would be quite content and healthy. Some areas take more effort and time than others to keep us contented and satisfied, and at different times in our lives certain of these may take more diligence and consideration than others. For instance, during our "bringing up family" years, financial and community involvement may take a hit and suffer. The assumption the Wheel of Life makes is that if we neglect any one area for a long period of time, we may find our life-balance goes haywire, and we lose control.

Most of our experiences probably bear this out. No doubt you know of someone who worked so hard on career and financial well being that he or she neglected the family, and as a result may have been successful in the career and financial areas, but "bankrupt" in others. How many people in hospital are probably there because of neglect of the physical or mental area of their lives? I suspect quite a few! You may decide you'd like to use a different set of areas. It is up to you, and we will give you the opportunity to *complete your own wheel* at the end of the chapter. For now, let's go to the next stage of this exercise, and use the 'Wheel of Life' areas I have already indicated.

Let's assume that a life in perfect harmony and balance is represented by a "10" on the rim or circumference of the wheel. To describe what a score of **10** for the "Family" area might mean: Family life superb. Lots of good loving relationships, experiences of laughter, close knit bonding, etc. A **10** in the "Finance" area represents having more than enough finances so that we have money at the end of the month and, can even afford to give a significant portion away. Life is not centered around our trying to make ends meet, but money is seen only as a commodity to ensure the rest of life can function. It's okay, by the way, to have money. We just don't want the money to *have us*, as our friend Zig says.

Continue this thinking for *all areas of your life*, until you have a fairly good Vision and feeling for what "the good life" really means to you. I took two days when I tried to describe my first balance. This was one of the most significant turning points in my whole life, and although the description has modified and been updated over the years, it has served as my focus for over thirty years. I am, in fact, living my dream for the most part, a dream which is so big it will take all of this life and much more to fulfill. Such is the power of taking the time to clearly "see" how you would like life to be for you.

Once we have described our "**10** lifestyle", we come back to our wheel, and take a brutal look at the facts. If "center" represents "**0**" (meaning we have no life at all in that area) and 10" is our idea of perfection, where would you place an arc for that life-area now, today, at this moment? Take a cold, hard look at yourself, and being as honest as you can, give yourself a rating, 0 to 10.

Let's say your "Physical life" is not what you would want at the moment. You know you weigh more than you ought, and could certainly do with some reshaping. Perhaps because your eating habits and your exercise routines are not good, you rate yourself as a 3. Lots of room for improvement!

Perhaps your mental life consists of watching TV, reading a few professional journals or magazines, and taking in a movie now and again. You may find yourself occasionally depressed, not looking forward to the work week, and regretting getting up on Monday. In short,there is much room for improvement when you look at your mental health. Let's say your rating is 5.

Then subscribe an arc on the "Mental" area half way towards the rim (5/10), and the "Physical" area about one third of the way (3/10). Get the picture? Continue the exercise until you have a *new wheel with a new circumference for each section plotted* within your Wheel of Life circle. Now create the new circle by tracing the edges of the segments – it is better if you use another color. This outline represents the *current picture* of your life balance.

Immediately this will give you a snapshot of those areas most in the need of actions to move towards a well-rounded wheel. The first time I saw this I had one of those 'Eureka moments' that caused our whole family to make some changes. Even if you have done this before, I suggest you and someone who knows you well complete the exercise on the pages at the end of the chapter, or in your journal/ computer document so you can take that cold, hard look at yourself and identify some changes that will improve your Impact Journey immensely.

So here we are, at what could be a significant turning point and start of your Impact Journey. I am aware that you might be tempted to say to yourself, "Nice idea, and I'll do that 'someday when ....'" – you fill in the rest: ...when the time is right, when I have more time, when the kids go back to school, when I'm not so busy and wrapped up in the latest crisis, when I am older, when the pressure is more, when the pressure is less, when the house isn't such a mess, etc. It takes rigorous effort to cross over this abyss of resistance and lethargy, as we described in the discussion on Comfort Zone, in order to begin a new course of disciplined practice and action. I know. I face this every day when I am attempting to write this book or do my exercises. The energy to break lethargy can be enormous.

Apply Maximum Power

When we were attempting to get the F4 Phantom into the air, we knew the time for full power was in the beginning. It takes more effort to get the wheels rolling, to move the aircraft from 0 to 155 mph than it does to accelerate from 300 to 500 when cruising at 20,000 feet. You will have to form new habits, and they all start with a disciplined decision to do something differently, for the first time – break our own world record – and step over the abyss. This will take your maximum effort, even though you may just be starting out, just like that F4.

You probably feel more motivated than ever and are "*perceptually ready*" to start this phase of your Journey. You have read some accounts from others who have gone before you. You have reflected upon the rationale for why the world needs impact, and why you need to be one of those people who can make a positive impact in your world. You have gained a fresh insight into why only you can make the difference with your unique combination and mixture of talents, experiences, motivations and beliefs. You have dreams and goals of what success would look like that fit only you. So why not make the most of the moment, this precious moment, and complete your Wheel of Life? This will form a vital step over the chasm of good intentions, I assure you!

Even if we have completed something like the Wheel of Life before – this is a new day, and new moment in time. Use this moment to avoid the danger of simply storing information in our head, and take that first step again! So now is the time, today is the day. Stop reading the book, and complete the following Creative Action Steps.

IMPACT Creative Action Debrief Chapter THREE

Do these before continuing to Chapter Four!

1. What ideas, thoughts and emotions do you have currently in your mind that:

· Excite and enthuse you?

· Are so big they need other people's help?

· Can do a lot of good for a lot of people, or influence people to do a lot of good?

Write here or in your journal or computer. We will come back to these later. Be very careful who you share these with, so for now, keep the ideas to yourself.

2. List three unique qualities you possess

   ·
   ·
   ·

3. What are the ideals you value most? List at least 5 of them here, and explain what they mean to you

   ·
   ·
   ·
   ·

4. Use the circle below to show your balance in life.

   · Follow the instructions provided earlier in the chapter

Figure 3.2 Your Current Balance In Life

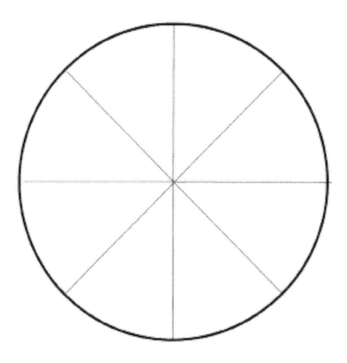

Four

Origin of the Impact! Program

⟿

Has the Wheel of Life Exercise revealed specific action steps to follow? We will build upon these action steps as we now roll up our sleeves and get down to the nitty gritty of the Impact Journey. In this chapter we shall describe the origins of IMPACT! and then provide some powerful tools that will help you in creating your own impact that makes a positive difference.

Where did IMPACT! come from? Was it the result of one 'Eureka" moment'? Hardly. Just as we indicated your own plan will evolve, IMPACT! was the result of many people's ideas, thoughts and contributions It is the result of countless hours of discussion, experimentation and thought borne out of years of helping people to improve their impact. Simon Wilsher and I owe a lot of the development of IMPACT! to Dale Carnegie, and the Dale Carnegie™ organization.

When we were exploring our Impact Journey even before it had a name, both of us were involved in running and developing Dale Carnegie programs in the United Kingdom. The way we got there from our respective Journeys from Zimbabwe for Simon, and the United States for me, could be a whole book by itself. Portions of the story will be told in the later chapters. We were both interested in helping people to better their lives. We were both Christians, and this meant that our Journeys were inextricably linked to doing what we felt Jesus would have us do; that is, being Christian in the business market place. We took the values we interpreted from our major source document, the Bible, and using these to began to build an organization that fulfils our view of why we are here on Earth. Not necessarily to "save the world," but certainly to make an impact.

After several years with the Dale Carnegie organization, Simon established his own company to offer programs that would help organizations, teams and individuals transform themselves. One of the first programs he developed, with the assistance of Carmen Harvey Brown, was entitled "PAC" and catered for individuals who wanted to improve their presentation styles and communicative skills. The power in the program was not the "how-to's," but the way in which people were encouraged to "have a go" at a different style of communicating, and then receiving feedback from the instructor or trainer, as well as the other delegates on the program, as to how they came across. To Simon and Carmen's delight, the change was sometimes dramatic.

One particular example was a scientist called Rob. Technically and intellectually very able, but finding the right words, especially under pressure was not his forte. The practice and coaching he received on PAC gave him the opportunity to experiment and discover how to be more articulate. Therefore he could use his scientific knowledge to even greater effect.

Soon after, I began my own training consultancy, with Simon's help and encouragement every step of the way. We cherished working together, and we had a combination of skills and experiences that the other could draw upon. So rather than paddle our own canoes, we chose to work together in developing programs and services that would truly help people grow and become more successful, wholesome and accomplished human beings. My role was to develop the PAC into a program that did more than simply improve people's presentation and speaking skills. We learned from listening to delegates, and our experiences in the Dale Carnegie years that there is a whole lot more accomplished through the program. Graduates declared that as well as improving their self-confidence for public presentations whether one-to-one, in groups or on sales interviews, their confidence to have a bash at other things was improved as well.

Delegates were taken around the Cycle of Experiential Development model and asked to choose an area to improve. Public speaking and thinking on one's feet under pressure, were frequently picked. As they practised and improved, they established momentum to tackle other fears and Comfort Zones as well. In fact, what we discovered was people were given a fresh SPICE for life! Hence "SPICE" became the acronym developed to help us and our clients focus on what the PAC would do for people:

S for self-confidence
P for positive attitude
I for interpersonal skills
C for communication skills
E for enthusiasm or emotional drive

The program then expanded from five to seven sessions, and we earnestly looked for a new name that would encompass what the program would do for the delegates and the client companies who embraced it. Simon first thought of IMPACT! as the name. To be fair, all of the staff and the people involved in the management and leadership of the organization played a part. The name IMPACT! was born, and for the past twenty years we have run IMPACT! Programs for dozens of organizations and thousands of people. We have run compact versions, extended versions, and it still represents most of the foundational principles, values and methods around which we orchestrate transformation programs for smaller, medium- sized and Blue Chip organizations in the UK, across Europe and in the United States. As we witnessed the amazing changes the delegates made to their family, business and individual lives, I felt God would want us to capture this process in a written form so those taking the program would have a reference book, and more importantly, for those who might never take a personal development course like this, they could use the book to help themselves make an impact in their worlds.

In the previous chapters, you have already been exposed to some of the exercises and thought patterns used on the IMPACT! program. Things like the Cycle of Experiential Development and the memory techniques for instance. As you have already experienced,

IMPACT represents a way of thinking about yourself, your life and your world. Hopefully by now you are convinced of the merit of making an impact and feel ready to do your part.

You have begun your journey by completing the Wheel of Life Reality Check, and have had some initial thoughts about areas for improvement. We will now dig a bit deeper, and begin to explore each part of the Journey, by first of all looking at what IMPACT! stands for, and use our discussions of each part of IMPACT! to provoke, inspire and inform you with exercises you can do that will help you develop your own unique Impact Journey.

Three Parts to the Impact Journey:

·   *Plan* for the journey
·   IMPACT! *core skills*
·   Continual *monitoring* of the journey

The Thirteen-Week Journey

In my earlier flying days, each flight was first created in our own minds, (as described earlier) and then secondly put into practice. Thirdly, upon completion of the mission, we would conduct a debrief of each and every significant portion in order to take maximum advantage of the learning opportunity provided by the flight. It may surprise you to know that very often for jet fighter pilots, the debriefing would last two to three times longer than either the planning or action phase. It was in the debriefing and resolution to "do things differently" next time that true learning and behavior change occurred. During this chapter, we will provide an overview of the three parts of the Impact Journey, then we will devote some time to each part with cumulative creative action steps to take that will encompass bite-sized learning. I suggest you take at least thirteen weeks to complete the journey, and use this book as a resource to return to time and again to record your learning, gain fresh insight and inspiration, and to reinforce your own understanding for what you could do to take the next steps in your Impact Journey.

Why spread it out over thirteen weeks? Remember I said in the description of the Cycle of Experiential Development, change most often happens gradually, by putting our thoughts into practice? The amount of practicing new things it takes to form a habit varies with each of us, but most behaviorists agree it takes many conscious applications of something new until it beds in and becomes ours. So give yourself time to go around the Cycle and this will increase the chances you will acquire those transformational skills and habits your Impact Journey will need.

Are you now ready for takeoff? "Redstick 34, you are cleared for takeoff, have a good flight!"

Plan for the Journey

What do I mean by a '*Plan*'? What happens to most plans? What are the barriers that keep us from effectively planning? It is often said *failing to plan is planning to fail*. If we do not plan, then we are on *someone else's* plan, and they may not have our best interests in mind, and be more focused on what is good for them, not us! I have previously described Gary's experience, which demonstrated we are given the power to create, then turn our initial concepts and ideas into reality by developing a plan. This is a process by which we *bring the future into the present, so we can better influence the outcome*.

It may surprise you to know most plans don't work – if we define "working" as bringing about the desired result exactly as we first of all envisioned. Plans, by their very nature, are movable and flexible steps in a process. The best ones "work" better than others because they are not so rigid and structured and allow flexibility. Plans need to allow new information to affect them, or keep abreast of current situations such as social trends, technology and feedback from those involved in implementing the plans. We can overcome most of the reasons most plans don't "work" by designing a planning process that incorporates that likelihood and even the necessity of changes during the life of the plan.

Some plans fail because they are *too elaborate*. It's like painting the Golden Gate Bridge in California, or the Forth Road Bridge in

Scotland! Before the structure is "painted," it is starting to rust at the other end, and we have to start over again! If we keep the plan simple, dynamic and easily implemented, we may stand a better chance of developing a plan that "works." The plan we are asking you to create reflects this.

Still other plans fail because we are *perfectionists*, and want every 't' crossed and every 'i' dotted before we embark upon the first step. If we develop a simple, dynamic plan that we can start to implement portions of right away, chances are during the writing and revision of the document, we will start to encounter enough early success and encouragement that we improve the likelihood we will continue the plan. "Every important journey begins with a single step", someone wiser than me once said. Let's develop the habit of taking early steps. 'Ready, fire, aim,' can be a great way to develop an effective plan for development. Perhaps an analogy might help our understanding.

During air-to-ground gunnery practice, before the advent of "smart" bombs and missiles, we were forced to use our own skill and aiming techniques to find and destroy the target. At 600 to 700 miles per hour, decision making and aiming time were at a premium. Once we had positioned our jet into the right airspace at the right time and the correct speed, our attention was focused upon our manual sight, a cross-hair that was projected upon a piece of glass through which we peered onto the outside world and then maneuvered the aircraft to face the target. But because of the inaccuracy of the sight, and the difficulty of maneuvering our jet into the right space at the right speed, if we pulled the trigger when the sight appeared in the cross hairs, we would more often than not shoot into space, or many yards away from the intended target. The way we dealt with this phenomenon was to track the bullets into the target. This meant we would deliberately aim below the target with our cross hairs, start to fire, then using the tracer bullets and puffs of dirt kicked up by the bullets as our feedback, and slowly maneuver the airplane by pulling the nose of the aircraft up so that the bursts of dirt and smoke were actually on the target. This was *ready, fire and aim* in real life. My theoretical view is effective planning is best done in the same way.

One Page Planner / VSOMA Planning Tool

Here is a dynamic, relatively simple and effective planning tool that is used by thousands to help them in many diverse areas of life. It is affectionately known by some as the **One Page Planner**. By others, it is the **VSOMA** planning tool, as each of the stages of the planning process are represented in the acronym, VSOMA – Vision, Status Quo, Options, Milestones and Action. Implement whatever works for you. Like any tool, it becomes more effective the more it is utilized, so why not try using it for your next holiday, business meeting, as well as your Impact Journey?

Notes on how to complete your plan and use the One Page Plan

1. Vision - First of all, create a Vision for what you would like to be, to have, and do in the future that would mean you are living a life of impact. Write in brief bullet points what you see, feel, and want the desired outcome to look like. Begin with the end in mind! (this takes helicopter view, big picture, "all things possible" thinking)

2. Status quo - Write down brief bullet points on the **threats, opportunities, weaknesses and strengths** that the current situation presents - factors <u>for</u> and <u>against</u> your being able to move from where you are <u>now</u> to where you want to be (<u>Vision</u>) Describe the current situation in your life, both externally and internally. Get brutal with the facts, as I described when you were introduced to the Wheel of Life.

3. Options - List briefly some of the options you could consider that might help you move closer to your Vision. - what will eliminate or reduce the impact of the threats, exploit the opportunities, minimize the weaknesses, and make full use of the strengths. Remember, green-light it! Anything will do for now, without reservation or trying to figure out how or whether this might be the best course of action.

4. Milestones - following the options step develop some milestones, the markers that help identify whether or not your actions are indeed getting you closer to the long-term, medium-term and short-term milestones you need to reach to realize and keep focused upon your Vision. What specific, motivational and measurable, agreed, realistic and time-phased objectives should be set? Set long-term first, and work through to short-term.

5. Creative Action Steps – finally, identify what Creative Action Steps you need to take NOW towards your more short term milestones. These Creative Action Steps are your most important tools that guide your daily behavior. They are the dynamic NOW "to-do's" that take into consideration all the current input of your changing world and yet fulfill your inner longing and desire to ensure you are moving closer to your Vision of the IMPACT! life. Answer the questions of the *what, who, when, where and how* that will move you towards your first short-term objective.

Here'a how to organize your plan on to One Page – follow the sequence suggested, then go back and fill in as things become more clear.

Figure 4.1 One Page Planner VSOMA

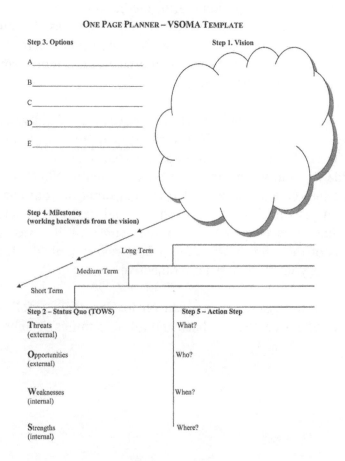

ONE PAGE PLANNER – VSOMA TEMPLATE

Step 3. Options   Step 1. Vision

A_____

B_____

C_____

D_____

E_____

Step 4. Milestones
(working backwards from the vision)

Long Term

Medium Term

Short Term

Step 2 – Status Quo (TOWS)   Step 5 – Action Step

Threats   What?
(external)

Opportunities   Who?
(external)

Weaknesses   When?
(internal)

Strengths   Where?
(internal)

Second Draft Action Plan
Use this for developing the One Page Plan into
a full blown plan

1. VISION- What is your Vision for your future? Describe it in some detail below:

2. STATUS QUO – Your current situation as of (Date)

Date

- Threats – (*external forces* that may prevent you from reaching your Vision)

- **O**pportunities – (*external forces* and influences that may help you reach your Vision)

- Weaknesses – (*internal factors* (personal) that may hinder you)

- **S**trengths – (internal factors that you have going for you – qualities and character traits that may help you achieve your Vision)

3. OPTIONS – things you could do that will help:

- Reduce the effect or risk of the Threats

- Exploit the Opportunities

- Minimize the Weaknesses

- Maximize the Strengths

4. Milestones /goals/objectives and steps to complete them:

- LONG-TERM

- MEDIUM-TERM

- SHORT-TERM

5. Creative Action Plan to accomplish short term objectives

- WHAT:

· WHO:

· WHEN/ WHERE:

· HOW:

IMPACT CREATIVE ACTION DEBRIEF CHAPTER FOUR

Complete these before continuing to Chapter Five!

1. Describe in a few words what completing at least the first draft of your One Page Plan has meant to you.

2. Where else besides your Impact Journey Plan might you be able to use the One Page (VSOMA) Planning Tool?

3. To what extent did the Wheel of Life follow this planning process? Can you see how natural a process it is?

Five

Impact! For Life

*

This chapter is called IMPACT! for Life as it is here I explain why each of the IMPACT qualities is needed and how to develop them. Then you have the opportunity to plan how you are going to develop the qualities for yourself. Congratulations, by the way, for the work you have already done to create your Impact Journey Plan. Like I said earlier, having a plan is great. Especially if you have generated a dynamic plan suggested by the One Page Plan you have just worked on. Now you need to work on the key elements for helping it become your reality. Here is my description of IMPACT!:

Interpersonal Intelligence
Mental Toughness and self-confidence
Passion with Purpose
Attitude control
Communication
Transformational Leadership

In our latest evolution of the IMPACT! Program, the core skills actually spell 'IMPACT'. As with SPICE and VSOMA, acronyms can help us when we are under the pressure of the moment (some people call these our "moments of truth") when we need to remember these skills. It is good to have an aide-memoir like an acronym to help us out. It will also help you to track your way through the book, and serve as a theme for capturing what are the key skills, tools and abilities needed to have a significant Impact Journey.

"Handles Raise, Triggers, Squeeze"

Another "war story" – I am very fond of these little memory joggers. Long before I read the Tony Buzan's books on memory, or became a student of how the mind works and records information for use later, I was taught that when we are under pressure and the mind starts to freeze for example during exams, in crises, and most certainly when flying in life-threatening conditions, we need some triggers that will help our instant recall.

One method we used while flying was something we called, *Bold Face Emergency Steps*. These were considered so important to air crews that certain pieces of information about what steps to take during extreme emergency situations such as having an engine catch on fire during takeoff have to be recalled instantly. We did this by memorizing by rote a series of steps for around 25 of the most critical aircraft emergencies. There were a lot more that we carried in a checklist, and still more we studied in the aircraft manual, yet the ones we really needed to have instant recall of were memorized. These were considered so important that we would review certain ones orally before every flight, and had to take a *Bold Face Exam* every week prior to our first flight of the week. So let's think of the acronym as our **Bold Face** critical skills that when under pressure we must have memorized for instant recall during our "moments of truth" we face every day. I still remember most of these: "Handles Raise, Triggers, Squeeze' - this is the potentially life-saving *Bold Face* procedure for canopy and seat ejection from an aircraft!

Let's briefly explain each here, and then we can get into the *how-to's* in the appropriate chapters.

Interpersonal Intelligence

*building relationships, gaining co-operation, helping others
to transform their behavior and attitude*

In Daniel Goleman's book, Emotional Intelligence, he encapsulated what many people who have devoted their lives to human psychology already understood, and what most of the 'Wisdom Literature' throughout the ages of history have maintained –

Our success or failure in this world owes more to our understanding of ourselves and how we interact with others than with our intellect and ability to grasp technologies, develop laws of aerodynamics, pass exams, etc.[18]

Interpersonal Intelligence, for me, goes one stage further. Yes, it's true our ability to be emotionally aware of how our interactions with others affects the outcome is vital. If we continually shout at our children or partners and those with whom we work, we will get a corresponding reaction that may not be the one we want. This reaction will, of course, affect how successful we are with them. Beyond this, there is something even greater. This we call Interpersonal Intelligence. It is emotional intelligence *plus* the ability to modify our behavior to gain co-operation and to help others to transform their attitudes and behaviors. It is what leaders are able to do, and followers respond to. To get along in this world we absolutely have to have Emotional Intelligence and if you want to know more about this, then Google-it and explore one of the 2 million references. If you want to really have an impact, then this will require you can do all three – *build lasting relationships quickly, gain co-operation* and *help others to modify and improve their attitudes and behaviors.*

Interpersonal Intelligence is used to make the most of the circumstances and people around you to gain co-operation that propels you and others towards worthwhile shared goals. By this I do not mean becoming a master of manipulation, where we trick others to act certain ways through some type of hypnotic trance or clever turn of phrase and body language. I define *gaining co-operation* as the genuine win–win arrangement where we find out where people are going or want to go, then see how by us helping them, they can help us move closer to where we need to be as well. The guidelines for both building relationships and gaining co-operation are not magical, nor are they the panacea for every human situation. Instead, they are common-sense guidelines based upon the best principles of human interaction and laws of sowing and reaping.

Beyond simply finding ways to work well with others, there is another level of human interaction that requires we go further. This level is the transforming of behaviors and attitudes. It involves engaging in confrontation and issue-resolution to remove blockages in ourselves and others to produce lasting change in the relationship and in performance. Leaders are there to inspire, coax, support and cajole others to improve performance for the common good of the organization or cause.

Leaders with Interpersonal Intelligence are able to improve both their own and others' performance by confronting difficult issues and challenging each one of us to change our attitudes and behaviors for the better. As someone who wants to make an impact in your life, I am assuming this will require you to become a leader, therefore you need this ability to help transform the lives of others. Let's move on to our second core skill.

Mental Toughness and Self-Confidence

being resilient, assertive, turning stress into success and significance

I have mentioned a number of times the importance of having clarity of thinking when under pressure. For me, this is Mental Toughness. We have already explored at some length the Cycle of Experiential Development and Comfort Zones, so I won't elaborate here. What I will comment on is the aspect of Mental Toughness and Self-Confidence as it applies turning stress into worthwhile activities and accomplishment. It is what one football manager in England coined as "bouncebackability".[19]

Recently I read a short article by Bob Gass in Word for Today[20] that stated, "Faith grows only in the soil of adversity! ... When young plants get too much rain, even a short drought can kill them. Why? Because it was too easy! During frequent rains, young plants didn't have to push their roots deeper into the soil in search of water so they didn't develop any strength. Now they have a weak, shallow root system and die quickly."

Faith and Mental Toughness go hand-in-hand. It means that when the going gets tough, the tough get going – not, 'go shopping,' as some would say! Jim Collins in his book "Good to Great"[21] describes the phenomenon of what takes organizations from mediocrity to greatness as being like the baby chick trying to get out of its egg shell rather than like a radical "change program" where change happens at a specific moment in time (as the media and so-called business analysts would lead us to believe). This is true of us in our personal transformation as well. We are not very likely to find instant success. It is much more likely we will struggle, have setbacks, feel disappointments, be misunderstood by family and friends, and yes even momentarily quit at some point. As I write this we are in the throes of unprecedented financial turmoil. Certainly things are as fragile and explosive economically as any time since the Great Depression of the last century.

If we cultivate our Mental Toughness and Self-Confidence by consistently moving outside of our egg shell Comfort Zone, as described by Jim Collins, on a frequent and consistent basis, we too will have the grit to rise above our own mediocrity and make an impact. We will explore in more detail how we can maintain clarity of thinking under pressure, and turn adversity into opportunity. We will develop our mental muscle and resilience to face the normal, sometimes negative and destructive downward pull that would keep us truly locked inside our shell.

Passion with Purpose

*having a burning desire attached to
a transformational cause*

If we are working on our Interpersonal Intelligence and skills with people, and developing our Mental Toughness and Self-Confidence, then where do we apply these core skills? Where do we get direction, focus and drive to help us to become a more fulfilled person? IMPACT, by definition, demands that *being* leads us to *doing* something. This we discover as we connect with our God-given Passion with Purpose. It is my firm conviction, backed up with faith and empirical truth, that we all have a purpose for living. When we discover what it is, and combine our Passion, drive and energy towards our Purpose, then such things as happiness, fulfillment, peace of mind and success all follow.

Laura Berman Fortgang, in her excellent book "Take Yourself To The Top"[22] defines having a Vision as a *compelling view* – one that pulls us on towards our destiny. Because our Passion with Purpose is bigger than us, it cannot be accomplished by ourselves without the help of other people and some "higher power." We are very likely, if not always, going to encounter obstacles, pain, hurt and suffering as we move towards our Passion with Purpose. Perhaps this explains why so few people really go for their Passion with Purpose, but instead settle for the easy life, going with the flow and living with unfulfilled dreams. Don't misunderstand what I am championing. Of course, there are times for us to "go with the flow", and seek peace, tranquility and an easy life. To my regret at times I have worked and strived well past the time I should have stopped and rested. But to dwell long term in this place can lead to atrophy.

Mel Gibson's cinema portrayal of "The Passion of Christ" was so poignant and graphic of the pain, shame, humiliation and sorrow felt by Christ as he approached his destiny. 'Passion' has as its root *suffering*, as well as the connotation of a *deep inner urge that is emotionally charged.* Why would we want a Passion with Purpose if it means all of this bother? The truth is without the passion, we fall short of living our best life. With the passion, we push through, as Bob Gass indicated, and as we discussed when explaining Mental Toughness. What a magnificent dilemma, to choose between the easy way, and living a passionate, purposeful life with the suffering and pain it may bring! In Chapter Nine, we explore this concept further, and help develop a strategy that unlocks your Passion with Purpose, and moves you towards both *being* the person you could be and *doing* what it is you really want to be doing.

Attitude Control

a habit of choices

You may recall from our earlier discussions that many personal development authors describe our greatest power as the power of choice we all have. I describe "attitude," our fourth core quality we need for our Impact Journey, as the pattern or habit of choices we make day after day based upon our beliefs about ourselves and our view of the world. Our attitude affects how we think, how we react to circumstances and how we behave towards others. Unless we choose to raise our attitude to our awareness level, it is the subconscious reaction we all take, our "mindset," or "frame of mind." It can be, of course, both constructive and destructive. It is described, depending upon our own attitude toward others, as positive or negative, good or bad. Usually, when people speak of someone having an 'attitude,' it is that they think the person with an *attitude* is being negative or destructive.

The fact is, as we delve deeper, we all have an attitude, and whether it is good or bad very often depends upon the impact it has on others, and our own reinforced behavior patterns. To be conscious we have an ability to choose our attitude can be a life-changing phenomenon! That's why we will devote a whole chapter on how to maintain an attitude that is positive and constructive towards our Passion with Purpose.

Communication

transmitting and receiving

If we have begun to more fully develop our Interpersonal Intelligence, Mental Toughness, Passion with Purpose and Attitude, then we have probably prepared ourselves to begin to communicate some of this to people we will need to accomplish our Impact Journey. When our Wilsher Group team is helping people to have an even greater impact in their lives and work, we discovered that there is a sequence. Before people are ready to talk with others, they benefit greatly from firstly understanding what they could become and have a clarity of Vision. Next step is to develop a Passion with Purpose.Finally they define specifically where they want to go and what steps to take to get there.

If we become competent at speaking to people, but are communicating the wrong things, we will only confuse, frustrate or at best produce cynicism. Ask anyone schooled in marketing, and they will state the package of publicity, marketing and promoting of our ideas will not bring us the desired results if we cannot first of all convince ourselves and others we have something worthwhile to say.

The other part of communicating, the receiving, is vital as well. Yet if we listen to people and attempt to take on board all of their ideas, frustrations, disappointments and emotional upsets, we only become confused and disappointed ourselves, and communicate to them there is no hope or way forward! It is vital we learn to communicate – to speak and listen to gain common understanding, embrace others' good ideas into our framework, appreciate what makes them tick and seek to find the win–win commitment that leads to success.

In Chapters Thirteen, Fourteen and Fifteen we will explore how we can become powerful communicators who can grasp the essence of what is going on within a meeting or gathering of a group of people or even one-to-one, and then take the appropriate action of listening or speaking that transforms the interaction into a mutually beneficial outcome. It is the difference between having people say, "That was some speech" to having them say, "Let's march"! It is what people with impact do all of the time.

Transformational Leadership

leading an individual or team towards a value-added,
win-win result, seeing the possibilities in every situation

An illustration from my own life – not that I understood at the time all of these principles of IMPACT! Somehow inside of me and my fellow cadets at the time, we fell into operating in an impact-full way that produced a sustained result that exemplifies Transformational Leadership.

During my time at the United States Air Force Academy, one of the most thrilling experiences for me was being the Cadet Squadron Commander of Seventh Squadron during our final year. The thrilling part for me was not simply because I was chosen out of 700 fellow classmates to head one of forty squadrons, but what happened to us as a squadron during that year and beyond.

Our squadron had a well-earned reputation for being terrible at athletics. When we became the cadet officers running the group of 100 plus cadets, this was unsatisfactory. Whereas we were one of the top ten or so squadrons in academics, we ranked at the bottom or near the bottom in intramural sports. In order to be classed as well-rounded cadets, we were required to become proficient at sixteen varied sports – from boxing and combative skills to squash and carry-over skills such as golf. Our Passion with Purpose, as I reflect upon it now, was that we wanted to replace that label of "non–athletes" with being admired for our achievements on the sports field. Perhaps some of my dissatisfaction with the way things were was I had always excelled in my growing up at both sports and academics. I saw they went hand-in-hand, and one fed the other. Therefore, I did not see we could either be good "brains" or good "jocks," but we could be both. First of all we had to focus upon balancing our sports achievements.

The opportunity we had was to identify the intramural, i.e., the competition between different squadrons and put together a winning formula that would mean we would be seen as one of the best at overall sporting prowess. The intramural program had seasons; an autumn season or schedule of sports, a winter schedule, and finally a spring schedule. Our first goal was to be the best in our Group (the Wing consisted of four Groups of ten squadrons each) in the autumn. The idea spread among my fellow cadet officers, and a plan was mobilized. We communicated this to the rest of 7th squadron, over half of whom had either been with other squadrons or were new to the Academy. The idea resonated with them, and a win-win desired result was born.

Not only did we achieve our short-term milestone of heading the Group when the tally was made at the end of the autumn schedule, we were number 1 out of 40 squadrons in the wing. We went on to win the Malanathy Trophy given to the outstanding squadron that year in Intramural Sports, and were honored at a parade prior to our graduation attended by all the invited dignitaries and guests. Having that banner at the top of the flagpole for the Seventh Squadron was a sense of common achievement where every member of the squadron played a part! (By the way, we did pretty well academically as well!)

The real impact and transformation, however, came afterwards. The cadets who took over the leadership of the 7th Squadron from us when my classmates and I entered active duty also set their sights at retaining the Trophy. They did. And so did the year following, and the year after that! What had originated in us as a unsatisfactory feeling about how things were, we used IMPACT! to develop a legacy. Firstly, we enaged our Interpersonal Intelligence to appreciate, adapt and connect to other people, then we were Mentally Tough on ourselves when things got tough (and they did!). Thirdly we had a Passion with Purpose and maintained a Positive Attitude for a sustained period. Finally we Communicated effectively through countless team talks and we became Transformation Leaders!

In Chapter Seventeen we shall explore how to do things in a transformational way and help you become the Transformational Leader your family, community, church, or organization require you to be. In Chapter Six we begin the journey of core skills development by looking at the 'I' in IMPACT!

IMPACT Creative Action Debrief Chapter FIVE

Do these before continuing to Chapter Six!

1. Complete what each of the IMPACT! letters represent in the spaces provided, with your own definition of each

I
M
P
A
C
T

2. Which of those attributes do you think and feel you have the most
of right now?

.

.

.

.

3. Which attribute(s) need the most work, and what would it mean to
you if you were even 15% more effective in that or those areas?

.

.

.

Six

The Stages of
Interpersonal Intelligence

⌒

Establishing Interpersonal Intelligence is a lifelong process and crucially it is a foundational core skill that is a prerequisite to earning the right to make an impact. Additionally, three stages of Interpersonal Intelligence are needed:

Stage One Interpersonal Intelligence

*Understand what it is you have to do in order to build
lasting relationships*

Stage Two Interpersonal Intelligence

*Fully engage in what others need so you can gain
co-operation when you need it from those with whom you
have built a strong relationship*

Stage Three Interpersonal Intelligence

*Work out ways to get both your needs, and their needs and
wants met, by exploring what we all have to do to change
our attitudes and behavior*

Stage One is crucial for *building relationships*. I vividly recall when I read Dale Carnegie's book, "How to Win Friends and Influence People",[23] the 'Eureka moment' I had that completely changed how I engaged with people. Mr. Carnegie related that before I can go about bossing other people to change various aspects of their behavior and attitudes, that first of all it starts with me! It is how I behave and think towards them, how I take the time to find ways of building bridges, engaging them in conversation and taking a genuine interest in them that lays the foundation for possibly getting them to work with me on something I want or need. What a foundational truth! Grasp this idea, if nothing else and you'll begin to see dramatic improvements in your Interpersonal Intelligence. We'll explore some guidelines and principles others have practiced to build lasting relationships.

Figure 6.1

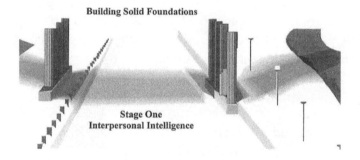

Stage Two, *gaining co-operation*, comes once we've built bridges and connected with the other person. Now we can begin to speak freely about what their wants and needs are, what ours are, and explore if there are ways of working and living that would bring about a happy solution for both. At this stage, *gaining co-operation*, we are hoping to find out where they are going, compare their journey with ours to look for similarities and synergies, then together work through options that will take us there until we reach agreement. Let's illustrate.

Supposing your new personal assistant wants to make a good impression, and in her eagerness to please all of the team in the office, some of the work you consider a priority is not getting done correctly or on time. You have to keep checking up on the work, and because you are not there for at least three days a week, some of your clients aren't getting the service you feel they need. You want satisfied clients. Your personal assistant wants to please everyone, so she, too, has a good motive and attitude, but on some occasions you are working to differing agendas. What could you do to correct the situation?

A. Tell her to give all of your work a priority, as, after all, she was primarily hired to act as your personal assistant, and to tell others their work will have to wait.

B. Tell her you are exasperated by having to check up on her work all the time to see if she's done it, and if she doesn't change, then you will have to consider other 'options'.

C. Ask your secretary how the job is progressing, and what she sees as some of the successes and frustrations, if any, at the moment. Praise her for the work she is doing that genuinely warrants praise, and especially for her attitude for wanting to get things right. Ask permission to make an observation, and when she agrees, tell her how you see things reference the conflict of priorities at times, how this makes you feel to have to check up on work, and your concern for keeping your clients satisfied. Ask her for her opinion as to what you together could do about the situation. Build upon her response, and then find a win-win-win solution – Win for her, win for you, win for the other parties who will be affected by the decisions and actions you agree.

Which choice would you make? It's a bit obvious, I know, but although c) goes much farther towards gaining immediate co-operation and keeps the relationship strong, it does take more time and thought. Some of us may be more focused upon a) or b) based upon our mood or attitude at the moment.

The essence of gaining co-operation is taking the time to find out what each others' wants and needs are, having a good enough relationship so we can explore options fully and express ourselves freely so that our feelings, fears, doubts and issues are aired.

Figure 6.2

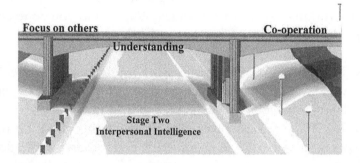

At Stage Three, helping those who are close to us at home and work to transform their own *attitudes* and *behavior*, we begin to address some deeper issues, where perhaps on the surface our interests are conflicting. Let's explore a hypothetical situation:

Your child is a loner. He keeps his thoughts to himself, has very few friendships and school reports suggest he is at risk for being bullied. On the surface, you are headed for conflict, and there seems little chance for resolution. To distinguish Stage 3 Interpersonal Intelligence from the previous two even further, let's suppose your relationship with your son is "dog eat dog." You are constantly yelling at him to "pick up your clothes, wash your hands before you come to the table, come to the meal the first time I call you, do your homework before watching TV," etc. If your relationship bridge is not yet built, then it is highly unlikely you'll be able to gain willing co-operation, and it will be almost impossible to see how you'll ever find a win–win solution to the permanent change of behavior you think is better. Let's explore each of these stages in more depth to see how to develop Interpersonal Intelligence.

Figure 6.3

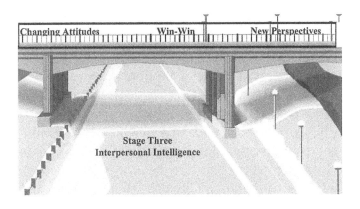

Changing Attitudes   Win-Win   New Perspectives

Stage Three
Interpersonal Intelligence

Stage One Interpersonal Intelligence

Build Strong Relationships First

Let's take first things first and begin to build strong and lasting relationships with people. It almost goes without saying, but in order to emphasize it once again, the first person to get to like and have a good relationship is with you. We have already looked in the previous chapters at the need to know yourself, and appreciate the unique person you are, in all of God's creation.

Assume you have an excellent relationship with 'me, myself and I,' and you can express your strengths, weaknesses, fears and doubts and still like your own company. Now let's focus on other people. First of all, check your own attitude and be honest – do you really and genuinely like other people? Do you truly want to build strong relationships with others, or are you happy to have only passing acquaintances and prefer to be alone? This part of the process is worth asking before you go on to finding ways of becoming Interpersonally Intelligent. Perhaps you have been so damaged and hurt in previous relationships, it is an incredible struggle to see how you can "open up" yourself to others again. If this is so, then I suggest you get some help from professional counselors and therapists that are trained to help you gain clarity and healing.

Another possibility is that your preferences or bias may indicate you do not want to be "everyone's friend", and you need a lot of space just for yourself. This is known amongst psychologists as our Behavior Preferences. Although we are all different, for purposes of finding ways of adapting and connecting with each other, we perceive people whose patterns of behavior are similar, so we can predict how they will respond to us if we behave towards them in certain ways. In fact, we all play amateur "psychologists" with other people subconsciously, so that we can learn to deal with people. Unfortunately, since it is a subconscious thing, sometimes our responses are not successful, and we get the punch in the nose we were not expecting. Most of what we learn through life is by trial and error, and most of it is by error! We end up with a number of individuals saying, "I just don't know what it takes to please so-and-so. I guess we'll just have to keep our distance."

On the other hand, we sometimes find with certain people, we just seem to "click." We immediately find we connect to their wave length, can find ourselves finishing their sentences (mentally, at least), laugh at the same kinds of things, and have common approaches to most things. Why the difference? Is it just true that forming relationships is "hit-and-miss", and there is no need to try to get along with certain people? Are there things we can say and do that might make it possible to work well even with people it seems we find rub us the wrong way most of the time?

There is good news. Psychologists have observed, (many observations go back thousands of years) that it helps if we see people expressing their preferences towards a variety of things in patterns.[24] The earlier work on these concepts indicated that there seem to be four predominant patterns that refer to:

·   The degree of dominance or lack of it we portray/prefer
·   The degree of influence or lack of it we prefer
·   The degree of security or lack of it we seek
·   The degree of compliance or lack of it we like in our lives

Carl Jung, a well known psychologist in the 20th century spoke of three spectra that he observed seem to cover most human behavior. He called these Psychological Types:

· The introvert – extravert dimension
· The thinking – feeling dimension
· The intuitive – sensing dimension[25]

We all, it seems, behave towards situations in observable ways which can be predicted based upon the range across the introvert – extravert, thinking – feeling, and intuitive – sensing dimensions in which we feel most comfortable. It is a "behavioral comfort zone" for want of a better description. This zone can change, just as we have seen in our other approaches to habits and skills development, depending upon our attitudes, circumstances, experiences, successes, failures, etc.

The most exciting part of this discovery for me, and for many other people, is once we see what our "natural" preferences are we can begin to understand ourselves better. We then can determine why we feel the way we do about certain people and situations, and make adjustments. We can also begin to see how others approach similar situations differently, and why. Therefore we can have room for us to explore our own preferences in light of others, and find ways of tolerating, valuing, adapting and connecting.

One of the best tools we have found to use with our clients and work colleagues is the Discovery Insights Report developed by Andrew Lothian Sr. and Jr. and their organization, Insights. They have developed a series of reports based upon the latest thinking on behavior preferences using Jungian Typology. Essentially, they describe our preferences in behavior "Colour (sic) Energies." They are the Cool Blue, Earth Green, Sunshine Yellow and Fiery Red energies. Whilst it is true that almost all of us display and can use any of these energies at times, most of us have a strong preference to at least two, and have one energy we portray most often to others especially when under pressure. Your "profile" of how you display these energies, both in response to others and also subconsciously can be quite varied from person to person. If you think you could benefit from further delving into this for yourself and other people in your life, then visit The Wilsher Group website on **www.wilsher-group.com**. There you'll find the valuable tools to really begin to understand yourself and how you interact with others.

Jesus, my main mentor and guide, once said, "Love your neighbor as yourself."[26] This was the second of His two favorite commandments. What strikes me about this statement is unless we love *ourselves*, we will really struggle with loving others. It is hard to give, be kind, take thought of and care about others if our tank is on empty. This has taken a long time for me to appreciate and understand, as one of my misconceived views of life was that, "If I just look out for other peoples' needs all of the time, then I won't have to worry about my own." That philosophy may work for some, but it left me on 'empty' on many an occasion. Today, as I approach my 64th birthday, I know for me to be at my best I need to look after my needs and interests as well, and only then can I truly serve and help others. I have people, including my wife, Heidi, who hold me accountable for this, insisting I take breaks and warn me when I have too much packed into my schedule. Another aspect of the Golden Rule is interesting to me. Jesus did not say "Treat others like you want to be treated." Love them, but treat them the way *they* want to be treated. Again, this reinforces my point of adapting our style momentarily to get in step with them.

Visit The Wilsher Group website on www.wilsher-group.com. If you want to explore this in more depth and find out how releasing it can be to begin to understand yourselves through this report, then click on to the provided link on the website mentioned. There is a charge for this service, but the 20-plus page report is well worth the investment.

Become Interdependent

We can all use our powers of observation to detect these patterns, and to use this information to adapt and connect even better. It takes a mature approach, and even children can learn how to spot these patterns. Stephen R. Covey describes this stage of maturity in our emotional development as the Interdependent stage. We have developed our Independence, so we can live with who we are, and now we can confidently begin to engage others who will help us through the mutually transformational Interdependent stage.[27]

Simon Wilsher and I like to think of it as a dance. If we are concentrating too hard on how we're feeling, are being mechanistic in our rhythm, what steps to take, etc., then we are operating independently. We will revisit this again when we discuss the 'Levels of Listening.' We may be able to get through the dance, but won't win any "Dancing With The Stars" awards. When we mature to the point that we can take our eyes, ears and minds off of what *we* are doing, and focus mainly upon the music, and the other person, getting into rhythm with both the music and the other person, only then can we dance. As Simon says, "Sometimes the best way to lead the dance is to move backwards. We need to be so in touch with the whole scene and what the other person is thinking and feeling we can allow things to not go our way to get the best results in the long term."

Here is an illustration: What I want – I want to go to the movies or theater on Friday evening. We haven't been for a while, I like the social side of the 'special occasion', and the contact with crowds of people in keeping with my preferred way of behaving. What my partner wants – an evening at home, nice meal by candlelight followed by relaxing with a good movie on TV. If I make the decision and act independently, I will force my partner to not get her way and we go out to the theater. I may 'win' this inning but 'lose' the longer game. She sulks all night, does not enjoy the theater, complains about the traffic, the seats, etc. and is less than amorous all weekend. If I had led the "dance" by going backwards a little, my partner may have gotten her way by remaining at home for the evening and then her demeanor would have been very pleasant and co-operative the rest of the weekend. This seems common sense, and yet how often do we consider the whole scene or bigger picture?

What is meant by being focused on the whole scene and with the other person? I try to recall this phrase as a reminder of focus:

"Wherever You Are, Be There!"

Perhaps you can picture times in you own life where you had many things on your mind – your job, the partner, kids, shopping, etc., and also trying to carry on a meaningful conversation with someone. You find your mind wandering here and there, floating and flitting along with no real pattern, yet not fully focusing on anything. I call it having a 'butterfly brain'. Or perhaps you have been on the receiving end of this with someone you know or love, when you have been trying to have a deep, meaningful discussion with them only to notice that the person although physically there is mentally somewhere else? What messages does that signal to you? One of the key ingredients of Interpersonal Intelligence to me is this ability to focus, to "be there" for that other person.

Very often when I am engaged with delegates on the IMPACT! Program or clients on important, transformational discussions, I am aware of the multidimensional communication and learning that is going on. The person I am working with in open discussion in front of the group is learning from how I am coaching them. Other delegates are learning from either how I am coaching the person, or from the experiences the person is sharing with all of us, or perhaps from both my coaching and the person's experiences. This requires refined focus – being present, giving my undivided attention to those people in the room. If I am also trying to solve the crisis back at the office and what to have for dinner, I will miss so much from what is being communicated. We will deal more with this in the later chapters on communication. For now, if we want to develop our Interpersonal Intelligence, *focus*! This remarkable experience of multilevel learning by developing people's ability to truly focus on what the people in the room are saying and doing has a synergistic affect of accelerating their learning. It is like creating 'in-the-zone' moments which athletes and sports people say help them perform at high performance levels.

We will discover so much with our ears and our eyes, with taking in the atmosphere and environment when with other people that we will instinctively begin to understand and connect with where people are, because we will "*be there*" with them, using our whole being. We will be able to find out what they want and need. We will recognize which of the patterns of behavior they seem to be displaying.

We will see through their body language and choice of words what is really on their minds and hearts. Even with all of this, we may still require the best way of all to find out what other people want and need. That is to *ask*! Yes, there is no law so far as I know against asking people what they want and need.

Sometimes, however, if the relationship is not built strongly enough yet, or they find handling straight questions too intrusive, then there are subtle ways to discover these things. We have discovered key "trigger questions" that help with the process, and these can be applied in many situations both at work and home. They are called, "Innerview Questions." That's right, the misspell is intentional. Although perfectly acceptable as Interviewing Questions for recruiting and job placements, they are also very useful in every-day life for finding out about what makes other people do the things they do. Here are a few of the questions.

Inner-View Questions

- What is the most challenging aspect of your job?
- What do you admire most about the people you work with?
- What do you do for fun/recreation?
- As you think back over your life there are probably many high spots. What is one particular achievement (not necessarily in business) of which you are particularly proud?
- Why do you feel that way?
- How were you able to do that?
- If a younger person came to you for advice before going out in to the world, what advice or philosophy would you give them?

Once you have asked the questions, and feel you can now fairly well indicate what it is the other person wants and needs, then make the time to feed it back to them, asking them to correct any misunderstandings you may have. Although many people I have coached expressed concerns about what the other person may say if they get it wrong, when I have made an attempt to truly understand the other person's wants and needs and genuinely try to relate back what I have heard, without reservation, even if I have failed miserably, people seem very pleased I have made the attempt. The worst thing that will happen if you use this approach is you will have strengthened your relationship with them. At best, you will be a long way towards gaining willing co-operation.

On the IMPACT! Program we assign a number of take-away exercises, and experiments that emphasize improving Interpersonal Intelligence, skills and awareness. When we first ask our clients to think of a situation in their lives where relationships could be improved, invariably the client focuses on a situation where they want the other person to change or co-operate. We then ask them to take a step back and simply work on the relationship building aspect. Once the relationship is improved they are much more likely to gain willing support and 'scratch my back because I scratch yours' attitude.

Remove Filters

On some occasions, as we are listening to others with our whole being, we may find their view of the world and the way they express themselves is so different from our normal approach, that we'll find our own filters and biases distorting what is really being communicated. Interpersonal Intelligence requires we recognize when we are filtering and we then need to adjust in order to get in step with the other person.

It helps if we have some tools like the Discovery Insights Report we discussed earlier. Therefore we are prepared for the ways other people's main color energies are displaying themselves. Even without this tool, if we have listened wholeheartedly, we can begin to use their words and type of language to communicate with them. Speak their language. Try to get in step with them, even mirroring their body language to display how much you want to see things from their point of view. We'll discuss this more in the communication section of the book. Another helpful technique is trying to imagine what it is they are describing. I create a word picture of them in their situation, saying and doing the things they are describing. Most importantly, for me, anyway, is to feel the emotion I imagine they would be feeling in that circumstance, even if the client may not be verbalizing those things.

Stage Two Interpersonal Intelligence

Gaining Co-Operation

"People don't buy facts and features. They buy benefits." Every book on selling and every seminar or workshop I have attended in almost 35 years of working in the people industry has drummed home this message. Although we aren't strictly speaking trying to "sell" anything to those with whom we would like co-operation, in a way we are trying to persuade them to do something that will aid us as well as themselves. So in fact we are "selling" them to "buy" our reasons for wanting their co-operation. What is meant by 'facts and features and benefits'?

Facts are those elements of our situation that will stand the scrutiny of investigation as being true. The day I am writing this is a Friday. Chances are you will believe this as true, and should you wish to check, you could ask others to verify its validity.

A 'feature' is something about the fact which highlights its usefulness, value, significance, etc. One of the 'features' of this Friday is the weather is cool and breezy. The feature describes what sort of day it is that might set it apart to the uninformed.

A 'benefit' is what it is about the fact and/or feature which is likely to interest the person whom you wish to "buy" the information you are stating. Back to the cool, breezy Friday, for instance, a benefit might be "so you can fly that new kite you just bought." Now it is only a worthwhile benefit to express if I were aware that the person in question was sincerely interested in flying his or her kite!

If we express our facts, features and benefits to get the help and co-operation from the other person, we greatly enhance the likelihood that they will delightedly help. Structuring how we say things in ways that get co-operation will be discussed further in the communication section.

The irony is, even without trying, if we have built a strong relationship and really understood the other person's needs and wants, and where they are coming from, we will find when we ask for help they will be very pleased to offer their assistance. The co-operation seems to be a reward for the way you treated them, and the desire they have to treat you in the same manner. It is almost a miracle the way it works.

The guidelines published at the end of this chapter will serve as an aide de memoire to help us choose an appropriate approach to building the strong relationship we desire with others, and then to go on to gain their willing and whole hearted co-operation. Why not try to develop your own list of tried-and-tested guidelines?

Stage Three Interpersonal Intelligence

Helping to Change Attitudes and Behaviors

Once we have gained people's willing and enthusiastic co-operation, we may find that we have already moved on to Stage Three – we are both getting our wants and needs met; our relationship continues to grow stronger, and we are being transformed as people. We may not need or even desire to consciously develop things differently. There may be times when we say to ourselves, "We owe it to this person to address certain issues that are keeping them and ourselves from being all we could be." How many of us know of someone who has a particular habit or way of approaching their world that seems to lead to self –destruction?

I remember early on when I was engaged by a client to help in a situation. Let's call him Chris. Chris had been employed previously as a service manager in the car industry. As we interviewed him for possible training and personal development, he voiced how frustrated he was with his boss, he was overworked and unappreciated, had recently married and wanted to spend time with his wife instead of sorting out people's broken-down cars in a highly competitive environment. We identified one or two areas we thought we could help, and then Chris decided he would attend a personal development program which he found very beneficial. As a result, he began to develop his confidence and self esteem. In fact, he concluded that he had outgrown the role and felt it was time to move on. He quickly found a new job with increased responsibility and challenging new work in a different industry and even better working hours at first. Then one day Chris called me in, and said, "Geo, I am just not happy. My boss just doesn't understand me, or appreciate me. Although it is a good job, I am working way too many hours, and hardly get to see Jean (his wife) and our new son Jonathan. I think I might have to find a new job. Can you help?"

Right away, as you can see from what Chris had said, I saw a deeper problem than simply the one that he had stated. So before I jumped in to offer Chris still more personal development of his management skills, I asked very directly, "Chris, what is different this time?" "What do you mean," he asked? "This sounds like a broken record (back in the days of things like tapes and vinyl records). It seems you said the same things to me about three years ago when we first met. The job is different, the boss is different, yet we are hearing the same things." The penny dropped for Chris. He saw that his job or the boss was not at fault, and that to keep running from job to job was not the answer, something else had to change. He needed to transform himself, not his job.

Happily, Chris decided that was the case. This was well over ten years ago, and to my knowledge he is still with the same company, now as a main board director. He learned to modify his behavior and attitudes, to stand up to his boss in a constructive way, and learn when to say "no" to extra hours that were degrading his home and family balance. So in the end, Chris, Jean and Jonathan as well as Chris's boss, all ended up with a Win. This is the desired result of Stage Three Interpersonal Intelligence. We do not stop at a Win –Lose result – where we win and others lose, nor settle for a Lose–Win result – where we lose and the other person wins. We don't even settle for a Win–Win result where both of us win. We look outside of ourselves to the bigger picture and look at all the relationships that are affected by the current situation and find a Win–Win–Win result. We feel we win, the other person directly involved feel they win, and others impacted by this relationship also feel they have won.

Test Yourself on Interpersonal Intelligence

How can we operate consistently at Stage Three in our relationships? For example, recall the story of the child who was in danger of being bullied at school? Isolation and poor interaction with classmates at the beginning of our school experiences can lead to real problems in later years. Therefore, we have to help that child to address this before it becomes a developmental issue. Take a moment to consider what you would do. Write it down somewhere, or discuss it with someone. Then come back to this book. What did you decide?

1. Nag the child incessantly over her lack of interaction with others.
2. Ridicule her, especially in front of other people. (This will really make a huge withdrawal from the "relationship bank" you have built up with the child).
3. Become a policeman to her, and acknowledge every time you see her to point out the error of her behavior, restating for the umpteenth time why it is bad for her to continue with this behavior. "Friends will laugh at you," "How can you possibly do well in school or at sports if you stay on your own all the time?"
4. Try something else?

In 'Don't Shoot the Dog!: The New Art of Teaching and Training,' by Karen Pryor[28] she states that during her time as a coach of people, she noticed there were at least eight ways of helping someone (or some animal, for that matter) to change her or his behavior. The title of the book comes from her explanation and example of getting the neighbor's dog to stop barking late at night. Each of her example methods of getting the dog to quit barking had consequences that might keep it from being a Stage Three solution. One of the methods was to shoot the dog! You can just imagine what that might do to friendly relationships with the neighbor. It is a great book to read, and I highly recommend it to anyone who wants to take their *Interpersonal Intelligence* on to a new stage. The person who recommended it to me, Kurt, attributed the book to transforming his relationship with his daughter. Thanks, Kurt, the book was a real blessing!

More Ways to Stage Three Interpersonal Intelligence

A sure-fire way to develop your Interpersonal Intelligence is to *catch the person displaying the right behavior*, and then feeding this back to them in a way which recognizes and rewards the progress they are making towards modifying the behavior. Back to the withdrawn child if we are to catch her when she was engaging actively with others, and reinforcing how well she is doing, congratulating her for her good choices, we will begin to see she will make this choice more and more often. She might even ask us for help in modifying the behavior.

Here is another – before we try to change that other person's attitude, first of all look at our own attitude towards them, and see if we can change that! When our family was younger, one of the things that used to get "right up my nose" as the English say, was when the rest of the family would leave the cap off of the toothpaste, and it always seemed that when I came to brush my teeth, there was this hard, dry lump of paste that plugged up the opening in the toothpaste and tasted awful! Time and again, being the first to arise every morning I would start the day with an attitude towards the boys and Heidi that went something like this: "Why is it that I cannot get those boys and my wife to put the top on the toothpaste? Time and time again I have told them how annoying it is, and yet, here it is again. They just don't seem to care. How can I exert my leadership as head of the house if they won't even do this little thing? I work my guts out to ensure they have plenty to eat, a warm place to live and this is the thanks I get. What else is going to go wrong today?"

Sound familiar? When I heard from Skip Ross[29] how damaging this negative attitude was, and saw how ineffective I had been at changing the situation, I decided to first of all change my own attitude about it. I began to laugh at myself as I approached the early morning tooth brushing, and say to myself, "I am comfortable with this. It is not a big thing, so I can happily live with it." Then I'd place the top back on once I had finished. My memory is a bit hazy on this, but I believe it was only a matter of a couple of weeks, I began to notice that the top mysteriously was put back on the toothpaste in the mornings! Either that, or it didn't seem to matter anymore! One way or the other, once I had changed my attitude, the "problem" with my family's attitude towards tops and toothpaste completely disappeared. Yes, you too, when adopting this approach to the small things that tend to set us off may find the other person's attitude miraculously transforms itself without you even raising the matter with them.

Before we move into developing our Mental Toughness and Self-Confidence, try the debrief exercises which will build strengthening foundations for your confidence and sharpen your impact.

IMPACT CREATIVE ACTION DEBRIEF CHAPTER SIX

Complete these before continuing to Chapter Seven!

1. Describe in your own words the different stages of Interpersonal Intelligence:

·   Stage One

·   Stage Two

·   Stage Three

2. What are three behavior preferences you like the most about you? Write them down and ask someone who really knows and cares about your success if they agree.

3. Think of a person you would be interested in developing an even better relationship with, and write her or his name here:

- What is the benefit to you if this relationship gets better? How about for them? How will she or he benefit?

4. Select from the Guidelines listed below for Building Effective Relationships the one you will put into practice as an experiment to see if it works, and write down your plan of action here:

STAGE ONE – GUIDELINES FOR BUILDING EFFECTIVE RELATIONSHIPS

- When asking 'How are you?', stop, listen and remember
- Smile when you meet or speak and enjoy yourself as much as you can
- Listen openly and intently
- Go out of your way for others – without hidden motives (go the extra mile)
- Bring good news, not always bad news or negative thoughts about other people
- Show respect for who they are, not just what they do
- Remember, and use people's names and other details about them
- Recognize and comment on people's successes or achievements

5. Select from the Guidelines listed below for Gaining Greater Co-operation the one you will put into practice as an experiment to see if it works, and write down your plan of action here:

STAGE TWO – GUIDELINES FOR GAINING GREATER CO-OPERATION

- Before seeking co-operation let's be honest with ourselves about our motives, and clear about desired results
- Respect everyone's right to an opinion even if we disagree
- Establish positive co-operation to date and areas where we think it could be improved
- If we have been found wanting in the past, admit it
- Let the other person save face if they have been wrong
- Be hard on the problem but soft on the person
- Ensure solutions go as far as they can to meet the needs and desires of the other person as well as your own
- Work together to find solutions, helping the other person to come up with ideas
- Avoid the argument stage of discussion but persevere in solving the problem
- Agree indicators of desired performance and when to review progress

6. Select from the Guidelines listed below for Influencing People's Attitudes the one you will put into practice as an experiment to see if it works, and write down your plan of action here:

STAGE THREE - GUIDELINES FOR INFLUENCING PEOPLE'S ATTITUDE

- Be thankful there are people who think differently – it makes life's tapestry far more colorful
- Accept that there may be legitimate reasons for their attitude
- Ask yourself how you would feel if you were in their position
- Identify the negative consequences of their attitude
- Help them see the effect they have on other people, especially those whose co-operation they need

- Help them find alternatives which may be more worthwhile
- Encourage them every time you see improvement
- Show understanding if you can – if you don't understand – ask!
- Be soft on people, hard on problems
- Finally, consider if your response to their attitude says more about you than it does about them

Seven

Developing Mental Toughness

O n our Nebraska, USA ranch in my youth I remember watching my father make repairs to our machinery that was needed to run a thriving agro-business. We had tractors, mowers, rakes, plows, hydraulic lifting machines, operating 'theaters' for capturing our cattle and then vaccinating, branding and loading onto trucks used for transporting to market. Because of the rough-and-tumble handling of the equipment from me and my brothers, from the sheer force of thousands of pounds of lively beef, things got damaged frequently.

We lived quite a distance from repair centers, and so invariably during our busy days, Dad would have to devote a great deal of his time repairing machinery. One of the most fascinating machines for me to watch was the welder. This electric or sometimes propane gas powered piece of equipment could take heavily damaged and broken pieces of metal and through hammering, heating, and still more hammering, make the metal stronger than it was before it was damaged. I asked, "Why do you beat the weld, Dad?" "To make the weld stronger, my son. The best way to strengthen the adherence of the new metal with the old is to beat it." There is a universal principle in those words. Whether it is metal or humans, we find we strengthen our character, and develop Mental Toughness through the trials, struggles and anguish of life.

*The "bad things" don't toughen us, but the way
we respond to them does!*

History is full of people who had the "X Factor" of a charismatic personality, but this factor did not make them a success. Quite the contrary. Think of Adolph Hitler. He was a great motivator with a powerful Vision that captivated many. Yet he had character flaws that led a nation to ruin, and almost destroyed Europe if not the World. On the business front, many of us are old enough to remember Robert Maxwell. Again, a very powerful and gifted entrepreneur, yet his flaws of character led to corruption, deception and finally to him apparently committing suicide because his "house of cards" crumbled before his eyes.

In one of the various circular emails I often get forwarded to me by my brother-in-law Robert was a test which asked a series of questions like, "Who won the Davis Cup three years ago?", or "Who won the best supporting actress in last year's Oscars?" Of course very few of us could answer these without some help unless we were particular fans of tennis or the movie set. Then the email asked a couple of other questions, like, "Name two of the teachers whom you really admired in school." Chances are we can all remember these. Why? The people who really impacted our lives were not necessarily the "personality" types, or celebrities, or even the most gifted. The people who mattered most to us and made a real difference were people of character, who took an interest in us, and who taught us through their example as much as through their words and works.

Character is what is developed through tests and time. I have personally been more inspired by hearing how ordinary people have coped with drugs and alcohol abuse than by the rich and famous who have achieved stardom. Stephen R. Covey captured it best for me when he stated in his "Seven Habits of Highly Effective People" that it is the *private victories* we have when no one is looking or even cares that *lead to the public successes*.[30] It is the recovering alcoholic who goes one more day without yielding to his or her craving which then leads to a generous, giving, loving member of society, or the abused child who uses his experiences to become an excellent parent that impresses.

Private Victories

One of the best places to start developing our Mental Toughness is through *private victories*. As discussed earlier, we begin the process of developing our character that makes an impact by first of all understanding and then changing our *defining beliefs* about ourselves and our world. For instance, let's say we have a defining belief about ourselves that "people don't like me because I am ugly." We will then find ourselves reinforcing this message by being overly sensitive to how people treat us. If anyone ignores us, or says some harsh words about us, or we see people talking and looking at us, we will automatically assume it is because they do not like us and are talking about how ugly we are. We will filter what we see and hear in the light of our *defining beliefs*.

When we look in the mirror we will see an ugly person people don't like. This will discourage us from smiling or looking at people in the eye. This shyness or withdrawal will likely be interpreted by others as if we do not like them or want to engage with them. Subsequently, they will turn away, ignore or reject us. This reinforces our defining belief, and so the message we send our brain is, "See there, it's true. I am ugly and therefore people do not like me." We can substitute "ugly" for fat, dumb, poor speaker, thin, bald, poor tennis player, etc.

The tragedy is the defining belief is simply not true. No matter what physical trait or lack of a certain skill or aptitude we now possess, we can overcome and sometimes even use this to develop a positive defining belief about ourselves which will yield public successes. The good news about defining beliefs is they can change. We can begin to change these beliefs by planting new seeds of thought into our minds when we encounter circumstances that could lead to our reinforcing of those limiting defining beliefs.

Figure 7.1

My self-image can at times be very poor. I get so intent on pleasing others that I have finely tuned my preceptors to notice those times when people were not always accepting of me. My imagination runs wild, and I see in every situation a reinforcement of "This person does not like me or what I think and do." It's better now, and here was one of the things that helped. Heidi and I had just left the security of the United States Air Force. We had little money, and hardly any business sense. We were living in a foreign country, viewed as 'outsiders,' and were trying to scratch a living through a business that required us to try to sell our products and services in a way that at the time was unconventional. We were inviting rejection and failure every day! You can imagine what this was doing to my self-image.

My loving wife saw the impact this was having upon me, and how it was making me become less and less active, more inclined to staying at home and busying myself with unproductive things, like counting the stock. She had heard on a tape or read in a book the power of the mind, and how we can change how we behave by changing our attitudes of mind. So she decided to do something about it. She bought a mirror, and took it to someone who etched "Yes, Geo, you are Terrific!" on the mirror. She then replaced the mirror in the bathroom where I shaved every morning with the "You are Terrific" mirror. Every day, I was forced to look into the mirror and have the message reinforced. Despite the rejection and failures we faced every day, I was, in fact still a good person, and at least *she* thought I was terrific! Wow, did this ever do me good! I was much more motivated to do the necessary things that were uncomfortable, and slowly over time I began to change the way I saw myself. Start to see yourself in a different light, and so will other people.

Keep Promises

How else can we begin to discipline our mind and develop that toughness? A very successful way for me has been to *keep promises* – first of all to myself, and then the promises I make to other people. If we say we are going to get up at 7.00 a.m. and exercise for thirty minutes before we go to work, then do it! If we tell our family we are going to be home by 6.00 p.m., then do it! If we begin to see ourselves as people who do deliver on the promises we make to ourselves and others, it will change our defining beliefs about our reliability, our effectiveness and our ability to do whatever it takes to keep the promises. It will help keep us from setting ourselves unrealistic goals, and from making outlandish statements that lead to disappointments for ourselves and others. This will then reinforce the message, "I am a person who can be trusted, and am therefore trustworthy." What a great start on building a character that will lead to public successes!

Skip Ross taught me a great lesson in Mental Toughness. Every time someone would say to him something negative or unproductive about "the way things were," he'd ask them, "Is that the way you want it?" "Of course not!" they would reply. "*Then why say it?*" he'd ask. It is called "Taking thoughts captive." We devote most of our time talking to ourselves. Our minds do not know the difference between the real experiences we have in life from the imagined ones we plant into our brain through our own thoughts. Therefore, if we feed our minds negative thoughts, we have "planted" some negatives into our defining beliefs. If we say to ourselves, "everything we eat turns to fat," then that tells our mind to ensure we eat things that will produce fat, and some people even claim it takes the good food we eat and turn it into the fat we say we "believe is our lot." So this leads to another way we can begin to develop Mental Toughness. Take control of our thoughts, and do not feed our negative defining beliefs. Change the words we say to ourselves about our perceptions of life. Skip calls this the Principle of Exclusion:

The Principle of Exclusion

Get rid of what you don't want so you can make room for what you do![31]

During my bewildering introduction to the world of computerization forty years ago, I remember as if it were yesterday the expression, "Garbage in, Garbage out," or 'GIGO' as an abbreviation. Our Computer 101 instructor was sharing an important truth about computer programming, which we were desperately trying to understand and learn. Although I never came close to mastering computer programming, the expression, "Garbage in, Garbage out" has proven a useful principle for life. If we allow our minds to be filled with garbage, then is it any wonder that what we produce as thoughts and actions later on is garbage as well?

As we have mentioned before, our minds are a remarkable piece of kit, yet they are for the most part, the product of what they have been fed through our experiences. This bank of ideas, thoughts, experiences and perceptions in our subconscious then feeds our conscious mind when we make demands of it to respond to a now experience we are having. If all our subconscious has to draw upon is garbage, then it is highly likely what we get out when we retrieve some information is garbage as well.

As an illustration – let's suppose we are asked to give a short presentation at a gathering of important people in the community. They want to hear our views on how we think the community should respond to the changes in the environment. We have strong views about this, and so impetuously we agree to give the presentation, which is a few weeks away. Then it hits us – we don't like giving presentations! In fact our experience bank of successful experiences of standing in front of groups of people and sharing our opinions has been less than 0! We have *never* had a positive experience, even back in school we were ridiculed by teachers and fellow students alike regarding our public utterances. This memory of *garbage in* now replays in our mind over and over again through the next few weeks, so when it comes time to give the talk we suddenly become so ill we call and send our apologies! This type of experience of reinforcing our *garbage in* thinking occurs over and over again in all areas of our lives, and sets us up to fail!

The good news is, we have a great deal of control over what we allow to go in, and can from this moment on begin to control our thoughts by replacing the garbage with good, healthy input! Where do we get this good input? It is abundant once we begin to look for it. I began in the Bible, when I read what God really thought of me (and everyone else as well). He says I am created in His image, to fulfill a good work.[32] I also watch what I say to myself – Yes, even my own thought life will create video images and PDF files in my brain. If these can be constructive, creative messages, then I am much more likely to be able to draw from them in a healthy way when my conscious mind instructs my retrieval system to pull out that file. Some authors and psychologists recommend "Anchor words and memory triggers" as techniques we can use as we choose to get us into the right frame of mind to deal with the moment of truth we are facing. It is a form of *"brainwashing on purpose."* The advantage is, we are aware of what we are allowing to go in to our minds.

This is very unlike the prisoner of war being relentlessly bombarded and hoodwinked into believing any sort of garbage the interrogator wishes to impart into our minds, and therefore get us to say or do whatever, including disavowing our own belief system. We can use "positive-choice brainwashing" to help us respond so much better to moments of truth, and thereby become the tough minded people we want to become.

Respond, Don't React

One of the most positive messages we can send our subconscious is thankfulness in times of duress and trials of our character. Philosophers and sages throughout our recorded history have generally all agreed circumstances, especially the ones that challenge and test us, do not make or break us as much as they *reveal us* – who we really are.

If we can "accept both victory and defeat, and treat both of these impostors the same"[33] and be thankful instead of resentful when "bad" things happen to us or those we love, we will form a habit of *responding instead of reacting*. I have heard in medical terms, when we *react* to our medicine which is intended to help us, the doctors will change their remedy, and try something else, as our bodies are *reacting* negatively to the potions designed to help us recover. However, when the recommended cure is given us and our bodies *respond*, it means the medicine is working, and we can look forward to a quick recovery. This analogy, then, as it applies to how we react to things or *respond* is very similar. Instead of quickly *reacting* in a spur of the moment way when faced with adversity, we need to *respond* by processing the information, and choose to *look for the good* in the situation.

Authors of "The Oz Principle" recommend remaining "Above the Line" rather than go "Below the Line."[34] In other words, be thankful, not resentful. This will help us spot the opportunity not the depressive problem we are presented with. This frame of mind can become habit forming, and infectious. If we remain *responsive* rather than *reactive*, we stand a much better chance of attracting the right ideas and the right people to help us, rather than attracting the nay-sayers and depressive sorts who spell out doom and gloom.

Laughter is Good Medicine

John Merrill, Peter McWilliams and John Roger write in their book, "You Can't Afford the Luxury of a Negative Thought" about the importance of having a good sense of humor. It is vital if you are to maintain Mental Toughness and Self-Confidence.

> *"Some people think laughter is a 'waste of time'. It's a luxury, they say, a frivolity, something to be indulged in only every so often. Nothing could be further from the truth. Laughter is essential to our equilibrium, to our well being, to our aliveness. If we are not well, laughter helps us get well. If we are well, laughter helps us stay that way."*[35]

I trust you have found as you have read this book that I believe in humor – good, clean, laughing-at-life-and-at-yourself kind of humor. My brother Bob has provided much laughter in our home when we were growing up, and now when we meet, the laughter continues. Here is how he described what it felt like facing a threatening illness in his life a few years ago:

"Well, I felt very shocked. The words from the doctor were heart stopping. My blood pressure must have risen a few points and my palms began to sweat. The shock turned to disbelief, anger. confusion and me asking," Why me Lord?" What have I ever done to have one of these moments in my life. Then I thought................ok maybe one little thing or two I had done in my life might influence a minor problem for me and I may be a little guilty of a small sin and expect this awful thing to be occurring today... but CANCER!! S%?%, I was dead!!!! Yep it was all over for me....shut out the lights the party is over, baby. Goodbye world!!! My poor wife sitting in the doctor's office must have been horribly upset too. She didn't say much either. As we gathered our senses and wits about us we then began to converse with the doctor and attempt a plan to cure this situation we were in. You know what, we did." Today Bob and

Marlene are well and happy, and living cancer free. He was given a new lease of life, and no doubt his ability to laugh at himself and the situation helped.

Find a Role Model

Perhaps you can think of a role model who exudes Mental Toughness and Self-Confidence. There are thousands and millions of people who exhibit the character trait of Mental Toughness for literally every walk of life. One of the most amazing people I have read about who has reminded me of Mental Toughness is John Wesley.

John Wesley had a dream to see the limitations and destructiveness of people's ability to worship God during England's feudal system and state governed church eradicated and replaced with a much freer worship of God individually. He believed we all can talk to God and have a personal encounter. We do not need interpreters from highly educated clergymen and women to dictate to us how we should believe. So he dedicated his life to getting the Word out to everyone who would listen. He was renowned for delivering five or more sermons in a day, and riding his horse for hours before sunrise and after sunset in order to arrive at the next location. He could hold a crowd of ten thousand people spellbound, well before the invention of microphones, by booming his voice in outdoor amphitheatres all across England. As a result, many came to a new revelation of who God is for them personally. Truly he was a man who was both mentally tough and self-confident. Did he have critics? Very many. Was he opposed? Yes, severely, by some of the most renown theologians of his day. Did it stop him? Not in the slightest. His view of life transformed the way we worship God today, centuries later.

More recently I have been impacted by another person, whose Mental Toughness and Self-Confidence inspires me as I think of him every day. He is Rich DeVos. Richard DeVos and Jay van Andel, his business partner of many years, were the founders of one of the direct marketing industries' major success stories, Amway. Established over forty years ago, Amway is a multibillion dollar international organization of independent business owners who provide a vast array of products and services in a highly competitive retail market.

It all started for them with a dream that they, like many people worldwide, would want to be in business for themselves. Rich and Jay themselves grew up in mid America to Dutch-American parents. They were taught that in this world there is no such thing as something for nothing, and yet in America at the time, they were given the freedom to seize whatever opportunity they could see and make something of themselves. Having successfully created their own business, selling one product, they struck upon the idea of helping other people do the same, the "American Way."

Therefore, they started the Amway business. Did they face opposition? Sometimes from their own families. Did they get criticized? All of the time. Did things run smoothly? Not likely. In one of Rich's most famous speeches, "Four Winds" he recounts how he and Jay faced trial after trial when the "North Wind" would blow and how this affects a sailboat. He also mentions the danger of the "South Wind" lulling us to take it easy and watch the money roll in. Both can be devastating to a venture, or if wisely addressed, both can propel us on to success.

These memories of hearing Rich talk about his experiences thirty years from when I first heard them still spurs me on. Part of my Mental Toughness and Self-Confidence comes from this. Who do you know whose thoughts, words or reputation can act as a confidence-builder to you?

Ben Franklin's Thirteen Attributes

Benjamin Franklin, author, statesmen and inventor, one of the most amazing men of the 18th and early 19th centuries had a terrific way of forming Mental Toughness into his character. He first of all reflected upon thirteen attributes he wished to incorporate into his character and behavior. Things like, Temperance, Humility, Thankfulness, Self- Control, etc. He would then focus on simply one character trait a week – reflect upon his application of this quality daily, and be brutally honest as to his ability to use and develop it into his life, asking other people to comment as necessary. Then the next week, he would focus on another of his top thirteen qualities and so on until after thirteen weeks, he had covered all of the attributes. If he felt he had fully developed the attribute as a habit, he would then replace that quality with another. If he felt he was still not "naturally" living that quality, then he'd simply keep it on his top thirteen hit list and repeat, if necessary, four times a year!

Now that is Mental Toughness, for even the most diligent of us. Where can we find these qualities we should be working towards appropriating into our character? We could take some psychometric evaluation to highlight traits and weaknesses to develop. We could incorporate the "Fruits of the Spirit" in Galatians 5 of the Bible. We could ask friends and loved ones to point out character faults to embrace. For most of us, the best person to ask is ourselves. You no doubt know in your heart of heart areas you need to focus upon. They could already be strengths you wish to strengthen as well as weaknesses to eradicate. If you can't think of thirteen, then I have at least one for you to start with – *humility*!

What does this mental discipline do for us as we continually work on our character development? Amongst many things, I believe it *gets us into action* to do something positive with becoming who we are meant to be. This in itself starts to build our own Mental Toughness and Self-Confidence. Our self-esteem, the sense of worth and personal value we intrinsically have built within begins to soar. Give Ben Franklin's method a try – if not for the rest of your life, then how about thirteen weeks?

Read Books

You will never find me too far away from books. I love reading books. Not just any books, but books that tell of the fascinating adventures people have at living a good life. I enjoy biographies, "how to" books, autobiographies, articles of business successes and trials, studies of successful people's lives in overcoming the lemons, tragedies, setbacks and disappointments. One of the greatest features of Rich and Jay's success with Amway was their use of human success stories and recognition and celebration of even the smallest of successes in people's lives. The thing that impressed and motivated me the most to want to "be like them" was how people encountered, faced and overcame their own personal battles. I remember saying to myself at one time, "But gee, I don't have a story of having to overcome trials like that." Now I *do*!

Set Stretching Goals

I believe one of the best ways of developing Mental Toughness and Self-Confidence is to *set a personal goal to stretch our Comfort Zone daily*. By now you know all about the Comfort Zone, but as a brief reminder, the Comfort Zone is used to describe the area or areas of our life and existence where we feel "comfortable." Not ill at ease, but relaxed, chilled, and even lazy.

Each of us has a Comfort Zone for each area of our lives, at home, school, work, sport, etc. We need them to give us space to recharge our batteries, renew our energies, and devote time to reflection and renewal. Yet our Comfort Zones can become highly destructive and dangerous places if we find ourselves trapped inside, or every time something unfamiliar or unexpected happens to us we jump back inside. Our Comfort Zones can become our habitat of excuses that keep us from risking doing anything new or differently. We can become stale, boring, flabby, and stuck in a rut. I was listening to someone recently who called it the "Sin of Passivity, and described it as a form of rebellion.[36] Strong words, but true. What's the cure? *Stretch your Comfort Zone daily*. Set yourself a goal to spend some time every day outside or at least on the edge of your Comfort Zone. This helps us build a habit so that the zone does not become a *trap*. Perhaps it is to say hello to a stranger. Maybe devote fifteen minutes to reading a book about a subject you are interested in. Perhaps it is going to the gym, learning a new language, or any number of things that force us to break the mould of daily rut living.

Strive to Be Excellent

Most of the highly-confident people I know have developed a keen desire to excel at some competitive game, become highly skilled at a hobby or pastime, or develop an expertise in a language, culture or art. To excel at something, we will have to seek advice from the very best, apply consistent Cycle of Experiential Development to acquiring these new skills, and raise our awareness of what is possible. Without this constant application to strive towards excellence, I would never have been able to say I have been part of establishing a million+ dollar business, earn a six figure income, or play golf with a single figure handicap, playing the best golf of my life at age 63!

Four Levels of Mastery

From my understanding of how we become a *master* at what we do, I believe we have to move through four *levels of mastery*.

- First of all, we need to be able to discover the language of the skill or competency we want to acquire,
- then we need to be able to understand what a good job looks like, and how to correct our behavior so we can transform a bad job into a good job,
- next we need to be able to do a good job ourselves, and be aware we are doing a good job,
- then finally, practice doing a good job over and over again until we can spot even better ways of doing it, and begin to add to the language and process for achieving that skill or competency.

Let's illustrate with someone who wishes to drive a car (this is the common practice in England). The first step is to learn the language of a car driver. This entails being able to recognize a car, describe why a car is not a boat, know the difference between a brake and a clutch, be able to read road signs, memorize the "Highway Code", and so forth. Some of this language we will acquire naturally just by being around cars. But some of it we will consciously have to learn through study and being taught by a skilled driving instructor. If we don't know what "Mirror, Signal, Maneuver" means before we take our first hands-on lesson, we're in for a real shock!

Now we have begun to understand the language and process for "car-driving." We need to be able to recognize when someone is doing a "good job" of driving a car. We may have acquired part of this by osmosis, by riding and watching others drive. Most of us who do drive are painfully aware we may not have truly observed the "good job" by simply watching parents and friends drive. Nevertheless, if we want to pass our test as a competent driver and obtain our license, we must be able to spot what a good job looks like to the minutest of detail. For instance, in a myriad of different situations from starting the car, shifting gears, doing a three-point turn, etc. This we do through observing, asking questions, trying to drive with our instructor, getting it wrong, making corrections and getting feedback until we can finally say for the majority of situations we are likely to face whilst driving, *that* is a good job. We can spot it instantaneously, and know what to do to correct inappropriate behavior to make it acceptable.

Then comes the toughest part. We need to take this *conscious competent* way of driving the car in a deliberate, methodical way and make it *unconscious, or automatic*. Our maneuvering at various speeds becomes effortless. Our emergency stops we do correctly time and time again, regardless of whether the instructor hits the dash or not. We stop when we are supposed to, not simply when told, and begin to be able to think and anticipate way ahead of the car, without having to worry what the feet, hands or eyes are doing to keeping the car traveling at speed in traffic! Wow! We have become *masters* at car driving.

We may have become so skilled, we begin to find new and better ways than we have been taught to do a three-point turn. We may find a smoother way to negotiate a sharp turn or set of stoplights. We may even desire to stretch our Comfort Zone even more by taking on a Michael Schumacher. We are so skilled as a car driver, we set new records, and help re-define what car driving means. Now we are truly masters of our skill and competency.

Does this take time? Certainly. It takes years. Do we just fall into it? Certainly not. We must become obsessed with improving our ability and skill incessantly. Is it worth it? Read about or ask those like Brunel, Armstrong, Branson, Michelangelo and Gates who have literally rewritten what competency really means in their chosen competency areas. That is Mental Toughness!

Develop a Powerful Vision

What role does our *Vision* have in helping us become more mentally tough? I believe it plays a great part. I trust your initial steps at creating your Vision have filled you with more confidence and hope about your future. Each of the people I have mentioned in the book so far who have had a significant positive impact upon others had a *Vision that would outlast and outlive* him or her.

Paraphrasing from Dr. Robert H. Schuller, one of the most impactful people I have ever known, let the strongest pull in our lives be the future, and may we go to our deathbed with our biggest dream yet unfulfilled. I believe I can say without exception, each and every one of us has a *purpose*, to use the power of our own imagination to connect with the God of the universe and create "on Earth as it is in Heaven." We will explore how to develop *Purpose* in Chapter Nine.

It just may be our part of the Vision is only one small part of the bigger Vision, but it is an essential, timely part only we can fulfill. That, then, becomes our focus. Produce the part of the eternal Vision we can see, and pass the remainder on to someone or some other generation to fulfill the whole. Knowing we are part of this creative process might just release some confidence and self-awareness in us to keep us making positive impact for a lifetime!

In Chapter Eight, we will explore even more ways to be the self-confident people we are meant to be, and overcome one of the greatest wastes of natural human energy known to man.

IMPACT Creative Action Debrief Chapter SEVEN

Do these before continuing to Chapter Eight!

1. How would you describe your state of mind when placed under pressure situations?

2. What has been your most significant test or trial to date?

3. What did you learn from the test or trial?

4. What can you put into practice this week to put your new knowledge into action?

Eight

Expanding Your Comfort Zone
For A Lifetime

"When faced with a mountain, I will not quit"
(Robert Schuller)

I was flying back home to Texas from a wonderful weekend in San Francisco – not with my wife and family, but in a T-38 Talon 2-seater with a student pilot. We had a "baggage pod" hung on the bottom of the aircraft, as it was a tight squeeze fitting anything other than ourselves in the cockpit. The problem was that there was a huge Texas size thunderstorm between us and home. We quickly calculated we did not have fuel enough to turn around, and, with some luck, if the storm tops were not more than 39,000 feet we could climb above the storm, and be home for dinner. So far so good – as we started to climb above the storm, we miscalculated how fast we could climb with the excess drag and weight of the baggage, and also the power of that storm to build clouds, hail, ice and up and down drafts at greater than 1000 feet per minute. As we reached the height of our climb, clouds began to engulf us. Our indicated airspeed was slightly above the stall, and with the buffeting of the wind gusts, we found we were in danger of losing one or both of our engines (they flame out). The only thing we could do was to start a slow descent into the clouds, try to keep our wings level as the storm raged around us. It got darker and darker, more wind shears, more up drafts, more

139

ice forming on the outside on the aircraft skin. We were in deep trouble. "How could we possibly explain the loss of the aircraft to our Squadron Commander? There goes my career" I thought. "No excuses, just poor planning", he would say. The only thing we could do besides pray (which I did!) was to trust in our gyrosystems that helped us keep our wings level and the aircraft in a slight descent. It all boiled down to our faith and confidence in a piece of machinery designed by people we never knew, and a series of electric signals built around some black boxes. Wow! Thankfully, as you probably already concluded, we survived. We popped out of the other side of the storm to bright, sunny skies without damaging the aircraft, returned home very coolly as if nothing had happened, and kept our "war story" to ourselves and our fellow fighter pilot buddies.

We have probably all had experiences where we had to keep mentally tough during stormy times. We have had to place our confidence in something outside ourselves, and well as in our own abilities and mental powers to overcome obstacles. This is the foundation for building a rock-solid confidence and self-esteem that helps us maintain a Mental Toughness that attracts others to follow our lead.

It really pays to remember these times you "made it through the rain" (an old Barry Manilow song I love to hear, as it was popular at a particularly poignant moment in our lives) or other sayings, pictures, triggers, etc., that you can recite or recall when under pressure. Here is one from Robert Schuller, the "Possibility Thinkers Creed."[37]

> *"When faced with a mountain, I will not quit! I will keep*
> *on striving until I climb over, find a pass through, tunnel*
> *underneath, or simply stay and turn that mountain*
> *into a gold mine with God's help."*

President Franklin D. Roosevelt said, "The greatest thing to fear is fear itself" during one of America's greatest traumas, the Great Depression of the 1930's. Some media people would have us believe we are approaching these conditions currently. He recommended, as do many other people who have developed their confidence during their lives, to *face the things you fear*. Consciously focus on the unknown, the undetectable disease, the irreconcilable difference, the business crisis, the lost sale, the angry customer if you want to develop your confidence.

"Feel the fear and do it anyway," is what Susan Jeffers proclaims in her book with this as the title.[38] If necessary, write the fears down and look them square in the face. As positive as some people claim I am, one of my greatest coaching questions I ask executives and managers who wish to do the impossible is, *"What is the worst that can happen?"* This was an important principle I learned early in my flying career, and poignantly expressed by Dale Carnegie, in arguably his best book, "How to Stop Worrying and Start Living".[39] Writing down the things we think would be the worst that could happen helps release an energy that will not only make us Mentally Tough, but also get us mentally focused to consider the risks, weigh the pro's and con's of anticipated actions and improve upon our situation. Give it a try the next time you have been kept awake at night, and feel immobilized by the fear and worry the situation causes.

Use the Fear to Turn Things Around

"The best thing you can do for yourself to get out of the money problems you face," said our banker one day, "is to sell your house and move into a rented flat. The bank can then take the proceeds of your property to pay off what you owe us, and you will be debt free." That, to me, was the worst thing that could happen – lose our family home, and not have a roof over our head. He made us so angry we stomped out of his office and never saw his face again. I immediately opened a bank account in another bank, and resolved to do whatever it took to show that bank manager a thing or two about managing money and getting rid of debt! Thanks to God, my family and friends, and a lot of hard work and effort, we were able to repay those debts in less than two years, keep all our commitments to other creditors and from that day over fifteen years ago have kept such a good check on our finances we have never found ourselves in that kind of situation again. I guess I should thank that bank manager for focusing us on what was the worst that could happen, and then mobilizing us to improve upon the situation.

Build Confidence by Developing Wisdom

Sometimes the most effective way of dealing with these seemingly insurmountable issues is to simply accept them. In AA circles, the fellowship has a great way of coping with "life as we know it" using the Serenity Prayer –

"God grant me the Serenity to accept the things I cannot change, the Courage to change the things I can and the Wisdom to know the difference".

How do we get the wisdom to know the difference? I think it is by getting the *serenity* and *courage* wrong a whole bunch of times! During our battles with alcoholism, our whole family got the balance between serenity and courage wrong many times – we tried exorcism, healing, hiding the bottles, denial, shouting, scolding, crying our eyes out – you name it. I can honestly say now, as many will attest to once through the crisis, the persistence, faith and hope we gained by never giving up has turned what the devil meant for harm into the best thing that has happened to this part of the Roberts family.

As we pointed out in the last chapter, Mental Toughness is produced in the caldron of chaos, fear, and inner turmoil. All the techniques, principles and methods used by those who have conquered their issues have started with stepping back from the situation and then getting a different perspective. One of the best tools our clients have found that helps, whether it be a personal or corporate issue, plan, or problem, is to gain an *Overview*.

Develop an Overview

The best way I find to convey the *overview perspective* is to relate to taking a holiday or vacation abroad. We probably can all think of times when we have suffered the stress of last minute packing, shopping and arranging for the well earned and yearned for break. Those last few hours are packed with all sorts of quick fire decisions, emails, telephone calls, etc. Then we jump in the car and head to the airport – wouldn't we know it, the traffic is worse than ever, we are cutting it tighter than we should have, and we're almost out of fuel – nevertheless, we finally get there, find we have to park miles away from the terminal, hump our overstuffed bags to the shuttle bus, who then deliver us to a queue that stretches out to the pavement outside! Finally, our bags are checked, we get through security having had two body searches. Our plane arrives, we get on board, and thankfully, despite all of the rush, hustle and bustle, we take off, high above the beehive of frantic activities below.

As we settle back with our drink, our loved ones around us and look at the ground 20,000 feet below, everything below looks so calm and tranquil. The world, somehow, takes on a whole new look, and we have a new sense the trouble we have just undergone over the past few hours is all worthwhile. We see things through *new eyes*. This is the perspective of *overview*. How do we get there without taking a helicopter or plane ride? Mentally, I believe it involves *looking up*, and *looking down*. By looking up, I mean to lift your eyes to the hills, to the Vision you have for your life or the situation you are facing. What would it be like if things went really well; if God were on your side? What if you knew you couldn't fail, what would happen to the situation you are facing? You may need to physically remove yourself from the workplace or setting that is entangled with the turmoil, go for a walk.

Heidi and I were involved in a critical situation – we found ourselves involved in an organization that was dragging us down; the debts were piling up, and we were working every hour we could. Something had to change. "Hon, let's go for a walk". And that's what we did. We were living in Norwich at the time, and the Highways Agency was building a new bypass just south of the city; not too far from our house. It was late in the evening, and we just set out, walking through the building site until we got on top of a new bridge overlooking Norwich city from a completely different perspective. Although much of the rubble remained near where we lived, when we set foot on an overpass bridge some half-mile away and looked down at the construction, it all seemed to make sense. We could see what the builders were trying to fashion. Miraculously, we also found our own overview in our own situation. All of the sudden, we knew what we had to do. We came home and immediately made plans to change our direction. This is the power of *overview*. Find a way to get above the helter-skelter of day–to-day living and ensure you *look up so you can look down*.

The Dreaded P-Word

Amongst my many failings I face daily is the dreaded "p-word." It affects many of us the way the "s-word" (shank) affects golfers. If we have any interest in golf at all, we have no doubt seen a very seasoned professional golfer at her or his very best turn to a quivering mass of gelatin after hitting a shank. Their energy, enthusiasm and focus is completely gone! For all of us, this can happen when the "p-word" infiltrates our world at home and at work. I suffered from it continually in writing this book. The consequences are it stops us dead. It drains our energy, it ruins our confidence and positive outlook. Yet it is completely controllable, once we know it is there. Therefore, the way it wreaks havoc upon us is by silently infiltrating our mind. Quietly and imperceptivity, it just places a thought there, just after we have made a decision to do something, say something or start a task or duty. Some people have labeled it a "Gremlin." It is far worse than criticism, because it is *internally-driven*. It can become so habit forming we will not even be aware of its presence. It has prevented the best song from ever being written; the best painting from ever being painted. It has kept more well-intentioned men and women from becoming the people they could be than any other factor. You have already guessed what the "p-word" is, haven't you? Yes, it is Procrastination. Putting Things Off. Someday I'll…, Maybe, One day, When I Get Around To It. Hesitant Harry, Meandering Mary. How do we overcome this menace which will keep us from developing the Mental Toughness possessed by people who make the greatest impact? Most motivational books and personal experiences we've had suggest these two steps:

Overcoming Procrastination I

Recognize it is there

When we continually find we are putting off doing something, or speaking to a certain person, or not tackling a particular situation, more often than not, procrastination is the culprit. You will know it is procrastination and not simply waiting for a more appropriate time to take the course of action because it will be the thing that flicks into your brain whenever you try to relax and forget it all. Yes, the things that detract from enjoying most holidays and weekends are the things we have been procrastinating over. They pop into your mind at the most inappropriate times when you are getting ready to call it a day, play with the kids, or go with your partner to a much-awaited special occasion. There it is – "You haven't filed your taxes yet", it says. "What about the spare room you promised you'd finish?" "You said you were going to do the planning to get ready for the Board Meeting tonight, and you haven't done it yet." It is a voice that sounds more grating than your worst in-law or parent. Nagging, nagging, nagging. And the longer you put it off, the louder and worse it gets. We waste so much energy, just trying to block it out of our minds.

Overcoming Procrastination II

Determine what it is about the things we are not doing that causes us to hesitate

Our procrastination normally boils down to one of these reasons:

· Terrifying – we simply fear either doing the thing, because it is uncomfortable or dangerous – more than likely, it is because we fear the outcome. Sometimes, it is not only the fear of failure that causes us to procrastinate; sometimes it is the *fear of success* that holds us back. What if it worked? We may have to behave more responsibly, or take on more work. This can keep us from tackling the task now.

- Trivial – the task is so unimportant it fades into insignificance; yet for some reason, it continues to invade our thinking and get in our way. Perhaps it is the result of a promise we made or commitment that reflects our relationship in keeping the family or work place going.
- Too big or too time-consuming – we know we "must do" and "should do" the task, yet we just cannot seem to find the time, all in one sitting, to get it done. People who paint, crochet or are authors know how this feels. In our fast paced lives, finding the time to do the things really important to us is a difficult challenge, and therefore we can easily find we put these items off
- Tedious – just like the trivial cause, items that are seen as drudgery, boring, unattractive and hum-drum can very easily be put off. They have to be done, and although can be easily done in a minimum of time, they just get left out of our planning and organizing. They can certainly cause some relational squabbles and unhelpful thoughts – even feelings of guilt.
- Don't know how – this cause of procrastination is probably one of the most common stoppers-of-progress. Rather than admit we need help and swallow our pride, we procrastinate over doing the task because we are unsure of how to do it, where to start, or who to speak to get the help we need.

By first classifying our "reason for procrastinating", we can begin to seek a remedy – just as any doctor would when we suffer a malady that requires a cure. Finally, once we have discovered what is causing us to procrastinate, we can apply any number of remedies. Here are seven that address most causes:

Seven Remedies For Procrastination

- Do the nasties first - take the toughest thing and do it first. Chances are it is not so difficult, and then everything else appears to be easy (or at least easier).

- Give it five minutes - tell your mind or inner voice, "Look, let's just do this for five minutes, then I will quit and do something else." Guess what? Once I 'give it five,' I will have started some momentum and I am more willing keep going. Try this next time you think of getting some physical exercise you have been putting off.
- Do–it–now - as with 'give it five,' the motivator 'do-it-now' can get us through the 'I ought to' stalemate and into the 'do' mode. Say aloud to yourself, 'Do it now' just after the 'I ought to…' thought comes into your mind. (Try NOT to do something after you have said, 'Do it now, do it now, do it now over and over again!')
- Give yourself a reward - let's face it, there are things in our lives we find tedious, boring and of little value, yet they have to be done at some point – for example the ironing, washing the car or completing tax returns. Give yourself a reward, however small, when you finish the task, not before you start. For example, 'I will have a cup of tea when I have ironed five shirts'.The reward helps us get through the inertia of 'not doing what needs to be done.'
- Ask for help - there are tasks we are simply not good at performing, dislike and feel we do not have time to do. Why not find someone who does have the time, is skilled at and enjoys the task, and ask for their help? Sure, it may 'cost you,' but not nearly as much as the energy-drain caused by procrastinating until you have the time.
- Use the 'sausage approach' - how do you eat a sausage? That's right – one bite at a time. We put off some projects and worthwhile 'ought-to's' because we simply cannot get our head around it or do not have the time to think it through properly. Like 'giving it five'- break the big project into bite-sized chunks which are digestible. Then go to work on it.
- Use the Churchill Method - Sir Winston Churchill was renown for many things, and one of his greatest qualities was his ability to make decisions involving highly risky and potentially life-threatening consequences for many thousands of troops during World War II. It is purported that

one of the methods he used to keep from putting off these momentous decisions, and mobilize people into action was to draw a line down a piece of paper. Then put on one side all the potential risks in making the decision. For instance, if they were to engineer a landing on a certain beach or area, he'd get those gathered to write down all the possible consequences if things went wrong. Next, on the same piece of paper, he'd have listed all the potential benefits or outcomes if the decision were made, and the beach landing worked out well. Then, he would weigh the pro's and con's, and decide. Although widely used now in many circles of decision making, sometimes it is easily overlooked as a way to keep from procrastinating over difficult decisions we all face. For more information on problem solving and decision making tools, visit www.mindtools.com

Hold Ourselves Accountable

Ironically, one of the best ways I know to build one's Self-Confidence, esteem and gain Mental Toughness is by holding ourselves accountable to someone or some other people. This applies especially when we share with them what it is we are learning. Our son, Tim, has recently applied this to his keeping fit. Although an habitual jogger, he was dissatisfied with his overall strength and tone, especially in his upper body. The jogs just were not working. Then eureka, up popped a plan. A friend of his from his church was starting a business as a personal fitness trainer, Tim was trying to encourage him to 'go for it', and they decided the best way to recommend someone is to be a product of their competencies. So Tim began sessions with his personal trainer, and sure enough, in just a few short weeks was already feeling much more fit and pleased with his workout routine. It applies to organizations and businesses as well. Almost any long-serving, growing organization that impacts the world has as part of its structure the formation of small groups or teams who share honestly what is going on in their world of work. It could be labeled, Performance Management, Personal Development Planning sessions, Cell Groups or Fellowship. In essence, these times of sharing are focused upon what we are learning about ourselves, and what we intend to do differently in the future. The degree to which they succeed is almost directly related to how honest these sessions are with people saying exactly where they are in life at the time, and to confess their faults, shortcomings and plans to change things.

Those who do not have this close knit network very often have a family, a church, or a coach or mentor they can use for this purpose. It does seem to be a vital part of Mental Toughness. On the IMPACT! Program, we have repeatedly seen the power of sharing and looking forward; holding ourselves accountable by simply confessing what we are currently going through. It is the best sort of exam we can personally take to check on ourselves. Hearing ourselves get out in the open what we are learning about ourselves and our journey through life makes us more self-aware. We find we are saying things we did not even know were inside, and once it is said, we can more effectively deal with things. Significantly, one of the added benefits in sharing with others is the degree to which we begin to take *ownership for the outcome*.

People are wired differently, and so different things cause uncertainty and jelly-like moments when our confidence erodes away. For many of us, one of the biggest obstacles to developing Mental Toughness is confusion and duplicity of thoughts and feelings that come from not knowing which way to move. Certain people thrive on this confusion, ambiguity and "not-knowing." For me, if this feeling lasts for over a week, and I cannot find an answer or way through, I begin to doubt myself, doubt there is an answer, and find it very hard to remain positive and forward-looking. This leads to inactivity, or at best, simply going through the numbers, putting one foot ahead of the other. This behavior is very unsatisfactory when it comes to making an impact. A powerful book by Patrick Lencioni entitled, The Five Dysfunctions of a Team[40] indicates one of the major dysfunctions in a team is lack of clarity.

Matt Perry, one of my colleagues at The Wilsher Group verifies this as he discusses with teams how to be World Class. He should know, as he has played International Rugby at the highest level for a number of years, and worked on high performing teams most of his career. "One of the four pillars of World Class teamwork is *role clarity*," says Matt. "We simply cannot operate at our best if we are confused or vague about what our role is on the team. When the pressure is on, and you need to be there to do your part at high speed, role clarity helps you focus on what it is you need to do to play your part. Without it, you let the team down, and the team lets you down. Confidence and trust that we know what we are doing go hand in hand in my view."

We have already seen how using the seven remedies for procrastination can help, as well as thinking, "What is the worst that could happen?" and trying to improve upon it. I also like to use Min Basadur's Simplex Method[41] for identifying the facts surrounding a fuzzy situation so we can begin to arrive at a solution. Here are my adaptations I use. Perhaps you could try to use these yourself when you get confused or stuck on a situation, and need to get back into control of the circumstances.

Seven Fact-Finding Questions for 'De-fuzzing' Situations

- What is it we know or think we know about the situation?
- What is it we don't know, but wish we did?
- What is so important about solving this problem?
- What is it we have already tried or thought of trying to reach a successful outcome?
- What would we have if we solved the problem or situation that we don't have now?
- What assumptions are we making that we don't have to assume?
- What are the most interesting or revealing facts that have emerged from the questions above?

I suggest you take a "fuzzy situation" you are currently facing, and have a go addressing this situation with the questions above, in that order, and see what you come up with. It may just give you some clues as to the best way ahead. It will certainly make you think more positively about yourself, and give you some insight to unblock the situation.

Believe in Yourself and Your Success

A vital ingredient of Mental Toughness is self-belief, I am sure you would agree. If we believe in who we are, we'll project this as we speak with others, and this will reinforce our own self-belief. I've already explained to you the "Yes, Geo, You are Terrific" mirror my wife gave me. That may sound strange, and may never be something you would ever do. Find, in your own way, a method of confirming your self-belief. It could be by quoting some phrases regularly about the kind of person you are, and want to become. Doing it out loud seems to work better than silently reviewing them. This process reinforces your psyche that those other thoughts that have led to self-doubt or criticism are not the only ones to store in the mind. If we begin to form other pathways in our memory system that reaffirm our self-belief, we'll be more likely to actually believe this rather than the limiting self-doubt images we have in our memory.

<u>Figure 8.1</u> Cycle of Experiential Development

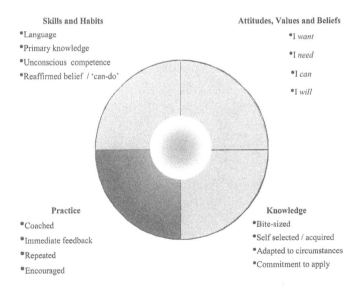

As we have illustrated in our discussions of the Cycle of Experiential Development, in order to grow any new skill, habit or

frame of mind, we need to *see ourselves as succeeding*. If not succeeding, then at least learning so we can go on to succeed. During our
review periods, hopefully the ones we hold daily with ourselves, we
will look for those things that we have done well, what new Personal
World Records we have had since our last review. Remember, it is
not so much we have achieved anything great, but simply we have
moved forward, learned something about ourselves and our journey.
We think this is so much a part of building self-esteem and confidence, we devote up to a third of the time with our delegates and
teams getting them to recount their successes and things which have
gone well. We then discuss them as a group, so we all can learn
and improve. Chris Sanders, a colleague and associate or ours, was
invited to come to one of these reviews at the end of a series of
IMPACT! and Leadership and Management Program sessions. He
was so amazed and uplifted by the experiences, he said, "This is
what I want to do with my life." Now he is a successful executive
coach and outstanding facilitator of transformational programs.

Give and Receive Positive Feedback

People who develop Mental Toughness devote most of their energies assessing and building upon their strengths. During the first
three sessions of the IMPACT! Program, we concentrate on giving
feedback only upon one's strengths. Let's think why. When we have
made ourselves vulnerable by stepping out of our Comfort Zone,
been open with people and tried something new, with a new group
of people, the last thing we want is to hear all the things we did
imperfectly.

Anyone can criticize. We all seem to be natural critics. It takes
very little skill to find things to be critical about. We have been
raised to spot defects in others. I am astounded by the lack of ability
most people have in giving and receiving feedback that builds and
improves people's performance. When I ask them about it, they say,
"We have never been taught. When we received compliments or
praise in the past, we found it was because people had a hidden
agenda, and were trying to get something out of us. We began to
see the way to survive in the jungle of school or work where people

are trying to score points at our expense, we learned to reject feedback, and to play the critical game in self defense." The result of sharing what we see as people's strengths is that we find they go on to develop even more strengths. Like peeling an onion or artichoke, as we become more aware of what we are, and what we share in common with others, the more we can see other strengths and skills we only hoped were there.

There is also a time to honestly assess what our strengths are, as measured by outside standards, so we don't go off with a Pollyanna view that leads us to self-delusion. Yet Doctor Timothy Harkness stated recently that, "It is proven that it takes 13 positive comments to overcome the impact of 1 negative comment."

We will now look at the engine, the afterburner that takes our Mental Toughness, confidence and skill set and gets us to take off and really make an unbelievable impact.

IMPACT Creative Action Debrief Chapter EIGHT

Do these before continuing to Chapter Nine!

1. Think of a confusing or ambiguous situation you are currently facing that requires some fresh thinking. Use the Seven Fact Finding Questions to help guide you through to an acceptable solution. Here they are again.

- What is it I know or think I know about the situation?
- What is it I don't know, but wish I did?
- What is so important about solving this problem?
- What is it I have already tried or thought of trying to reach a successful outcome?
- What would I have if I solved the problem or situation that I don't have now?
- What assumptions am I making that I don't have to assume?
- What are the most interesting or revealing facts that have emerged from the questions above?

2. Keep track of your accomplishments every day for a whole week, and reflect upon the strengths these represent.

3. Go out of your way to point out strengths you see in others, and record what they say or do when you tell them what you see or sense. You may be surprised!

Nine

Passion with Purpose

~

Find The Missing Ingredient To Energize Your Purpose

We have looked at ways we can become more Interpersonally Intelligent, and seen the importance of developing our Mental Toughness and Self-Confidence. If you have done the exercises, you will have a plan or Vision for your life, and have looked at how you are going to remain balanced in your approach. We have seen the value of gaining an Overview Perspective to maintain our Mental Toughness.

Another ingredient is needed to help us focus our people skills and character qualities to truly make a positive impact. Unbridled, this factor leads to extremist terrorism and radical fanaticism. Properly managed, this core ingredient can be the difference in whether or not we achieve our goals and dreams. We call it having a Passion with Purpose.

'*Passion*', by its own definition, is a highly emotive word. It can be frowned upon by the self proclaimed sophisticates as twee, or something confined to the football supporters. It causes fear and revulsion in some who have seen the negative consequences of zealots who sacrifice their own lives and the lives of many innocents for a cause they believe in. Every war is fought at least at some level because people find that expressing their passion justifies their atrocities. Let's look at its definition, and find out how we might channel our *passion* effectively, rather than totally suppress it as an irrelevant and dangerous emotion.

When we "Googlesearch" for *passion*, we are referred to the recent film by Mel Gibson, The Passion of Christ. This is soon followed by a number of dating and sexual attraction references. According to Wikipedia, the free online encyclopedia, '*passion*' is the emotion of feeling very strongly about a subject. Its root is in the French passio – suffering. The three possible definitions the online dictionary gives are:

- suffering; particularly in Christianity, the crucifixion of Jesus
- great emotion
- fervor, determination

The meaning we intend in *Passion with Purpose* is a combination of all of these. Does '*passion*' require suffering? Certainly, at times. Your journey will not be without its trials and tests. The core skills of Mental Toughness and Self- Confidence require it. Does Passion with Purpose require great emotion to overcome the tendency within us to go along with the crowd, not rock the boat or remain within our *comfort trap*? The "I believe" portion of getting us to break out of the comfort trap necessitates our fervor and determination. Passion works for us best when it comes from within; an inner drive or emotive force that culminates in a new way of thinking and acting that compels us to do the things we find uncomfortable.

Tapping Into Our Passion

How do we tap into our Passion? How can we combine it with our purpose, so it is properly channeled, and not running loose, causing havoc and turmoil among those with whom we live and work? Here is an example from my own life:

"We're off with Leslie, Bernice, Pearl and Oscar and their families to the Black Hills of South Dakota!" said my mother when I was about 8 or 9. Boy was I excited. As I have learned in subsequent years, I really enjoy being around people. I truly love to have fun and experience new things. My family is extremely important to me, and this combination of aunts, uncles and cousins were at the top of my list of people to have fun with. When they all got together, it was a laugh every minute! The trip was fantastic, and for me, life-changing. Funny enough, it had nothing to do with the people we were with. My life changing moment came when we attended and participated in a "Passion Play" in Spearfish, South Dakota.

As of this writing, the Black Hills Passion Play has been going on every year for nearly 70 years. Like the more famous play in Oberammergau that is performed every 10 years (since 1634), the Black Hills Passion Play portrays the life, death and resurrection of Christ. Although I had heard of Jesus' life and death before, to see it portrayed vividly in a 3 hour drama did something to me. I found myself being transformed by the message, and I made a commitment right then to believe. This commitment to belief in Jesus Christ being who he says he is started a *passion* within me that has helped shaped who I am, where I live, and what I do with my time. There have been waverings along the way, and times when my commitment has fluctuated. But at the heart level, this belief permeates almost every important decision I make.

Let's go back to the Vision

We discussed in the last chapter the need to know yourself well, warts and all, and to define what it is you are good at. In Chapter Three the putting together of a Vision of your life that excites you, is written uniquely for you and by you. If you have not completed your Vision for your life, then take a few moments to review the last part of Chapter Three and complete it now.

As you reflect and read it, does the Vision invoke Passion? Do you feel inspired by it? If not, then re-write it until it does. Share it with someone who knows you well, who can give it a sympathetic hearing, and see how they respond. If they want to clap when you have finished, then it is probably passionate. If they yawn and shake their head, you'd better think of a re-write!

Here is a quick checklist to see to what extent your Vision *evokes* Passion:

· Does the Vision describe how the world will be a better place as a result of your impact?
· Does the Vision describe how you are using the strengths and skills you identified previously?
· Does the Vision describe specifically the people groups, regional areas or specialist subjects your life will impact?
· To what extent does the Vision scare you, as it seems impossible at the moment?
· Does the Vision need the support, help, and efforts of other people?
· Does the Vision get you to say to yourself, "Without the help and intervention of a Higher Power greater than my own, I am doomed to NOT achieve it"?

What Can Be Achieved When We Channel Our Passion with Purpose?

Mike and Diane Schlimgen made a powerful impact upon our lives, and continue to make this impact upon others as they pursue their Passion with Purpose. Shortly after we met them in a small cottage near Campsea Ashe in Suffolk, UK, they introduced us to a small business opportunity that was to change our lives forever. For the princely sum of £7, we "invested" our lives into a part time direct marketing venture called Amway. That event, more than any other, helped shape our lives for the next thirty years. What attracted us most to share a business venture with virtual strangers in the undeveloped part of a country we have lived in for only a year was their Passion. This was remarkably demonstrated to us, not by the words but by their actions when they encountered an obstacle that would have provided most of us a good "excuse" not to go for our dreams.

Mike had declared to us that they were going for broke, and intended upon building their business to an unprecedented level in that portion of the United Kingdom. They declared a level of monthly turnover they hoped to achieve with their team, part of which was us! In the space of a few months, their declared goal was to grow their business by 250% in their spare time. Mike worked seventy to eighty hours a week in the United States Air Force as a Helicopter Paramedic, subject to no-notice alerts that he had to be able to respond to within thirty minutes. Daunting as that was, there was also the factor we lived in a rural part of Suffolk, knew very few local residents, and were seen as "foreigners", who quickly labeled us remnants of the "Over-paid, over-sexed and over here" Americans from World War II days.

Within a week of us "Starting our new business," Mike was involved in a helicopter accident that meant he was confined to a hospital bed for the next six months. Amongst other injuries, he suffered a break to his lower leg in thirteen places. Doctors believed he would never walk normally again. He went through numerous surgeries that resulted in one leg becoming 2 ½ inches (6 cm) shorter than the other. He was, understandably, in constant pain that required strong pain killers. Diane, in the meantime, was raising a family of three, and was expecting the fourth child in a few months as well! Mike and Diane had an advantage that most of us just don't have. They had a Purpose filled with Passion. Their goal represented more to them than financial achievement, being recognized as achievers by their peers and family or as a career improvement. For them, they felt "called" by a Higher Power to go for their goal. And this they did.

In order for them to achieve their dream, despite Mike being confined to bed, they had to recruit and train a number of part time distributors who would offer their product line of thirty products or so, and then encourage them to recruit and train others as well. How could they do this with Mike in the hospital? Very easily. Mike convinced the hospital that they could move the hospital bed to their home, and Diane would be able to help in his convalescence. This they did, and so from the bed, Mike grabbed a telephone and began ringing those he knew to come over to see this fantastic business proposition he was promoting. In a few months, despite the obstacles, Mike and Diane achieved their *Vision*. They have gone on to become much- loved and well-respected leaders of a church in

Texas. Mike and Diane still promote the power to overcome to those who believe in their dreams!

Have a Burning Desire

I'll never forget the first time I read Napoleon Hill's book, "Think and Grow Rich." This was one of the first books we fledgling part-time business owner's were encouraged to read, and for good reason. Mr. Hill devoted over twenty years of his life at the behest of well known entrepreneur and philanthropist Andrew Carnegie to explore, "What was it that made successful people successful?" So Hill interviewed thousands of people who had achieved a modicum of success at the time from all walks of life and work. Although dated when trying to relate to the stories of people he describes, it is a classic book in terms of identifying principles of success that have withstood the test of time.

One principle caused me a great deal of consternation and challenged me to investigate it further. 'Desire' must be so strong that you must be willing to burn bridges that might lead to retreat or other opportunities. According to Hill, unless you get to the point your dream or Vision obsesses you, you are not likely to achieve it.[42]

He applied his principles to the achievement of money, and this gave me the most trouble as I have difficulty in countenancing that people's *passion*, their obsession, should be financial. The attraction does not need to be monetary. Money is not in itself a bad thing, but to obsess on the acquisition of money for money's sake can lead to a very unbalanced, and in the end, unproductive life. This does not negate the principles Hill outlines, it simply focuses, in my opinion, on the attainment of money as an end itself.

Benjamin Disraeli, one of the most renowned British Prime Ministers when Britain was a dominant world power in the Nineteenth Century was purported to have said,

"Man is only great when he acts from passion."

Another famous quote whose author is anonymous is:

"The whole world steps aside for the man who knows where he is going."

People Inspired by Passion With Purpose

Both quotes can inspire us to develop this magnificent obsession, which drives us beyond what we now think as possible. One of the other people who has influenced my thinking and gave me an example of Passion with Purpose is Skip Ross.

Early in our business career, Mike, mentioned earlier in this chapter, suggested we develop a habit of listening in our spare time to talks from successful entrepreneurs and motivational speakers as a way of developing ourselves. One of these early tapes was called "Dynamic Living" by Skip. He outlined in this set of six 1.5 hour tapes a way of thinking and behaving that if followed would change our lives for the better. And so it did. As I heard, digested and applied Skip's "Formula for Dynamic Living," I began to see myself in a different light. I remember thinking, "You know, I wish one day I could begin to make the impact Skip does on people with what I say and do."

Skip became a role model for me, and to this day, I very often hear myself saying things to other people I first heard Skip say to me. Whenever I get down, and let's face it, all of us do at times, one of my methods of recovery is to replay those tapes again, and get myself sorted mentally. What a deposit he has left to keep my passion burning! What can you do to keep your light lit?

Many of us have heard of James Dyson. His passion, as we know, was to invent a different type of vacuum cleaner. His product has become so popular, that instead of saying, "We must get this room cleaned, someone grab the Hoover", we are now as likely to say, ".. someone grab the Dyson." (£3 billion sales worldwide by 2002[43]) Mr. Dyson believed so strongly in his innovative vacuuming process that he overcame dozens and dozens of attempts to get the product licensed and to find a financial backing. Hundreds of people told Mr. Dyson his product would never work and he approached bankruptcy before his successful breakthrough. That is what Passion will do for someone who is *committed to a Vision*.

Reverend Jeanie B was driven by Passion with Purpose. Jeanie was a contented housewife and mother going about her daily duties. She was prompted to take up a counseling course offered by her church because she had to settle one or two issues from her past with guidance from skilled counselors. After much consternation, heartache, and tears, Jeanie began to deal with these demons of the past, and found herself with a new focus on life. She was so thrilled with the 'release' that she decided she wanted to devote the rest of her life to helping people get better emotionally and spiritually. Hence she began the process of becoming a Vicar in the Anglican Church. All these examples hopefully will serve to get you to ignite your Passion with a Purpose.

Psychiatrist Viktor Frankl's "Man's Search for Meaning"[44] powerfully illustrates the vital need for us to have a Purpose with a Passion, especially when faced with life or death decisions. Dr. Frankl survived the WWII holocaust and wrote about his experiences from the psychiatry point of view. He concluded that he and other survivors had one thing in common over those who died in captivity before being selected for the gas chambers – they had a Passion with Purpose, a meaning behind their existence that drove them to look for solutions and keep their hopes alive despite the filth, cruelty and degradation they faced. His book will inspire you to ponder issues to your life's meaning. Here are some taster quotes that might prove useful –

> *"It did not really matter what we expected from life, but rather what life expected from us."*

also

> *"We needed to stop asking about the meaning of life, and instead to think of ourselves as those who were being questioned by life - daily and hourly. Our answer must consist, not in talk and meditation, but in right action and in right conduct. Life ultimately means*

taking the responsibility to find the right answer to its problems and to fulfill the tasks which it constantly sets for each individual."

also

"A man who becomes conscious of the responsibility he bears toward a human being who affectionately waits for him, or to an unfinished work, will never be able to throw away his life. He knows the "why" for his existence, and will be able to bear almost "any how."

Zig Ziglar, another hero of mine whom I have previously mentioned, in his book, "See You at the Top",[45] uses the words, 'desire' and 'enthusiasm' as the ingredient for success in life. He defines 'desire' as, "...the ingredient that changes the hot water of mediocrity to the steam of outstanding success". He says that '*enthusiasm*' is the internal hope from within that not only drove the first century Christians to challenge the authorities across the Roman Empire and face martyrdom for their cause, but it is also the drive that will empower us as well. It is the *iasm* of *enthusiasm* – '*I Am Sold Myself'* that convinces ourselves and other people that we will overcome any obstacle we face. It's not that we must create or invent it, but as Viktor Frankyl says, "The meaning of our existence is not invented by ourselves, but rather detected."[46]

It goes without saying that people who tend to have the most passion have a profound faith in something greater than themselves. 20th Century Norman Vincent Peale was one of these men. Reverend Robert H. Schuller was another. Even in his 80's he is actively involved in the Hour of Power TV program that has impacted the world for the better with his Possibility Thinking Creed we mentioned earlier. Although living our lives in the United Kingdom some 5000 miles from his Crystal Cathedral, I have remained keenly devoted to the church's Hour of Power television broadcast every week. The reason is the messages these people of Passion with Purpose have provided has helped us keep our own purpose burning brightly, and give us a reason for the hope that lies within.

The extraordinary Richard Branson's magnificent obsession is challenging the giants who monopolized air travel, banking and a myriad of industries. He dares to believe there are better ways, and pioneered efforts to create a more level playing field – the result? Millions of travelers now can fly across Europe at much less of the cost necessary a couple of decades ago when nationalized airline companies dominated air travel. The fruit of this for Lord Branson? Knighthood, and a balance sheet in the billions of Pounds Sterling. Plus a life full of making a positive difference.

Other names perhaps not household names who had a Passion with Purpose have changed our banking world for the better. Messers A.P. Giannini and Dee Hock were just two individuals in the early days of credit cards and paperless transactions who rewrote the rules for how to conduct commercial and personal payments without the use of paper currency. The result? Literally billions of transactions occur every hour worldwide, from computers that are as powerful as any known in the world. All because two men dared to believe that there must be a better way![47]

People who have Purpose and Passion seem to be in the right place at the right time. Take for example the founders of Domino Printing Sciences in Cambridge, United Kingdom. Founded in 1978, the company forged the technology in the UK for using inkjet printers to imprint European legislated coding onto manufactured products. Once the technology was developed, they seized the opportunity to become a world leader in providing ink jet and laser technologies offering total coding and printing solutions. Variable data such as bar codes and traceability codes are printed onto products in industries such as food, beverage and pharmaceutical.

In the late 1980's Domino recruited a couple of entrepreneurial business oriented accountants, Nigel Bond and Andrew Herbert, who could see the potential of the business, and who were able to build, with the hard work and efforts of many people across the world, Domino's base to a multimillion pound business. They made it possible for manufacturers world-wide to meet the requirements of packaged coding on their products at affordable prices. We take this for granted now; but forty years ago it seemed inconceivable that manufacturing could comply with coding legislation that provides instantaneous recognition in virtually every known language. It takes men and women with *purpose and passion* to make these impossibilities possible.

Martin Goymour, the Chief Executive and son of the founder of Banham Zoo and related businesses used his Passion with Purpose to propel the family business on to a whole new level. Martin's entrepreneurial father, Harold Goymour, had taken advantage of the major presence of US military establishments in Suffolk, UK after the Second World War to provide them with a variety of homes. The tenanted USAF service families required refrigerators, washing machines and televisions for their new homes but they were then relatively expensive to purchase and in short supply in the U.K. but were soon provided on a rental basis by Mr. Goymour, a former baker by trade.

Then in the 1950's Mr. Goymour Snr. realized that it did not pay to send the fruit produce from his farm to the wholesale markets and engaged upon selling the produce direct from the farm, a then novel approach and an untapped potential. To encourage visitors they were made welcome to explore the farm and its animals including various aviaries housing a collection of ornamental pheasants. Other exotic animals and birds followed until staff were needed and he seized upon the idea to start a Zoo, in the middle of Norfolk, far away from any large conurbation. Would this really work? Now enter Mr. Goymour's son Martin.

When I first met Martin, he was just beginning to take over some of the aspects of his father's role. He had the determination and drive to make the Goymour Group of businesses flourish, yet had never committed plans to paper. Martin came on a LAMP (Leadership and Management Program) we were running that helps people to get to grips with their Vision, their management and leadership style and how to unlock the potential and power in themselves and their staff. Once the 'Goymour Group Vision' began to crystallize Martin began to share it with the team. Over the next few years, Martin and his team were seriously mobilized to move things on with Purpose and Passion. Now, some 20 + years on, the Goymour Group have grown Banham Zoo to be one of the leading Zoos in Britain, specializing in exotic animals and those that are in danger of extinction. They have since also acquired and developed Africa Alive!, a wildlife park in Suffolk, with village shops, restaurants and even car boot sales to give the people of East Anglia and visitors from all over the UK a truly amazing experience! Recently the dream has expanded to include a golf course and Dinosaur Park as well. Their Passion with Purpose lives on.

"The secret to success is find a need and fill it."[48]

"You can get everything in life you want by helping other people get what they want."[49]

Want a *Passion with Purpose*? Live those two quotes for a start!

Meet Peter Tucker

One last story, and then we'll help you get down to work on your Passion with Purpose. Peter Tucker was the son of very good friends of ours, Tom and Vivien Tucker. Early in 1980 Tom and Viv's friend Brian Leaning wrote from Perth, Australia and told them of the Amway business opportunity. Tom then contacted Amway UK who suggested ringing us, as the nearest Direct Distributor. We explained the business to them and the Tuckers started their own business with our help.

Tom was already a successful site manager and engineer for a local construction company, but had some unfulfilled dreams that only came to the surface when we encouraged them to set some goals and make some plans. One of their dreams was to be able to travel the world, and experience different cultures before they were too old to enjoy it.

Our friendship grew as we began to work with Tom and Viv. One of the ways we helped Tom and Viv was to encourage them to go on a training and development program to help them to learn to speak in public and improve interpersonal skills. Tom was a natural public speaker, but Viv, bless her, really struggled. She would get so filled with nerves, and spoke so quietly that to have to stand in front of a group of people and explain some of the products we used in the business frightened her speechless. Over the weeks, Viv learned to overcome her fears, and nowadays, although not a fervent nor eloquent after dinner speaker, she has the confidence and communicative skills to hold her own in any situation. Now enter Peter.

Following Tom and Viv's success with the program, Tom asked if we would help with Peter. Peter was a fairly typical teenager. He was very popular with his peers but was somewhat shy around grown-ups. He lacked a certain amount of self-confidence when relating to grown-ups on a business level. He had started an Amway business and was keen to succeed but needed to overcome his fears and nerves. He had his dreams and set his goals in the business. Of course, Tom and Viv wanted to help him succeed. As they had experienced what the self-development program had done for them, they felt it would help Peter with his self-confidence, personal relations and communication skills

With some persuasion Peter embarked on the same communication program as his parents. Peter, at eighteen years old, was the youngest by far. Standing in front of thirty strangers and learning to speak for just two minutes without notes was an enormous challenge. Peter was determined, despite the fact that he was so nervous before each session that he was physically ill. This went on week after week, for nearly 3 ½ months! Finally, on the last session, Peter was able to stand in front of a room full of strangers and family, and get across a clear message with Passion about how he wanted to fulfill his dreams, have his own car, join the Royal Air Force and become a leader. He brought the house down and there were few dry eyes in the place.

At the conclusion of the course Peter's parents helped him achieve some of his dreams. He moved out of the family home into his own apartment. They helped him buy his first car, albeit only a second hand one, but it was his pride and joy. Then tragedy struck. Only ten days or so after getting his own car he was taking some fellow cadets from the Air Training Cadets to play in an inter-company rugby match when there was a tragic head-on collision on a notorious accident black spot just outside his home town. Everyone survived but Peter, his heart was ruptured by the force of the impact.

At 18 years old his life, now filled with a new confidence, beckoned before him. All of his dreams and activities he wanted to fulfill were snuffed out in an instant. That is not the end of the story.

After the funeral and months of mourning by Peter's family and friends, Tom and I met to reminisce about Peter, his life and how he grew through stepping outside his Comfort Zone. A new dream was born in us that day, and that was to ensure that as many young people like Peter, who suffer from lack of confidence and inability to communicate effectively have the opportunity to live the dreams, purposes and ambitions that Peter was unable to fulfill. Peter, this book, and every development program we run is for you! I pray that before I die, we will see a national if not international curriculum for young people that gets them to believe in themselves and the Passions that lie within.

"Put everything you've got into everything you do!"

I first heard this expression made by Skip Ross while listening to him explain his concept on Dynamic Living. It described one of the Principles of Success he explained for living this dynamic life. It was called the Principle of Enthusiasm.[50] As we discussed in Chapter Three, a fulfilling life is one in which we look to for Overview, Balance, as well as Focus. Our experience says that once you find your Passion with Purpose, you will be able to see how it impacts on other areas of your life as well, and how it might look. For instance, if your *passion* is helping the homeless, then this very easily could become a business or career interest as well as a way to get involved in the community. Therefore, at least two of your "Wheel of Life" goal areas are being addressed with one set of activities. Very often the same can be said if your Passion is helping your family to grow and become worthwhile citizens, it might lead you to become involved in the school as a governor or part time classroom assistant. Getting fit and combining time with the family can also go hand in hand towards the same goals and activities. If you can develop a Passion with Purpose Statement so it encompasses nearly all the areas of your life, then life stops being such hard work and becomes a fulfillment of your dreams and goals.

So many people striving for fulfillment and purpose devote far too much time looking *inwardly* instead of *upwardly and outwardly*. Very often the answer comes in seeking God's purpose for us, and even if we do not believe in God, then get involved in giving yourself away. Many years ago I first heard the saying, *"The Secret of Living is Giving."* I have practiced it for years, and observed others who have devoted themselves to reaching out and helping those less able than themselves lead much richer and fulfilling lives. What local interest group could you support with your time, thoughts and prayers that would love to use your gifts and abilities? Why not give them a ring, get involved, and see if after three or four months you have reached a deeper level of satisfaction? In the next chapter we will get down to the nitty gritty of actually completing our Passion Plan using our One Page Planner from Chapter Four.

IMPACT Creative Action Debrief Chapter NINE

Complete these before continuing to Chapter Ten!

1. Who would you add to the list of people who have displayed Passion with Purpose?

2. What is it about this person / these people that inspires you?

3. What one question would you wish to ask one of the passionate people mentioned?

Ten

Defining Your Passion with Purpose

W riting something down can be intimidating. There is a sense of commitment that comes from seeing something written down from our own hand. I have often thought what would have happened to humankind if we had remained solely oral communicators rather than developing a written language. What do we have now we would not have had if someone had not taken the time to write down thoughts, ideas, dreams and visions?

Leonardo de Vinci, for one, was an amazing capturer of thought, ideas and visions. Michelangelo was able to see human forms in blocks of granite, and then took the time to chisel the form out of the rock. What excuse could we have for not completing the relatively simple exercise of carving our thoughts out of the granites of our minds on a word processor or on paper? If we are afflicted with the inability to write, then perhaps we could at least record our thoughts orally, and then have someone transcribe them.

Without further explanation, take a good thirty minutes, right now, to reflect and capture your first thoughts as to your Passion with Purpose at the end of this chapter in the space provided. Or, should you be someone who has a word processor to capture your thoughts, transfer over the headings from the book and place it in a Word document you can use to capture your thinking. Struggling? Then answer these questions in short statements, and then later transfer to the pages at the end of the chapter.

1. "What is it you want, what you really, really want?"

2. If you were completely free, like a bird on a beautiful "blue sky" day, what would you try, think or do? Write down your first thoughts here.

3. Is your Passion big enough? Will it out live you? Will you need lots of help to bring it about?

If you could not answer any of these questions, then answer this question: '*What would make your idea so big it would outlive you, and you would need lots of help from God and everyone to bring it off?*' How can you make the above statements come alive? How can you describe those ideas and thoughts so they are vivid in color, sounds, tastes, etc? Let's say you have a statement that says, "I want to help the aged in my community." Take that statement and convert it using vision, sounds and tastes.

> "*I am walking into a purpose-built center for the elderly. The walls are brightly colored in an ocean blue. The windows are large, and surrounded by colorful curtains that invite the eye to have a look outside. I hear laughter in the corridors, and coming from the lounge. There is ample seating of well designed, comfortable easy chairs. The mouth watering smell of freshly baked rolls wafts through the building, and we hear the chef shout, 'Dinner is served, come and get it!'*"

That may be a bit over-the-top. Attempt this yourself taking some of your statements and converting them into statements that involve your senses. See how it makes your Passion come alive. How does that look and feel now?

Now, let's have a go at infusing the statement/vision with a sense of urgency. Take a statement that starts with "one day I will or would like to ....." According to those who know how our brain works, the mind tries to complete the picture you give it. If we signal to the brain we "one day will do something or other", the mind interprets that as, "Whew, I don't have to do anything now. If my master wants to do something someday, and not now, then I have already satisfied her 'I will or would like to.'"

Alternatively, if we tell our brain, "We are ....." this signals to the brain, "Hey, you have got some serious work to do, brain!" We are *speaking the truth in advance*, and since we are not yet there, we need to get a move on." Take your statement that is "one day I will," and convert it into the *present tense, as if it were already true. How does that strike you? Can you sense the extra energy conveyed in the statement now? Isn't it less likely to be ignored and not acted upon?

Here is another test of your vision – is it positive or negative? Another truth about how our brain works – The *mind only sees the picture, not* the *'not.'* For instance, if our vision statement is, "I am not tired all of the time", supposedly the brain focuses on the tired and not the not tired. It is much better and more powerful if we say,

"Today, I am getting stronger and stronger, and have more than enough energy to cope with what life throws my way."

For those of us who have played golf for a few times here's an example to illustrate. We are facing a tough shot over what is known in the golfing world as a "hazard" – this could be water, sand, a tree or bush – anything that stands in the way of us having a clear shot at the target, which is the green where the hole is. These "hazards" have a way of reaching out or up and grabbing our ball, seemingly holding on to it forever. And funny enough, the more we concentrate on the hazard, instead of the green or target, the more likely we are to bring the hazard into play. The reason is our brain tries to complete the picture we give it, and it does not see the "*not.*" Therefore, we are saying to ourselves, "I don't want this ball to go into the water, it is the best ball I have." Guess what picture the brain has? Yep, you guessed it, there is that ball flying straight into the pond with a big splash!

It is far better for us, when playing golf, to look at the target regardless of the hazard. Not that we blindly hit at the tree as if it weren't there, but we look at the hole between the branches, and not at the branches. Adapting this to our vision – use positive, what-we-want–to-happen language, not negative, what we don't want. Now give it a try with one of your statements.

When you read your statement, does it invigorate and inspire you? Remember, at this point, it is *you* who needs the inspiration and invigoration. This is not for dissemination to others just yet, and I will explain why. Before I do, go back and re-write your entire Vision using the *present, positive tense*. When you do, you will have a series of statements that will propel and compel you to its completion. As many a psychologist would say,

"We cannot consistently perform in a manner that greatly differs from our view of ourselves."

If we have a view of ourselves performing and living as captured in our Purpose Statement, then this frees us to go ahead and be that person! How powerful! How wonderful! How amazing!

Be careful who you share your Vision or Purpose Statement with. Remember, there are 'dream-stealers' that do not want you to change and become someone else. Not that they are necessarily against you, in fact, very often they are telling you to "Not get your hopes up" to keep you from being disappointed or getting hurt. That's the dilemma – in order for us to become people of high impact we need to grow, change and reach out and up. In doing so, we open our lives, hearts and minds to experience struggle, setbacks, confusion and yes, even hurt. Is the alternative 'playing it safe' every day? Should we stay in bed, take the easy route, keep our heads below the parapet and never risk failure? Not if you truly are going to become the person you and the world need you to be.

Have you ever heard of the Johari's Window? Two fellows named John and Harry (hence the Johari) observed that we all have a part of us we are aware of and so are others, another part that other people are aware of us that we are not, thirdly, part of us we are aware of that we don't let others see and finally, part of us that neither we or others are aware of.

'Johari's Window' can be viewed nicely as a matrix:

Figure 10.1 Johari's Window

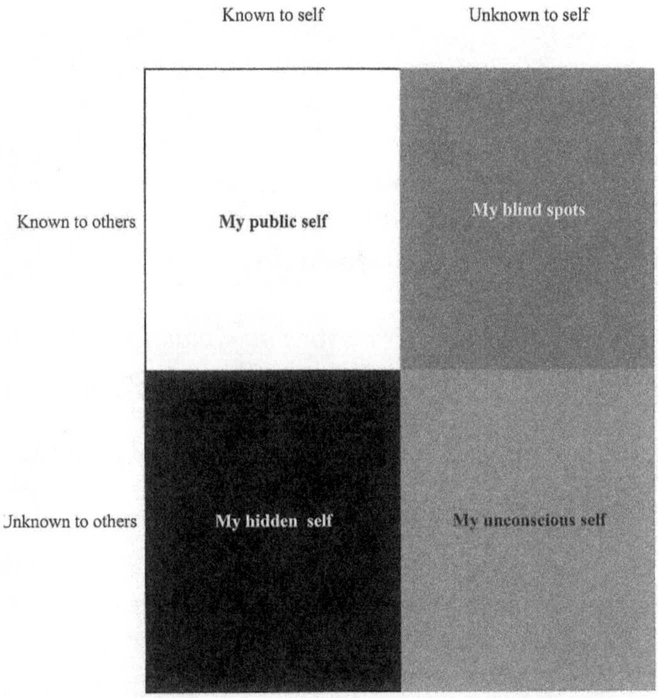

	Known to self	Unknown to self
Known to others	My public self	My blind spots
Unknown to others	My hidden self	My unconscious self

Of course, these are not equal quadrants – depending upon our awareness of ourselves, our willingness or propensity to share freely what we are thinking, saying, feeling, etc. Others may be more aware of what we are than us. We can use this model to explore the challenge of changing as we become more aware of who we are. As our part of the window expands, others begin to see us differently than before. If they are not ready for this, they may not like or feel comfortable with the increased size of our awareness window. This forces them to have to make changes or rearrange their perceptions in order to cope with the 'new us.' Besides wanting to protect us, they are also wary of these new changes, and the potential conflict within themselves which demands that if they want to keep the relationship alive, they have to be as willing to change as we are. A film my wife and I were watching the other night illustrated this perfectly. Sarah, a white, middle class girl was attracted to an African American from the lower echelons of an inner city. The boy, Derek, had a sister and a friend who were desperately trying to protect him by pulling him back into "their world". Sarah was confronted by the sister, and her reply was, "But I thought there was only one world!" It's a great movie, called "The Last Dance".

My wife informs me that sober alcoholics frequently find it very difficult to keep their partner after they enter recovery. The partner who lived with them prior to recovery finds it very threatening and demanding to be asked to change as the alcoholic has done to remain sober.

Be gentle on those around you as you begin to live your Purpose Statement – start the change process, and then if they ask "What on earth is going on?", then you can carefully share the new you, why you are making the changes, and share the benefits you're feeling, and what the helpful consequences are for your relationship with them.

Let's explore what *God-given Equipment* you possess that you will be using to achieve your Purpose.

1. List here the skills and talents you know you have – none of this fake modesty here – you know you have some God-given skills and talents, so write them down.

·   Skills

·   Talents

2. What is it you really *like doing*? When do you feel most fulfilled and on-fire? Write these down.

· Like doing

3. If your skills and talents are characteristics you have worked on and developed, there are also areas that you were gifted that somehow were *'just there'*. Perhaps you are a quick runner, and easily run faster or farther that anyone in your peer group. Maybe you have beautiful hair, nice teeth, smiling eyes – and that's just in the physical.

· Physical

4. What about your *emotional gifts* – you love being with people, you are a good problem solver, and love to serve other's needs. Perhaps you find you can anticipate a situation and bring corrective action before something gets blown out of proportion and difficulties arise – this is what Jesus called being a "peacemaker."

· Emotional gifts

5. How about your *spiritual gifts*? Do you find yourself at "one with nature." Are you most spiritually alive when you are reading or contemplating? How would you describe your spiritual gifts? Write these down.

· Spiritual gifts

6. What about your *mental capabilities*? What abilities have you acquired through study, and what subjects fascinate you, thrill you as you explore and keep you occupied for hours? Is it exploring the internet about space travel, numbers and logic? Perhaps it is in your

ability to create images, seeing stories in pictures, or your ability to use words effectively to describe things? Whatever they are, capture them here:

· Mental capabilities

7. There are probably skills you have acquired through your *life's experiences* – school-related, working at home, through hobbies, interests, sports or socially. Perhaps you have a particular job that has helped develop some skills and habits, like good time keeping, being organized, quick thinking, problem solving, etc. Write down these here, even if they are a repeat of what you have already written. The more times these come to mind, the more likely that these are well-developed in you. Have a go, brainstorm all that "life" has taught you.

· Job- related

· Hobbies/interests

· Sports and social

STOP READING NOW - Go to the Passion Plan at the end of the chapter once again and complete the reality check and T.O.W.S. portion.

What went on inside of you as you once again reviewed your current situation? What are the strengths that can propel you forward, towards your life of fulfillment and impact? Now let's see what role your personality may have in making you the person you are and can be even more of.

William completed an IMPACT! Program a number of years ago. When he was yet a young man, he was told that he was a poor communicator by a well meaning teacher or parent. This dogged him for years. He devoted much of his time in "correcting" this behavior, yet always being convinced that he was a poor communicator. However, once participating on IMPACT! with other delegates, he began to see that he was, in fact, an excellent communicator. He quickly learned how to open, structure and convey meaning and understanding when he spoke. He was an excellent listener, able to perceive the views of his audience. This helped him become skilled at extemporaneous talks. In fact, as he applied himself back in his working world, he found people responded very well towards his style of communicating, and he was asked to speak on behalf of others on a regular basis. His drive to overcome a labeled weakness propelled him to improve his communication substantially. Let your inner drive shape who and what you are, so that you *make the positive difference you know is possible*!

"Inner motivation is the strongest – it drives us when outer motivation fails or is not there"

IMPACT CREATIVE ACTION DEBRIEF CHAPTER TEN

Do these before continuing to Chapter Eleven!

1. Complete the Passion Plan First Draft

Part Two of my Passion with Purpose Plan First Draft

2. My Reality Check and TOWS to date:

 · Responses – What I think, do or say when under pressure:

 What other people close to me say:

·   Easy and Exciting – Those things I do that come easy, and I find exciting to do

What other people close to me say:

·   Attributes – What attributes, education, experiences and qualifications have I gained and what are the gaps still to be filled?

What other people close to me say:

·   Like – What do I like doing? Who do I like to be around? What do I dislike or find tedious and boring?

What other people close to me say:

3. A look at my **TOWS**!

·   **T**hreats to my Vision becoming a reality

·   **O**pportunities I have currently to move me towards the Vision

·   My perceived **w**eaknesses to overcome

·   **S**trengths to work on

Eleven

Success or Failure, Gain or Loss – It is Your Choice!

~~~

Hanging in our home in a place I see every day as I arise and get ready is a beautiful painting my wife did for me, with this anonymous saying:

> *"This is the beginning of a new day, God has given*
> *us this day to use as we will. What we do with today is*
> *important, because we are exchanging a day of our life for*
> *it. When tomorrow comes, this day will be gone forever,*
> *leaving in its place something we have traded for it.*
> *We want it to be gain and not loss, good and not evil,*
> *success and not failure, so that we shall not regret*
> *the price we have paid for it."*

My older brother Dick has applied 'conscious choice filter' with his physical fitness. In earlier stages of his life, Dick was a pretty heavy smoker, and allowed his physique to deteriorate. When his son, Zack, and daughter, Melissa became interested in running while in high school, he fancied having a go himself in a "veteran's" athletics event. Dick had a great time participating, and it was something he could have in common with his kids. Dick starting running, and running, and running. He has competed in marathons and as regular as clockwork arises early each day to begin his workout routine. Recently, he discovered he had prostate cancer. Did this cause him to go into a tailspin and say, "Woe is me?" To the contrary. He kept himself motivated by talking about how quickly he could get back to his running following the operation. He had faith that the surgeon would do his job well. He did. Within a few weeks, Dick returned to running his twenty miles a week! Was he lucky? Maybe. Something tells me he increased the likelihood he would recover immensely by exercising his power of choice.

Now Dick is 65 – guess what? He was actually recruited by a very successful bank in the Midwest of America to start and run a new real estate division – in spite of his age – in a very mature market, the threat of recession and downturn in the property market. Dick has never been happier! A new venture and opportunity to operate his *power of choice*.

The habits we choose to create have a vital impact upon who we are and what happens to our world. How do we choose which habits we keep? It is really quite simple – not easy, but simple. Which habits do we need that will help us move towards our goals, our Passion with Purpose and things we want in our life? Which habits free us rather than restrain us? Which habits build our character and power to choose wisely under pressure? If we make a list of these, and then consciously choose to make our actions and thought processes in line with the habits, we will be developing the best habits for us. Let's not think that it is simply a cognitive process. As Dr. Timothy Harkness, a psychologist and physiologist whom we met recently says, "You cannot isolate the mental thought processes from the spiritual, emotional and physical. If you want to change, you are best able to do so if you focus your mind, body and spirit all into the process." That's why we get the most likely transformation of our choices when we combine the passion with the thought – Body and Soul.

Looking beyond at what choices and habits will lead you towards your better future, remember to use the perspective Skip Ross calls the "Principle of Exclusion" introduced earlier :

Principle Of Exclusion

"Get rid of things we don't really want or need to make room for things we do"[51]

Skip states that in order for us to make room for the things we want in our lives, we need to get rid of the things we don't want. Applying this to habits, if we can stop our natural reaction to certain situations/stimuli, then choose to replace those with something we do want. Suppose we have a habit of keeping things, accruing material, and then hanging on to them long after their "best by" date. We are not talking here about wisely using the possessions, and getting the most out of them. We are speaking of worn out clothes, ill-fitting trousers, shiny suits, dresses long out of fashion and wide lapels on jackets. Things, quite probably, you will never wear again and fill our wardrobes, drawers and closets. We hang on "just in case" we might one day need these things and fear we may return to times of scarcity. The habitual fear of losing needs to be addressed. We can begin to change this habit by using the Principle of Exclusion.

Clearing our closets and wardrobes may trigger our brains into thinking perhaps we are not going to fall into hard times again. We may start to believe in an "abundance mentality instead of a scarcity mentality." If we believe in abundance, then we can behave more generously. We can take our time to live life in balance, not rush and work every hour God sends.

Another choice we can make is to become like those with whom we associate, depending upon the significance we place on their opinions, interests and ideas. If we see them as people we value, trust and have a close affinity, then we will unconsciously begin to acquire their attributes, ways of thinking, etc. If these significant others are positive, encouraging, and expect the very best from us, then we will be more likely to grow, develop and challenge ourselves to live this way. One of the ways of explaining this is with the Law of Expectations. Psychologists and educationalists alike agree that the expectations others have of us can provide a powerful influence in who and what we become. We probably all have heard or read of the Pygmalion Effect.

The Law of Expectation

The Pygmalion Effect[52]

The Pygmalion Effect is one big demonstration of the effect teachers have on how well students learn, showing they can double the amount of pupil progress in a year. Robert Rosenthal and Leonara Jacobson (1992) mention research that showed that ten seconds of video of a teacher teaching without sound allows students to predict the ratings they will get from a teacher. Similarly hearing the sound without vision and without content (rhythm and tone of voice only) were enough too.

This is powerful evidence that teachers differ in ways they cannot easily or normally control, but which are very quickly perceptible, and which at least in students' minds, determine their value as a teacher.

The Law of Expectation made the damsel in "My Fair Lady" into a lady despite her previous lifestyle. The military use this in turning ordinary civilians into hardened soldiers capable of risking their lives in combat. Negative expecations also influence how we behave. We will start to think, develop the attitudes and behave like the people who have expectations both good and bad of us. We can, however, apply the Principle of Exclusion, like with old clothes, and get rid of those influencers we don't want to make room for those who do. It might be painful, but if we are serious about making an impact, then we perhaps need to consider discarding some of the people whom we have chosen in the past to be our role models. This doesn't mean disowning parents, or discarding loved ones. It simply means we need to consciously devote our time and attention to those who will build and not those who destroy.

Tim Ayres, a good friend, namesake of our younger son, and fellow combat pilot during the Vietnam War in the 70's, was given an "opportunity" to apply filters to what he allowed to go in. On his second tour in Vietnam, he was shot down during a combat mission in North Vietnam. He survived the ejection from his F-4 Phantom when it was hit flying low over the enemy's position, and then after a brief escape and evasion Tim was captured. During his captivity,

Tim was subjected to brainwashing, indoctrination, punishment and torture. Despite the tough time, he was able to "filter" out those thoughts that he felt would lead him to compromise his country, his belief systems, his fellow captors and comrades in arms. When asked after his return how he was able to resist the attempts to influence him, Tim says, "I trusted my country, my God and family. I knew they wouldn't let me down and I sure didn't want to let them down."

The Law of Frequency

In addition to The Law of Expectation (Pygmalion Effect) we can use the "Law of Frequency" to help propel us towards our passion and purpose. It is quite simple, really. All we have to do is to spend *quality time* with our dreams. The more we acquaint our brain with what it is we truly want, reinforce our Vision of our future, it will have the same effect as if we had friends and associates telling us "You can do it"! Yes, become our own best cheerleaders. If we talk ourselves into believing that our dreams are possible, then we are more likely to see these come true.

Nathan and Lucy, our elder son and daughter-in-law went through the turmoil of having their home 'super-sized,' nearly doubling the living space for their growing family. No doubt you have also experienced the turmoil of a similar trauma which can precipitate lack of peace, sleepless nights, disruptive behavior in children, and strain on family relationships. All this happened to Nathan and Lucy. When they were near breaking point the builder announced, "I am sorry but your kitchen installation will be delayed three weeks." You can imagine how they may quite rightly have reacted. They had been inconvenienced without a kitchen for months, understandably resulting in strife and confusion. Yet despite the unwelcome news, Lucy remained calm and took it on the chin. The builder was so impressed he offered, "Lucy, because you have not caused a big fuss, I will give you a brand new stove and oven you had not ordered." Lucy was thrilled and told me, "Geo, I believe that oven is God's way of honoring my attitude control. I coped with it because I just kept my focus on the dream of everything being completed, our boys in their new bedrooms and all of us sitting in the new kitchen and dining room enjoying a nice meal."

Focus on Business Dreams As Well

Keeping focused on your dream works in business as well. A few years ago our business was on a serious downturn. We engaged the advice of a consultant and he concluded, "I do not expect you will be able to prevent bankruptcy in the next few months." Simon and I suddenly became very focused on a new short-term objective – survival! We both felt that the devil himself was out to destroy us, so we decided to quote daily some Bible verses which claim God's protection:

"Use every piece of God's armor to resist the enemy
in the time of evil, so that after the battle you will still be
standing firm. Stand your ground, putting on the sturdy belt
of truth and the body armor of God's righteousness. For
shoes, put on the peace that comes from the Good News, so
that you will be fully prepared. In every battle you will need
faith as your shield to stop the fiery arrows aimed at you by
Satan. Put on salvation as your helmet, and take the sword
of the Spirit, which is the word of God."[53]

To this day, I mentally and audibly put this armor on. It seems to empower me to start the day with the right mental framework. During those 'moments of truth' when life does not seem a 'bowl of cherries' (or if it is, why is it I am left with the pits?), we generally have to dig deep to keep our attitude constructive and serving us well. If we have not created a habit of thinking well, we can be sure that under pressure, we will revert to some destructive negative thinking about ourselves and how tough life is to us.

Heidi, my wife challenged me on this just recently. I have been traveling a lot all over Europe in the past few years, and as things have worked out, we have had a great deal of things going wrong. We have had lost baggage, delayed departures, delayed returns, poor nights of sleeping, bad weather, diverted flights – you name it!

Sure enough, I began to verbalize that my next flight must certainly follow the pattern. *I was expecting bad things to happen.*

Thankfully, Heidi gave me a wake-up call by saying, "Honey, shouldn't you be thinking and verbalizing what you want to happen, not what you don't want? Won't this give you a better mindset?" She was spot-on. I immediately changed what I was saying, and pretty soon, I once again believed things would go well on my next flight. Surprise! It actually did go very well, and I am in a much better frame of mind to face the future of travel!

This 'framing of our thinking' can be very effective. It is like *speaking the truth in advance.* It does not guarantee we get a more positive result, but it does get us better prepared to enjoy whatever comes, and I am convinced that in the long term it helps us attract better things into our lives. Faith, in essence, is believing things we cannot see, but we are hoping for. It is agreeing with God what He says about things, about us, about our future is true, regardless of how things look at the present. By choosing to have faith, we pave the way by preparing our minds to see more opportunities and things we want in the situations we face every day. We are "perceptually ready" to learn things, bounce back from disappointments and generally be happier to be around. An illustration might help.

Suppose you go out and buy a certain outfit, car, type of home, etc. Chances are once you do, over the next few days, you will notice how many "other people" have the very same outfit, type of car, phone, that you do! Because your antennae are tuned-in to your new possession, you then become aware of others like yours. This tuning-in for those things we hope for is another illustration of faith in action.

By this time hopefully we are becoming increasingly empowered to believe we can change our lives by making choices to permanently alter the way we think and behave. We then *make a habit* of *making the right choices*, especially when we are under pressure, have too much to do, and are feeling the heat of the moment.

Compass or Clock?

We all know of people who are ruled by the clock and not the compass. I was recently speaking to someone who headed a large church in a major city in England. He had learned to be a super efficient multi-tasking expert. On a scale of completing things on his to-do list, he would have rated himself 8 or 9 out of 10. Question: Was he happy? Was he contented and productive? In his words, "No!" He was devoting most of his time doing things others expected he 'should be' and 'ought to be' doing. Most of the time these activities were so far removed from his Passion with Purpose that he had to take two or three days off frequently just to recover! He felt guilty just taking some time to do some reading and reflection! What a pity! He was driven by a clock instead, as Covey would say, by a compass.[54] So what is the difference?

'Ruled by the clock' means we are *driven by efficiency, not effectiveness*. We see how much we can get crammed into every second of living. We become addicted to the urgent. Ruled by the compass means we measure our productivity by doing the *right things*, not necessarily how many things we do. It is not how many trees we cut down in the forest, it is making sure we are first of all in the right forest, and cutting the right trees (with a sharpened axe!). The *direction* of our events and activities is more important than the amount we do. This is a completely different mind set, and frees us to make and keep the priorities that lead to purpose. From now on, when you are planning your day, week and month, think *'compass'* when you plan, and *not 'clock'*. Make decisions when under pressure that answer the question, "Will this move me nearer my goals and purpose?" not "What can I cram in and get done quickly?"

Priority Check

In "Putting First Things First," Dr Covey emphasizes setting goals in each area of life, or role we play, and then *plan backwards*. Start with the long-term goal first, and work back to the medium-term and short-term. Then set a *weekly goal* in each of your key roles, and plan enough time in each to ensure you get at least those activities done. That way, if you have eight roles, and you accomplish eight key tasks, not only will you keep your life in balance, but you will also keep your activities aligned with your overall *purpose*.

When we choose to live in alignment, we also choose to let go of jumping from activity to activity, depending upon who is shouting the loudest, or who is shouting the longest. We can learn to say 'No' to living solely by the expectations others have of how we should behave and what we should be doing with our time. This is what our harried and worn out church leader did, *and you can too! Make living your Passion with Purpose a habit by choosing to do the right things, on purpose*!

IMPACT CREATIVE ACTION DEBRIEF CHAPTER ELEVEN

Do these before continuing to Chapter Twelve!

1. What areas of your life are prompting you to make deliberate choices?

2. What exactly is it you are going to do?

3. What will 'success' look like when you have done what you wrote in No. 2?

4. How committed are you on a scale of 1 to 10?

5. What would make it a 10?

6. What changes do you need to make to your Passion with Purpose Plan? Go back to Chapter Ten and review what you wrote, then revise as necessary.

Twelve

Developing an Impact! Attitude

"**B**oy have you got an attitude!" Generally speaking, when we say, "Someone has an attitude", we generally mean they have a destructive or negative one. It is infectious, and is guaranteed to spread doom, gloom, fear and doubt wherever it goes. It is a lens that distorts ours and others perspectives so the world fills us with concerns. We can become neurotic and paranoid. Of course, we can also have an attitude which is constructive and positive, as we indicated in the last chapter. Attitude determines our Altitude. Attitude is the state of mind that is determined by the momentum of choices we have made. Let's look at some other ways we can build and maintain a helpful and constructive attitude.

As mentioned previously, reading our purpose, roles and goals daily helps significantly. So does monitoring our progress. Remember, every experience we have can move us towards our goals, or give us something we can learn from. Either way we succeed. We can live without viewing life as being completely full of failures. So long as we are not addicted to perfectionism, we can see each event, activity and experience as a chance to progress and learn. This frees our attitude to look positively at the future, not dread it.

Personal World Records

On our IMPACT! Program, we ask people to share their "Personal World Records." Let's face it, we are all world record holders, not just the athletes who compete in the Olympics. Each of us has an opportunity every day to set some Personal World Records – doing something new, stretching our Comfort Zones in some way. Why don't we naturally do this, without consciously stepping out and up? I believe it is because *we love the steady state*. Our minds are prone to want to operate in this "life as usual" state, where we can operate subconsciously. After all, we think this gives us an easy and stress-free life. We all know this just isn't so. As airplanes are meant to fly, so we are meant to stretch in order for us to live life to the full. It takes *consciously stepping out of our Comfort Zone* to make us build and maintain a positive attitude.

Recently, I stepped out by sponsoring a golf day for people I know, but doing it differently. I felt one of the things I treasure the most is my faith in God. I felt compelled to share this with people I know and appreciate, and get those who wouldn't necessarily go to church a chance to hear others explain the benefits of having an active faith.

I started with a confidently positive attitude – how could I fail? Then I spoke to others who did not share my enthusiasm – they countered my zeal with, "What if …. happens? Or suppose people don't want to pay that much for playing golf? What if you cannot get a speaker?" All of these were good questions, but having started with positive, out-of-comfort-zone energy, soon I was sweating and regretting ever sticking my neck out. That is when I had to rely on maintaining a constructive attitude. Instead of pulling the plug on it all, I prayed even harder, asked more people, became more animated and active in ensuring the day was a success. And it was a success. Christians who rarely associate with non-Christians participated in the day, and vice versa. One of the participants who loves his golf now loves the Lord and is making huge steps in his spiritual journey. Want to build and maintain a positive attitude that serves you well under pressure? Step out of your Comfort Zone regularly. Experience the *risk of failure!*

Culture and Climate of Innovation

Another attitude-developing activity is to develop within yourself, your team and organization a *culture and climate of innovation*. To be innovative requires more than anything an approach to life that says, "There has got to be a better way." So much of our way of life that has produced the standard of lifestyle we enjoy in our society has been the preponderance of innovators who have not been content with sitting back and enjoying life as they found it. Instead, they have been *constructively discontented* with the products, the processes, the level of thinking that led to the status quo. Want to have a stronger positive attitude? Try innovating – start with *constructive discontent* of the unsatisfactory elements you find in your day-to-day world, and ask, "In what ways can we make things better?"

Secondly, do what innovators do, and use *"green-light thinking."* Albert Einstein once said the level of thinking that is used to solve the problems we face must be different than the level of thinking that created the problem in the first place.[55] Green-light thinking is to keep the ideas flowing, while suspending judgment, until you have a whole raft of ideas to choose from. If we stop to analyze every idea as it appears, we lose momentum, stifle our creativity, and find our attitude starting to slip. It is vital, for our attitude's sake, to feel we have many options we could choose from, not just a few. It is back to abundance mentality again, not scarcity thinking.

Once we have a large group of ideas or options (Edward de Bono says we need at least twenty five before we start to be creative)[56], we can start to analyze and judge or group the ideas. Some of them will undoubtedly be useless and irrelevant. Some foolhardy. Within those ideas that survive our scrutiny will be a gem of an idea that could sustain our enthusiasm to press ahead, and keep us positive.

Another approach to build our habit of keeping a positive attitude could ironically appear the opposite of being innovative. The concept is to just *go with the flow*. Rather than continually fight against the current, sometimes it is necessary to keep a positive attitude for us to "let go" and go with the flow.

My perspective on this goes back to my flying days, when we were in a tough situation in the air – threatening thunderstorms and airplanes don't mix too well. Despite intensive preflight planning and intelligent regard for precarious weather, every pilot can run into an unpredictable weather condition that means we run out of ideas, airspeed and/or altitude at the same time. In those conditions, we were taught that rather than turn around and try to miss the line of storms associated with a front of weather, we should pick a direction perpendicular to the front and press on, relying upon our in the cockpit "attitude indicator" to keep our wings level, not lose any altitude, and ride the storm. Believe me, if we tried to rely on our senses, our internal feelings and what our brain was telling us to do, we would have fought and struggled to stay clear of the clouds, flamed out our engines or entered a "stall", all of which would have plunged us deeply into the heart of the storm, icing, fierce gusts of wind and a much more hazardous situation. Trusting our "attitude control instrument," disregarding our emotions of escape and our bodily senses of preservation, was the best course of action—"*go with the flow.*"[57]

W3

We have already mentioned feedback is the food of champions. This is especially so when it comes to building and sustaining a positive and constructive attitude. If we surround ourselves with people who know us well, and devote quality time to getting regular feedback using the W³'s :

W1 What is it I am doing well?
W2 What is it I am not doing so well?, and
W3 What can I do differently or better next time?

The *W³* can help us learn from our experiences and keep a sense of moving ahead, not going back or stagnating. We have discovered that giving regular and immediate feedback to people who are consciously exploring different ways to improve their communication skills and presentations has yielded profound and rapid growth. This, of course, has affected their view of themselves and their ability to change. Hence they have gone on to make even more changes and build an even more positive attitude.

Watch Your Talk

The language we use when reviewing our mistakes and efforts that don't get the desired results is another area to look at when developing a positive attitude. We of course need to be honest with ourselves, yet avoid berating ourselves as failures, good for nothing, self deprecating language that reinforces our limiting beliefs. Instead, the next time you have a failure, instead of saying to yourself, "I am a failure," try something like, "That didn't get the results I wanted. *What can I learn from that*? How can I view this in a way that will help me do better in the future?" It may even feel at the time like we are a failure, but we need to keep our attitude positive by phrasing the matter in a way that builds, not destroys, a positive self belief system.

Recently, I had a chance to exercise a series of events as learning opportunities instead of failures. My heart, the doctor told me, had an artery that was 70% clogged. It was causing angina when I ran and exercised strenuously, so was giving me a cause of concern. Quick as a flash, I was in the hospital, and gave my life, literally, into the hands of skilled cardiologists who performed a very difficult and amazing angioplasty. I now have two pieces of wire mesh in one of my arteries. It keeps my heart muscle fed with oxygen when needed, and I am thankful that this has at least temporarily reduced the likelihood of a heart attack. Now part of me, the Gremlin, would love to rub my nose in it and get me feeling guilty. I must be a poor eater and have an unhealthy lifestyle, otherwise, how come my artery is furring up? However, I refused to go down this road of negativity. I have reviewed the facts and yes, there are things that I can change about what and when I eat, my lifestyle choices and how stressed I let myself get. I can use this experience to learn some vital truths that hopefully will increase my longevity and keep me active. This will come about as I choose my attitude to learn from experiences and not listen to the nay-sayers who would get me to condemn myself and reinforce my limiting self beliefs. Do you want to make a more positive difference in your world? Then build an attitude of learning from experiences, not dwelling on regrets of previous circumstances.

Successful people, in fact, rarely use the word, failure. They experience "hiccoughs," "minor blips" and "things we can learn from." They also cut out limiting words like "impossible". We can learn from this if we, too, want to emulate the attitude of successful people. It is reputed that in every Tiger Woods interview, arguably the best golfer who ever lived, he very seldom gets down on himself even if he has not met his extremely high expectations of himself. Instead, he focuses on what was good about the round and what he is going to do to be even better the next time out.

Positive mental attitudes are formed also with other modifications to our language. Instead of saying, "Someday I'll," when we have made our minds up to do something, we set goals and time related activities and ask people to hold us accountable to them. In addition, we talk to ourselves as, "I am the kind of person who keeps commitments and looks forward," not, "I can't seem to get around to doing the things I should."

'*Should*' – that's an interesting word. How do you feel about yourself when you say, "Should." Try it right now. Think of some activity you know would lead to you having a more positive impact in your life. Now, say, "I should ….." (fill in the spaces). What thoughts do you have? Does it inspire you to get on with it? Probably not. When we coach people to make changes in their lives, we advise them to eliminate "Should's." Instead, try saying, "I could." So repeat your "I should" statement with "I could …... Now, what do you feel? It is not so pressuring is it? It doesn't seem to haunt you so much? That's what most people say. The 'could' leaves the option open until we are more convinced that is the right thing to be doing. Once we are convinced both mentally and emotionally that the course of action we have stated is the one we will do, then we replace our could with will. Much more positive and likely to motivate us to act as we really want.

We have already discussed previously one of life's deadliest diseases – the "hardening of the attitudes" – another one even more deadly is the "PLOMs." PLOM means the Poor Little Old Me disease. Like all of these mind sets, they are habitual – most people who have the PLOMs don't even know it! They go through life thinking their perspective of "Life is the pits" philosophy is normal. The irony is that *life is more or less what we make it*. Jessie B. Rittenhouse wrote a poem that reminds us of what we can make of life –

"My Wage"

"I bargained with Life for a penny, And Life would pay no more. However I begged at evening, when I counted my scanty store. For Life is a just employer, He gives what you ask. But once you have set the wages, why you must bear the task. I worked for a menial's hire, only to learn, dismayed, that any wage I had asked of Life, Life would have willingly paid."

Sober thought, isn't it? To live life as a victim, when we could live it as a victor, means we cannot afford the PLOMs. Instead, we can choose the attitude that I am a goal-setter, goal-seeker and goal-maker. And then regularly review your SMART goals.

Action Makes Goals Achievable

Co-Active Coaching[58], a book and model devised by Laura Whitworth, Henry-Kimsey House and Phil Sandahl have added a different twist to the acronym, "*SMART*" goals. They suggest replacing the A – "Achievable" with "Action – oriented". The ratio-nale is that holding ourselves accountable to not simply set goals, but to DO something and move forward gets the focus off ourselves and our problems, and onto changing things. Even if we don't perform perfectly, one thing is certain, our action will produce some results – something we can review, and at the very least learn from. Yet my experience is that the doing almost always yields more success than one would anticipate, and we will be surprised at the progress we have made. These "*quick-wins*" around the Cycle of Experiential

Development build a momentum that can't help but give us better results, and get us out of the PLOMs.

Keeping our commitments to ourselves builds our self-esteem and helps us keep a positive attitude. The more times I set commitments and best intentions and actually keep them, the more likely I am to see myself as a victor, a finisher and do-er. This positive self-talk and then doing can be habit forming, and thereby reinforce long-term behavior.

I attended a fascinating AGM (Annual General Meeting) very recently. The golf club to which we belong has had a very successful year. More members, better food, facilities and customer service – in almost every way a club can be managed, the year was a good one. Yet during the Question and Answer period, the atmosphere became heavy and changed the mood completely. We left wondering, what had happened to leave us with such a bad taste in our mouth from the meeting? Then it dawned on me – the Q&A session was totally focused on the W^2 – What did not go so well, rather than a balanced view of all W^3's.

The Ninety-Day Criticism Challenge

Skip Ross says we could all gain a much more positive mental framework if we would devote at least ninety days to totally eliminating criticism from our lives, especially our criticism of those people closest to us. He went so far in protecting his attitude, that during one period of his life, if he was engaged in a conversation where people started criticizing others who were not present, that he would stop them and say, "Excuse me, I appreciate you and would love to keep our relationship flourishing. Three things can happen as a result of us sharing time together. Either I will become affected by your attitude, you will become affected by my attitude, or we'll part company. Since you choose to focus on the negative, critical elements in life, I cannot afford to allow your views of life to affect mine. Therefore, we only have two other options. The choice is yours." The results were that people either changed when discussing things in his earshot, or Skip very forthrightly would excuse himself and part company. It takes courage and self-discipline, yet is so empowering when we do. Why not take the ninety day challenge for yourself?

Here's how it works – select a person close to you, who means a lot to you, and for the next 90 days, totally eliminate all criticism of that person. That means saying nothing critical either to that person or about that person for ninety days. It goes even further. Not only shall you not *say* anything, the challenge is to totally eliminate *all* criticism – that means controlling your *thoughts* about that person as well. Do as St. Paul suggested in his letter to church members in Philippi – "Summing it all up, friends, I'd say you'll do best by filling your minds and meditating on things true, noble, reputable, authentic, compelling, gracious – the best, not the worst; the beautiful, not the ugly; things to praise, not things to curse."[59] A great place to practice this is with someone close to you – at work, at home, at school. Even your pastor, if you go to church. Especially at AGM's! The rest of Skip's challenge is this – if, for any reason, you don't make the full ninety days, then all you have to do to complete the challenge is start over! It will, guaranteed, change your life for the better.

Jim Janz, a very successful businessmen from Canada has a great way of dealing with depressive and negative thoughts – whenever things don't go his way, he finds circumstances getting the best of him, he says, "I cannot afford to get negative and dwell on how terrible life is treating me right now. What I'll do is save them up until *Thursday at 4 O'clock*. Nothing very much happens at 4 O'clock on Thursday, so I'll save all my moans and groans until then." Not so surprisingly, Jim found that by 4 on Thursday, the problem and with it the negative feeling had disappeared!

St. Paul advised his friends in Thessalonica to:

"In everything give thanks"[60]

This grateful attitude also keeps us from dwelling on the negative. I appreciate more and more as I gain more of life's experiences the joy of living, and the joy that comes from giving thanks. Look in your BAG – (**B**lessings, **A**ccomplishments, and **G**oals) regularly, it can transform your approach to life.

Figure 12.1 – What Is In Your Bag?

BLESSINGS (THINGS, PEOPLE, EVENTS YOU ARE THANKFUL FOR)

ACCOMPLISHMENTS, ACHIEVEMENTS, ACTIVITIES

GOALS, PRAYERS, HOPES, DREAMS & EXPECTATIONS
FOR THE NEXT FEW YEARS

With your new-found Interpersonal Intelligence, Mental Toughness, Passion with Purpose and Positive Mental Attitude you are ready to make a significantly positive difference in how you communicate!

IMPACT CREATIVE ACTION DEBRIEF CHAPTER TWELVE

Do these before continuing to Chapter Thirteen!

1. Record at least one of your daily successes and achievements, every day for a week and write them here, however small you think they may be

· Success One

· Success Two

· Success Three

- Success Four

- Success Five

- Success Six

- Success Seven

2. Record your response to this exercise here:

3. Person I shared this exercise with:

4. What other actions to build a more positive attitude will you apply? (Set a SMART activity to make it happen!)

S

M

A

R

T

Thirteen

Mastering Communication

~~~

Have you already found your genius of expression through some medium such as art, music, or some other media? For most of us, these means of conveying our feelings, thoughts and ideas aren't well developed. All of us have a way of transferring our ideas, thoughts and feelings that we have used since we first drew a breath. Daniel Goleman in his book, Emotional Intelligence[61] says that one of the major differentiations of those with emotional intelligence and those without is their ability to communicate effectively. It is rare indeed to find people who have made a positive impact in their world who have not been skilled communicators. Yet it is a vast subject, one that is maligned, addressed, criticized in more board meetings, family meal times, school lessons than practically any other subject. Let's explore some aspects of communication that can help us become even more effective at this vital skill. First of all, what is communication, and what is its purpose?

What is communication?

I immediately think of my days in flying to illustrate what communication is. When in combat in Vietnam, the aircraft I was flying had six different transmitters and receivers. Picking the right transmitter was important, or we would be speaking to the wrong person. Some of the channels were not usable, because either the North Vietnamese would send interference signals to "jam" our signal, or some of the transmitters were line of sight, so when we were behind a mountain or too low in the trees meant we could not get our signal through to the right receiver. Even the weather would interfere.

In order to communicate effectively, we of course need to have a transmitter and a receiver. Yet any old transmitter or receiver doesn't work. The transmitter and receiver need to be powered, tuned in to a specific channel that matches, and devoid of interference with other signals, obstacles, etc. that mean the signal sent is received.

For instance, for takeoff, we need permission to taxi. So we need to be tuned in to "Ground Control." We ask permission to start up and taxi, but we wait until we get clearance from them. Still, we don't start taxiing until we acknowledge we have heard them say we are cleared. "Barky 14, you are cleared to taxi to runway 35, winds are 300 @ 10 knots." "Roger, Ground Control, Barky 14 is cleared to taxi to runway 35." Even then, communication has not really happened. The only way Ground Control can determine whether or not we have really understood the message is when they observe our aircraft moving towards the runway. This is effective communication - transmit, receive, be tuned-in, right signal, acknowledgement, and action

Transmission Levels of Communication

Let's say the purpose of communication is to "convey or transfer thoughts, ideas and/or feelings so that the listener(s) understand fully what is transmitted." If this is so, then we might do well to explore communication as it appears in different levels. These levels are:

- · Level 1 Facts
- · Level 2 Opinions
- · Level 3 Feelings
- · Level 4 Values
- · Level 5 Beliefs

Here is a method I find helpful to decipher different types of the words we use for each level.

Communication Level 1

Facts

As we begin to communicate with someone with whom we are unfamiliar, generally, our conversation centers on factual elements. The weather. What brought you here. Where you are from. Who is in your family. How much it costs. What size it comes in. (Get the idea?)

When we contemplate why this might be so, especially when we are encountering someone for the first time, we want to test the ground and find out a bit about the other person(s). It is our way of holding the person at arm's length, getting the measure of the person, to see if they are 'safe' to be around. All the while we share these facts, our subconscious is busy detecting and deciphering the signals through our senses about this stranger, to determine whether we should fight or flight, or whether we should like this person or not. Unless we are really confident, we'll stick to this first level for some time. (Particularly those from more reserved cultures or with more introverted personalities).

Communication Level 2

Opinions

"Nice day, isn't it?" This might be a foray into the second level, our opinions. Less safe than facts, opinions begin to make us vulnerable — our opinions might not be shared by our fellow conversationalist. We generally keep to less risky opinions like the weather, time of day, how our favorite team did at their last outing, etc. Again, our subconscious is working overtime to determine how well our opinions are being received, and building our trust levels to perhaps even share more risky opinions. Unfortunately, so often this can be the only level which many people conduct their communication in much of their lives. They lose such a rich experience of intimacy that comes when we truly become honest, open and trusting in our communication. It is at these other levels we really begin to have an impact. Our work very often is with technically competent people who find it most difficult to communicate at levels deeper than one and two. Only when they get really provoked, do they delve into the deeper levels, and then usually it is in a pique of disgust or anger that puts the continued relationship at high risk.

Communication Level 3

Feelings

Look out, at this level, we really begin to engage and understand or misunderstand each other. Feelings open us by making us even more vulnerable to the other person(s). At this level, we find our clashes of perspectives, beliefs and values are first detected. If we like the Blue Team instead of the Red Team, we could be ridiculed. How we feel emotionally about things differentiates us from our fellow humans. We have different opinions, we can almost live with this. But to have people we value and love express displeasure with our feelings, we can get damaged and hurt. Unless we learn how to handle our feelings, and more importantly how to communicate our feelings of other people's views and feelings, we can withdraw our emotions, and our subconscious mind says, "It's not safe to share our feelings. Better keep them to myself and only communicate facts and opinions."

When our emotions are engaged and really aroused, we tend to explode with them, saying things we regret later, or worse yet, letting our actions speak for us through tantrums, brawls or knife or gang fights. It is my observation most dysfunctional behavior starts when feelings are not communicated effectively. There are still two other levels to explore.

Communication Levels 4 and 5

Values and Beliefs

I've put levels 4 and 5 together because they are detected in communication very similarly, and for most of us we do not really know whether we are speaking from our values or our beliefs. Conversations that involve our values – what matters most to us, what we hold most dear to our hearts, really opens us up. It intensifies our communication around who and what we are, not just how we feel about things. The stakes get very high. Yet there is even a more vulnerable level. What we believe about ourselves, our world, who we are, why we are here – may be the most intimate of all areas. At this level, we not only share our bone-deep thoughts and feelings, but also how badly we feel that we don't always honor them. It is at this level we confess our faults, fears and agonies, hopes and dreams. Perhaps most of us might communicate at this level with very few people on odd occasions. Certainly not share at the belief level with every person or every moment. So picking the right level of communication appropriate for the right person, right moment can be a tremendously important but tricky skill to develop.

Communicating More Effectively

A few years ago there was a terrific beer commercial that sums up what happens when we dare to communicate at the third and fourth levels. The beer supposedly "refreshes the parts other beers can't reach." For me, effective communication is designed to enhance and/or enrich the depth and level of understanding by the transference of a thought, idea, feeling or belief – broaden or deepen our understanding. This happens best, and arguably only, when we can engage at the feeling, values and belief levels. Until we can comfortably and accurately communicate at these levels, we constrict our ability to have deepened understanding and learning.

In practically every organization from a family, community, civic authority or government, when we ask, "What is the one aspect of your life you wish to see improved, or what would make your company or family work even better?" The answer invariably is "We need to improve our communication." So what causes our communication to go badly? One reason we have already explored; we do not communicate appropriately *at the right level,* or *at the right time.* Another is we simply don't communicate at all!

Avoiding the Void

When we avoid communication, we humans are at our worst. We assume when communication breaks down, especially with those with whom we live and work, something is wrong. We fill in the void with feelings like, "I have done something to upset my mother." "He doesn't like me." "I have difficultly relating my feelings to others." The truth is that as time passes, we all continually add to our experiences, our thoughts, our emotions and all that makes us who we are. If we don't express ourselves to others regularly, we drift apart; misunderstandings form, our relationships dry up like a river bed whose upper flow is cut off. I don't know the exact statistics, but we all know of marriages and relationships which end not through too much communication, but too little, especially at the emotional and values and beliefs levels. Daniel Goleman says in his book, Emotional Intelligence, "Simple neglect, studies find, can be more damaging than outright abuse"[62]

Tuning-In Our Receiver

It is more than simply communicating to each other. If we truly wish to make an impact, we need to communicate appropriately. And it starts with us learning to listen, seeking first to understand, rather than being understood as Stephen Covey expresses.[63] One of the greatest impact skills in communication is to develop our *ability to listen*, really listen at the feelings level. How do we practice this? Our approach is to look at both the attitudes and behaviors we take when interacting with others.

For instance, if our attitude towards the person we are communicating with is, "I already know what you are going to say, and I could complete each of your sentences for you," then chances are we will behave in a way that stops listening to the person right away, and we devote our time preparing our responses instead of listening to the words and the 'music' of what the person really is trying to say. Another example – suppose our communicating partner is saying something that is challenging our attitudes, behavior and beliefs about an issue, our natural reaction is to go defensive, and start to prepare our argument. We are *listening with our agenda in mind*, not necessarily hers or his. Our attitude is one of, "I will listen to you so long as you do not make me feel vulnerable or challenge my belief systems." Yet to truly communicate at the 3rd, 4th and 5th levels mean we need to approach communicating with an attitude that says, "I will continue to listen to you and will allow your views and what you say to influence how I see things."

What would happen in most conversations with those who matter to us if we adopted these types of attitudes and behaviors? We in The Wilsher Group have developed a series of attitudes and behaviors we set as ground rules to effective communication, especially when we are in disagreement – see what you make of these.

The Wilsher Group

Ground Rules to Effective Communication to Resolve Conflict

Attitudes

- I assume in good faith that you will be sincere in your expression and are not coming to the discussions with any hidden agenda
- I believe you to be sane (this means you have a valid reason for saying and doing the things you do)
- I truly want to see things from your perspective because I value you as a person and care about our relationship
- I am committed to finding an agreeable solution which will keep our relationship healthy
- I am open to influence and prepared to change the way I see things

Behavior

- I will listen openly and allow your point of view to affect my view
- I will speak to help increase understanding, even though it may make me feel vulnerable

· I will ask questions and summarize your point of view until you agree I am stating things just as you currently see them (Reverse Advocacy)
· Let's work from agreement slowly towards areas of disagreement, at an agreed pace

Why not sit down with your significant others and develop your own "Ground Rules for Effective Communication"?

Selecting the Right Signal

One of the blessings and yet one of the curses within the modern family, business and organization is the preponderance of emails. The blessing: We can communicate almost instantaneously with people all over the world for next to nothing. Even when we are traveling, and only have a mobile phone or text making service for our use we still can keep in touch instantly. Yet who among us has not had strife and misunderstanding spread when we opt to send an email or SMS message instead of picking up the phone or going to see the person, sometimes only a few meters away?

One of our clients (let's call her Mel) rang me recently about an incident which happened on a training program she was attending. Rather than communicate by:

· not attending further sessions of the program
· sending a message of complaint via someone else
· sending an email

She picked up the telephone and gave me a call. We were able to isolate the problem and the cause. The problem involved a third party. Then I had a choice to choose the right signal

· send the third party an email
· wait until Mel was absent from the next session and explain her absence to the third party
· get someone else to handle the situation
· have Mel call the person herself.

Instead, I talked to the coach myself and then we held a conference call where all parties – Mel, the coach and I could openly discuss the incident and arrive at a positive solution. The result – a happy client and much better communication!

The Mighty Written Word

How can we improve our communication when writing? I think first of all it is important to write it, read it, get someone else to read it and give us feedback, then occasionally for certain sensitive communication to sleep on it before we send it.

My good friend Simon Wilsher is a master of the written word. He ponders over it, uses the language of the other person and rewrites important documents a number of times before he pushes the button. The result – generally the recipient says, "Simon, that is exactly the situation, and you have captured accurately the context and facts surrounding how I think and feel about the situation. For that reason, we can work together." *The written word has power*. It is worth taking the time to ensure we get it right so we convey exactly what it is we want to say, with the right tone and words to provide clarity and understanding.

When Face-to-Face is Best

What, then, is a good guide to decide whether we communicate face-to-face or at least by telephone rather than write? Our experience says, if the risk of misunderstanding is high or if the relationship is apt to being damaged if we get it wrong, then it is best to go the face-to-face route, if possible. If not, then at least telephone and actually speak to the person – do not simply leave a message. In fact, only the most skilled of listeners and communicators can get by with dealing with sensitive issues over the telephone.

Until your listening skills are honed to the point of hearing *both the words and the message behind the words*, and you are bold and assertive enough to bring to the attention of the other person what you think you are picking up, even if it is controversial, then I suggest you go eyeball-to-eyeball.

Remember how big our optic nerve is in comparison to our aural nerve? Approximately eleven times. Since our visual sense is so powerful, we neglect using it at our peril. The other person's eyes, posture, what she is saying with her limbs could completely negate what we are hearing with the words she is speaking. Face-to-face allows you to immediately interpret whether or not what you are saying is getting through. And if you detect some dissonance between what she is saying and the body language she is producing you can immediately clarify.

This is especially important in different cultures. In some cultures, the nod of the head actually means "No", or, "I don't understand a word you are saying." As you might remember from our discussions on different personalities, the way they communicate the same message might be completely different. For instance, someone with lots of fiery red energy, may show his lack of confidence by speaking louder, coming across quite aggressive. Someone who communicates earth green energy may display his lack of confidence by saying "yes" to stop the argument even when he means no, and later demonstrates this by his actions. That is why we cannot afford to just take on one set of signals. We need to *use all of our senses*, both physical and inner, to detect what is really going on in the other person's head and heart. Complicated, isn't it?

Is the skill and art of communication a natural or trained attribute? Psychologists have debated this for years. Suffice it to say, regardless of how well we can communicate now, we can all get better at it if we are willing to go around the Cycle of Experiential Development. That *we have been endowed with the seeds of greatness* means we can learn to do things better, including speaking and listening. This is a new day, so why not take one of the ideas discussed in this chapter, and practice your communication?

How to Improve

Ask someone who knows you and cares about your progress in life to give you some feedback. You might ask him, for instance, "John, I am working on my ability to communicate more effectively, as you will appreciate, it is very important if I am to achieve some of the aims and goals I have in life. Would you therefore be prepared to give me some feedback and make some observations about how well or how poorly I listen, and how well you think I get my messages across?" Then make it easy for John by scheduling regular informal chats where he will feel secure in making his observations. We will become nicer people to be around and better communicators when we discipline ourselves to be open to improving our communication.

We are taught by master coaches that in order to help someone through a situation, we need to not only operate at levels three, four and five as we communicate, we also need to *listen with their agenda in mind, and not our own.* This means we must see things from their point of view, hear things with their ears, feel things from their heart. This, believe it or not, is a skill we can all develop. Building genuine rapport and caring deeply about that other person are attributes that work 100% of the time if we earnestly want to develop our ability to listen, as we discussed in the chapter on Interpersonal Intelligence.

Improve Your Public Speaking

Want yet another way to improve your ability to speak and listen? Frequently offer to give a presentation or speak to groups of people! There is something almost magical about the impact on us of speaking to groups if we truly want to improve our communication. Our IMPACT! Program's success in transforming people is largely achieved through having delegates communicate their ideas and give feedback to others in a group situation. The group does not have to be big, but if it can be eight to sixteen, you are likely to find you can hone your skills and develop your communication powerfully and quickly. Why does it work so well? I cannot honestly say. All we know is people when communicating to a group become more transparent, vulnerable and open to receiving helpful feedback than in any one-to-one situation.

When we are asked to coach even high level executives in communication, we almost always insist we see them operate in a group, and then try to use the group experience to sharpen their skills. The result? Time and time again we consistently see when people learn to communicate effectively in group situations, they remember the techniques better than any other way. They then are able to transfer this to working one-to-one, whether written or oral much, much better.

Just a Minute

Here is another exercise you can practice. If you ever had access to listen to BBC Radio 4, you will no doubt remember a very popular program for years called "Just a Minute." On the program the host invites celebrity guests to take a word or topic and speak about it for a minute without hesitation or repetition. If a fellow contestant spots a violation, they beep in, and then having stated what the violation was proceed to speak on that topic themselves. It is hilarious and good fun, full of wit and good humor.

5 W's

What, When, Where, Who, Why

Here is something not quite so demanding, but nevertheless very useful thing to practice. When you are in a conversation with someone, and a topic in introduced, think to yourself, "What experience or incident comes to mind about that topic could I speak about for a minute?" Then, when it is appropriate for you to speak, start with one of the 5 W's listed above and relate your experience, including any lessons learned or interesting conversations that happened during the incident. Then notice people's reactions – did you keep them engaged, interested or amused? At what point did they turn off or interrupt, if they did? You don't need to dominate the conversation, or speak for longer than a couple of minutes, but at least you can practice your skills in conveying messages in an interesting and effective way.

Why We Need to Get Better

We can readily adapt and connect with at least 25 to 50% of the population instinctively. Yet our aim as excellent communicators who want to make a positive difference is to ensure we adapt well to all personalities. This includes transmitting, receiving and sending the right signals which 'tune in' to our listeners and then getting the appropriate response.

Summary

Communication is a vast subject, and none of us become masters of it. We are all just practicing to get better. If we learn to communicate at levels three, four and five more effectively, we are more likely to reduce the occurrences when we are misunderstood or damage our relationships. Our attitudes and behaviors, especially in tricky or sensitive situations are crucial to arriving at a favorable outcome. Finally, it takes practice, feedback and a willingness to discipline ourselves to developing this important core competency if we are going to make the positive difference we desire. Let's now turn our attention to how to speak more effectively.

IMPACT CREATIVE ACTION DEBRIEF CHAPTER THIRTEEN

Do these before continuing to Chapter Fourteen!

1. Which level of communication do you most normally engage in when meeting people for the first time?

2. What sort of person do you find makes it easier for you to communicate on the third and fourth levels?

3. What could you do or develop that might make it easier for people to "be open" with you?

Fourteen

How to Speak So Others are Compelled to Listen

~~

We know instinctively to be an effective listener we must care about what is being said and the person who is saying it. Do you know how important it is to *care* when speaking? Dale Carnegie, author of "How to Win Friends and Influence People" plus other classic works on personal development, first said what I think is at the heart of speaking effectively. It is summed up in *earning, caring, and sharing*.

Earn The Right

First and foremost, ensure you pick the right topic to speak on. *Earn the right* to speak about your subject. We've all witnessed the opposite, when a speaker has not taken this step in his preparation to speak. He fumbles, comes across poorly, lacks enthusiasm, charisma and panache. The listeners are bored, wanting to change the subject and generally dismiss the speaker quickly. If it is a formal situation, then they may be more polite and sit there, although more than likely their mind is somewhere else. We earn the right by sharing from our experiences, our studies, or the personal experiences of others we agree with and support. Dale Carnegie suggested we know forty times more about your subject than you can possibly speak about. Good advice. Here is some more advice he shared – never tell them everything you know or you will put them to sleep or bore them.

Care

Secondly we need to *care* about the subject. So it is not enough just to have studied or researched our subject before we speak. What we are presenting must evoke that passion within us that means we'll convey this positive energy when we speak to others about it. I have listened to thousands of people speak on thousands of subjects over the years, and believe me, one of the quickest ways to lose your listener is to drone on and on about something in which you do not believe or care about. Do the opposite, *develop a passion and excitement about your topic, or pick another topic.*

Share

Thirdly, be *eager to share* what it is you are saying. Some of the topics you may know a lot about and be excited about may not be appropriate to share unless you are eager to do so. For instance, I have been married for many years, to one woman. There are many things I care about that concern our marriage, yet are not topics I would be eager to share. Therefore, I could not speak well on those topics. The same for you. Certain things you have experienced and studied, that you care about are not for sharing with just anyone. So let's be sure to first of all select the right subject to share with our listener(s), and do so with care. Remember – earn, care and share.

Six Honest Men

Here is another tool for both effective speaking and writing that we owe to Rudyard Kipling, the author and journalist of centuries past. He is credited with the saying,

> *"Six honest, working men taught me all I knew. They were what, why and when, how, where and who."*

When you think, "What do I have to say about the subject or topic at hand?", think of the Six Honest Men. For instance, let's say you were asked to speak on your favorite sport, perhaps rugby.

Rather than wade in explaining the rules of the game, use the Six Honest Men questions, and just answer them.

"What, Why and When, How, Where and Who"

"What I like about the sport is the physical side of the game. I like the physical side of the game because when those players start running at each other across the pitch, the ball carrier is challenging the defender to take him down. This cannot be done any other way than looking at their center of mass, keeping your eye on it, and then running at that center. If you hold back, or stop to think you might get hurt, you will not be in the proper hitting position to tackle him. It takes guts, stamina, and concentration. When I was working with the Bath Rugby Club team, I watched them practice their tackling. It was most effective when the tackler threw themselves fully into the tackle, driving their legs, wrapping their arms securely around the ball carrier so as to drive them back. That was a good tackle!"

Now see if you can spot the Six Honest Men in that paragraph. Some might be explicit, others implicit, but the answers to those Six Honest Men form the framework of that communication.

Here's another thing to try. When you want to capture the listener's attention, start with an ORI – observation, reflection, inspiration. Example:

Observation, Reflection, Inspiration

Observation – "I was watching my wife play golf the other day, and noticed how rhythmically she was swinging. The ball was propelled forwarded like a shot from a gun, and yet the effort she seemed to take in making the swing was minimal. It was of little surprise, then, that she played well, had fun, and could not wait until the next game."

Reflection – "As I reflected upon this and its application to communication, it seems that we can sometimes try too hard, and force ourselves to try to think of the right words, rather than 'go with the flow', and simply say the first things that come out of our minds and hearts."

Inspiration – "So in our session today, as we polish our communication skills, let's remember, like the golf swing, we can get in a rhythm and let our subconscious 'gut feel' determine what it is we are to say next, simply say what first comes to mind and let it flow."

Tuning-In

As we discussed earlier, unless we know what channel the other person or persons are on, there is no way we can deliver our message effectively, despite how well we say, structure, or put energy into it. Tuning-in is a preparation thing to do as well as an on-the-spot response to what is going on at the moment. Great speakers know their audience. They can instinctively tune in to the listener's favorite channel, WIIFM – **W**hat's **I**n **I**t **F**or **M**e. If we can weave into our opening few words things that connect with the listener's benefits or interests, using their words if possible, we are well on our way to gaining their favorable attention and interest. Example - "Charles, you said recently that money is tight. If we could find a way to save you an extra $200 per month, would you be prepared to explore it?" Of course he would. You have his attention.

First Three Words

When we are delivering our message, we need to keep in mind that our listeners are able to process information at least two to four times more quickly than we can speak. Therefore, once we have made our point with the last topic, we then need to smoothly transition to a new thought, idea or experience in order to sell our overall proposition and keep their attention. One method I picked up from Steve Manning[64] was to ask yourself a question you think the audience might want to hear the answer to, then to think of the first three words or "picture thought" that come to mind that answer the question. Then, structure a series of sentences or paragraphs which relate. Keep it action focused, using words that stimulate thought and word pictures in the mind of our listener. Form good bridges from the last thought, and then move on. Here is an example:

Suppose you think the listener might be asking, "Why should I learn to speak more effectively in front of groups"? As you contemplate this for a few minutes, the words "fear, power and passion" come to mind. You might then start your speaking with, "How many of us know one the greatest fears most people have as shown in numerous polls is public speaking? Conquering this fear is nature's best way of building our confidence and power to get messages across, regardless of the size of audience. Each of us has a passion for doing something worthwhile with our lives, yet so often we die with our passion inside of us because we fear we might fail. Yet very few of us will ever get our passion outside of us unless we learn to overcome our fear of speaking in public, and build the self-confidence to succeed."

That's how simple it can be to construct your topic in bite-sized pieces. If you had previously been making your point about what communication is, then you could introduce the topic on "Why should I learn to speak more effectively to groups" by saying, "So communication, then, is the process of conveying a thought, idea or picture from one person on another through a medium both the transmitter and receiver have tuned in, and what better way to do this than when speaking to groups of people, face-to-face." This bridge then introduces our listeners to the next question, "Why should I learn, etc." Get the idea?

Use Your Audience's Knowledge and Experiences

Listeners' lives are filled with countless experiences, and we can use this fact to help us ensure they relate well to and actively listen to what we are communicating. If we are excellent listeners, we'll know how to open their menus of topics by relating experiences we have had which we share in common. With footballers, we speak about football and sports. With music lovers, we speak about music, instruments, etc. It really is that easy. A great way to engage them is to first of all ask them a question that relates to their interest. Let's suppose you are speaking to a young person who is into the latest high tech gadget to do with mobile or cell phones. And what you want to convey to her is how much better it is if she would keep her room tidy. You might then start your conversation with, "Ellie, what is so fascinating to you about the 3G technology now available on most phones?" She will then tell you what she thinks. You might then ask, "What kind of structure and order do you think the technical people who made 3G work had to use?" Hopefully, she will hypothesize they had to use a lot of structure and organization. Then you might bridge with, "So if you want to be able to be as creative and inventive as these people, what is wrong with practicing some order and structure in your bedroom?" She will probably just laugh, but at least you have made your point, and kept her attention. Who knows, it might even sink in!

Laughter Has a Place

Use of laughter is a great way of engaging our listeners and helping us to keep attention. Unless you are a great joke teller, use jokes only once well rehearsed and tested on smaller audiences or friends. The best humor is the quick-witted kind that arises at the spur of the moment, during your conversations.

The safest and best type is when you make yourself the butt of your own jokes. Zig Ziglar tells on his "See You at The Top" tape series of being confronted by a lady prior to a speaking engagement who accused him of being nervous about the occasion. Zig replied to the women, "Certainly not! I may be excited, but I am not nervous." "Yes, you are" said the lady. "What makes you say that?" replies Zig. "What else would describe you being in the ladies' toilet then?"

One of the ways I introduce laughter in my talks/facilitation sessions in the United Kingdom is by making fun of my American heritage. I politely ask, "Can anyone pick up a slight twinge of American accent?" Of course, I have quite a broad Mid-western American accent, so I always get a twitter of laughter or a least a smile or two. This also serves to connect me to them, as I then go on to explain, "I may not speak with the best British accent, but having lived in England for over thirty years, I certainly listen in British, so you'd better watch what you say!" Very often I am partnered by someone from the U.K., so I then claim, "I have brought John with me to interpret if needed!" As you can understand, if you use unique or "out of the ordinary" things about yourself, and then turn it into laughter, you will more than likely keep your speaking entertaining and keep your listeners attentive.

Focus upon their WIIFM

Remember, the listener is usually at the WIIFM level of listening. This means they are listening with their *own interests, wants and needs in mind*. They are focused on *themselves*. Want their engagement? Get them involved in what you are saying. Ask questions that bear upon an interest of theirs. Use their name often in a conversational style. This will require before the event you get to know their names and discover possible areas of interest. Then when you are speaking, you might ask, "So Jo, in what ways will being a more effective communicator help you improve the chances for promotion you are seeking?" Believe me, if this is genuinely what Jo wants, you will have her fully engaged.

Using the Laws of Learning to Communicate

One of the greatest aids to my being able to make a positive impact through engaging in meaningful conversation I discovered through reading a number of books on the Laws of Learning. These "Laws" are based upon theories of how the brain works and stores information, and are found in many books on learning. We have already explored some of these in previous chapters, and we know spaced repetition is good for us, so here they are again! I use an acrostic to help me remember them.

Poor Richard Finally Asked Kelly Out Virtually Every Rainy Season.

The first letter of each word reminds me of a "law" that I can then use to help people to learn or remember.

Poor – Primacy
Richard – Recency
Finally – Frequency
Asked – Analogy
Kelly – Known to unknown
Out – Outstanding event
Virtually – VHF – WIIFM
Every – Expectation
Rainy – Rhyme
Season – Steady state

Law of Primacy

The First Time

Behaviorists and psychologists have proven that the first time we hear of a piece of information it forms a synapse in our brain that is linked forever. And the first time can be the most powerful. One example of this is when someone is asked to repeat the sentence, "The moon is made of _____." Invariably, most people answer "cheese," or "swiss cheese" or something like that. Now why would grown, educated people reply with that? Chances are, the first time they heard their parents answer the question, "What is the moon made of daddy," the reply had something to do with cheese. Try it on someone, if you don't believe me!

Law of Recency

The last thing in is the first thing out

How many times have you awakened in the morning humming a tune you heard just before you went to bed at night? How often have you had thoughts the day after the night before that reflected something you had just read, heard, etc., just before retiring? That is the Law of Recency at work.

Law of Frequency

Over and over and over again

This certainly works if you want to remember something for exams, your password, shopping list, take the time to say it or at least think it over and over and over again. We know this as "rote memory," and it works very well. Someone once said the way to get a point across is to "*Tell the person what you are going to tell them, then tell them, and at the end, tell them what you* told them." It is a classic way of structuring a longer talk or conveying complex information.

Law of Analogy

Using a picture thought to convey a 'just-like' connection

We already know the power of visualization. We use it when we want to energize our passion, so why not use it to get others to connect to what we are saying? Analogies and metaphors very often get our ideas rolling into the minds of our listeners simply and effectively. It's like "Water off a duck's back." (Sorry for the crude example.) Hope it worked for you, though!

Law of Known to the Unknown

Taking people's thinking from some piece of information or thought that you know they know to something that is new to them will help them form the links in their memory

It will make sense more easily, and therefore stick. If flying a super-sonic aircraft is related at all to driving a car, then pointing out to a person the similarities will help the learner grasp the new concept of flying. Going from the known to the unknown. It's the way our brain works, so use it when we converse with others.

Law of Outstanding Events

An experience so engaging by its out–of-the-ordinary
or un-expectedness that it causes the person
experiencing the event to say, "Wow!"

On the detrimental side, having or witnessing a car accident forms such a strong synapse in our brain it may haunt us for the rest of our lives. Physical and mental abuse as a child are examples of this. On the other hand, helpful experiences that are pleasant and memorable serve as excellent ways of reinforcing a message in our brain, or making it easy for our audience to remember. In our work we tend to use multi-level learning experiences where there is a lot happening all at once as a way to make the experience memorable.

Putting people on the spot, and gently asking them to step out-side of their Comfort Zone then getting them to practice something with all eyes upon them really reinforces the message. How can you use this when you speak? Do something unexpected! *Give them something to remember*. Engage their senses of taste, touch, smell, hear, or see all at the same time! This leads very nicely into the next law.

Law of VHF – WIIFM

Visual, hearing and feeling senses lead more effectively to
tuning in to people's What's-In It-For-Me"

There are two parts to this law; the first one is to ensure you get people engaged *visually*. We have described earlier the necessity to ensure our message and our body language are in concert. At the same time, ensure they *can hear you adequately*. Use your pitch, pace, pause and intonation in ways that keep the person awake, not put them to sleep. Thirdly, put elements into your speaking which *involve them emotionally* – develop your emotional power so you can take people with you. Then add the really powerful part of this law – the WIIFM. We've already discussed the relevancy of "**W**hat's

In It For Me." Combine WIIFM with VHF and we can use this law to capture and keep people listening to our every word.

Law of Expectation

If we expect people to respond, they probably will, and vice versa

The Law of Expectation is also known as the Pygmalion Effect as we discussed briefly before. Pygmalion, for those unfamiliar with the story, was a mythical person who sculptured a woman rather than try to find one. Over time, his treating the statue like a woman was recognized by Aphrodite as "real love," and rewarded Pygmalion by bringing the statue to life. The Pygmalion Effect, then is the "teacher expectancy effect." The stronger the expectation is of the teacher that the student will perform in a certain way, the more likely it is that the student will indeed perform in this way, either good or bad.

How does this apply to our speaking? If we expect our listeners will want to listen to us, find us interesting, and are positive we have something to say, we will be more likely to present ourselves well, and therefore get a positive response. However, even more predictable is the likely outcome if we think we have nothing to say, that the listeners won't want to listen to us, then we won't speak well, will come over poorly and therefore reap the expectation we had – a *self- fulfilling prophecy*. What is the conclusion – obviously, *expect to speak well and we'll be more likely to do so*.

Law of Rhyme

Use of rhyme, music and rhythm leads to improved memory

Using rhyming words such as poems and in music, even rap, helps us to remember more, and to help our listener's remember what we said. Speakers and sermon writers for years have tried to help their listeners by using words that rhyme or are spelled with the same first letter as "hooks" around which to hold the talk together. For instance, we could help people remember the importance of building relationships before we attempt to tell them something we know will help them by summarizing with, "People don't care how much you know til they know how much you care." The rhyme and sing song of the saying helps it stick in our mind.

Law of Steady State

Breaking the mold

Like the Law of Outstanding Events, breaking the principle of the universe of momentum will cause people to sit up and notice. As Sir Isaac Newton stated, "every object will remain at rest or in uniform motion in a straight line unless compelled to change its state by the action of an external force."[65] The German language calls this phenomenon, Gestalt. It is sometimes known as inertia. The way this can help in our communication is to *get out of sync with what the listener thinks will happen next*, break through the routine of what might be said and be provocative. This jolt of the steady state will certainly get our listeners to pay attention.

Warming Our Listeners

Want a surefire way of warming the listener to what we are saying? Speak modestly about yourself, and build up your audience with genuine regard. I can recall countless conversations with people who try to convince me they are important and famous, rich and worthwhile to listen to. Instead of warming to them, and holding them in high regard, I thought, "How arrogant and full of pomp." (That's the clean version!) It makes very hard work of taking seriously whatever it is they say. Yet the opposite is true. Dale Carnegie said, "Give people a fine reputation to live up to"[66] as a way to build a strong bond with them. Do it sincerely.

When you speak about yourself, speak modestly, play yourself down, point out your faults and foibles or at least your "humanness" if you want to get the listeners to warm to you. Of course, don't over-do it or you will appear insincere, and turn your listener off, not on. It was said Winston Churchill when appearing before the

Congress of the United States after WWII started his talk by stating how humbled and honored he felt by being asked to appear before Congress. This resulted in Senators and Congressmen giving him a standing ovation.

The Eyes Have It

One of the ways to convey our sincerity, and show our listener we mean what we say, is to *look at them squarely in the eye*. They say the "eye is the window to the soul." It's like we can look right inside a person when we carefully look into their eyes. Allowing the other person to look into yours has the same effect. Few of us can fake sincerity when we are eyeball to eyeball with someone. Of course, like all of these ideas, to coldly stare is not what we are talking about here. It is simply allowing our eyes to naturally connect with our listeners. Very effective when we are attempting to convey emotion or convince them of our sincerity and genuineness.

Getting Back on Track

We have all probably had the experience when our listener quit listening. Let's face it, most of us have never been taught to listen, and when we do listen, we listen at the level with US in mind. That means even the best listeners will wander in their attention to what we are saying. What can we do to ensure we are connecting, and keeping them glued to what the conversation is about? Simple. Let *them* speak. In fact, force them to speak by asking them a question. One of the most amazing pieces of information I can remember getting when I was learning to communicate more effectively was that *if you want to guide the conversation, then ask questions*. Get the other person speaking. People generally answer the question you ask, therefore, asking the questions leads the conversation. If you want to find out about the other person, then ask her about her family, her work, what she does for recreation, or what she might do if she had extra money.

How many of us would love to be asked these questions, and then have someone genuinely listen to what we say? Practically everyone. They will leave your encounter thinking, "My, what a great conversationalist you are," when all you did was *ask the right questions*!

Conveying Technical Information

Use diagrams, schematics and drawings to help get your point across. Very often, when we are in communication with someone our goal is to convey some technical information – at least it appears to be technical to him because he has not got your level of expertise about the subject. How do we ensure we get the message across effectively? Some tips – First of all, one picture is worth a thousand words.

Keep it simple. Chris Bradley, a very dear friend of mine, is a chartered accountant who has made a good living in making accounts easy to understand for non-financial people. One of his favorite sayings is, "To explain simply is to know profoundly." If you use simple language, explain carefully and simply any words or concepts not familiar to the listener, then you will help them to connect with what is being said.

Organize your thoughts in a logical order. Go from beginning to the middle to the end. Arrange it chronologically. Go from something they know to the areas they don't know – remember from the Laws of Learning? Use examples as a way of making technical information interesting and understandable.

Use analogies, as described in the Laws of Learning. If I were to try to convey to us, for instance, what makes an airplane wing produce "lift", I would try to illustrate by saying, next time you are riding in a car on a nice day, roll down the window, and put your hand straight out into the wind, like a wing. Then, turn your hand slightly so that the angle of your hand is up. Watch what happens. Your hand will want to "fly" up. Tilt the hand down, and again, observe the results. The hand will "fly" down. The air pressure that makes your hand go up and down is the same air pressure that supports the Boeing 747.

Narrow your technical information to the 'vital few, not the trivial many.' The first time people hear something new, they need to have it simple, and not too in-depth. There will be time for them to find out more, if they are interested, later.

Last of all, *summarize often*. At each stage of a technical explanation, bring the listeners with you by summarizing what you have covered before commencing some other new information. Better yet, ask them to summarize. That will ensure they have taken it what you have presented.

How to Get Others to Take Action

When you want to call someone to take action on what you are saying, it seldom works just to say, "Do it because I told you so." It might work with your three-year-old, but soon enough, even those who love you dearly will balk at being told what to do "just because." Human beings respond best when the action is justified in some way. One great way of getting someone to do something is phrasing what it is you want her to do by *providing evidence that supports the benefits* of them doing it, and avoids the consequences of not taking the action you suggest. Dale Carnegie called these "Incident, Action, Benefit" talks. They work wonders.

Incident, Action, Benefit

Let's suppose you want a member of your team to stop trying so hard to please everyone. How could we persuade them to do this by using the structure, incident, action and benefit? First of all, we *start with the action we want him to take*. Make this short and positive. Rather than saying the action is, "Stop trying so hard trying to please everyone," we will rephrase this as a positive action such as, "Focus on doing what is right, regardless of what others may think."

Then we work on the *benefit*. The benefit may seem self-evident, yet all too often we assume others know the benefit, when they don't. Specifically state the benefit you think he will get when he "Focuses on doing what is right." There are probably a dozen benefits, so just pick one you feel applies to the person at the moment. It might be, "You will build clarity and focus in your own judgment." Now that you have identified and clarified what action you wish your listener to take, and the benefit if he does, we need to search the archives and synapses of our brain to recall an incident or experience –something you heard or something you observed—that illustrates your action and benefit.

In the example above, we said our *action* was, "Focus on doing what is right." Our *benefit* was, "You'll build clarity and focus in your own judgment." The *incident or experience* that comes to mind for me was recently when I was listening to someone who was not getting the results he wanted – he was new to his role, had sold himself well in the interview that he could "do the job" and introduce a large amount of new business to his company. Let's call him Roger. Roger was manifesting all sorts of behavior and attitudes that said, "I'm trying to please everyone." He would start one thing, then bounce over to another. He wanted to introduce a whole group of new ideas despite only being in the role a few weeks. He was stressed, could not maintain his attention on anything for longer than a few minutes.

Finally, I asked Roger, "What is it you are afraid of?" This stopped him in his tracks. He pondered a moment and then said, "I am afraid I might fail, and the owners of the company will not like me because I am not performing the way they expect me too." After some more discussion, when we asked Roger to put into words what he really thought he could do, he relaxed, became much more focused, and was able to make significant decisions and take actions that did help him achieve the success he expected from himself. If I want you to take the Action we stated earlier, can you see how the Experience I related would help you see the relevance of doing so? To what degree was it more convincing than if we had just said, "Stop trying so hard to please everyone."?

Hopefully, you get the point. Let's summarize –

· Think and clarify what *action* you want people to take
· *Memorize* it if you can
· State one *benefit* in words that connect with the listener(s)
· Think of and then tell an *incident* from your own experience that makes the point

Following your story, state both the *action* and the *benefit* in that order to persuade them to do what you are saying. The *action – benefit* summary will have so much power and influence, and really stick in your listener's mind.

In the next chapter, we will look at how to make longer talks with impact for communicating more complicated or bigger ideas which require the input and action of others.

IMPACT Creative Action Debrief Chapter FOURTEEN

Do these before continuing to Chapter Fifteen!

1. Write down at least 3 things you feel you could speak about that meet the ECS criteria:

- Earn the right through personal experience and/or study
- Care about what you are saying
- Share what you have learned or experienced because you care

2. Who is it that you'd like to share at least one of these with?

Go ahead, do it now, by telephone or face to face, then record your reflections here.

3. Try using the incident, action, benefit process to persuade someone to take action. Record what happened here:

Fifteen

Presenting With IMPACT!

Giving Longer Talks or Presentations

What do we mean by a longer talk, and what makes it different besides just being longer? Longer talks generally mean we are asked to speak, or have the opportunity to more formally convey an idea, message, course of action or plan, and very often this is to larger groups of people. It usually has a number of points that need to be made. The message might be complex or technical. The "longer" talk means by definition that it may last from fifteen minutes to three hours or more. I know of one presenter, Zig Ziglar, who held a group of us spell bound with life changing information for eight hours, and never once used a note! If we aspire to make an impact in the way we communicate, then we must learn to present with impact. Therefore, it will involve us having to plan even more carefully what we are going to say, the structure we use in presenting, as well as how we present it.

When the pressure is on to perform, we need to plan carefully what we are going to say, back up our points with supporting evidence, and then sell the message! Here is a sure-fire planning method – the Six P's because Prior Planning Prevents Poorly Performed Presentations!

The First of the Six P's

What is the Purpose of your presentation?

What reaction do you want from your listeners? What do you want them thinking, saying, feeling and doing as a result of your presentation? Write it down, make it precise and clear. Know why you are talking. Keep it simple. When preparing to deliver a message, idea or thought we need to identify whether we want to:

- persuade
- educate
- convince
- entertain
- justify
- reach a decision
- take action
- influence
- motivate
- gain consensus
- test the idea
- clarify

and many others. We need to be able to put our purpose into a clear statement of intent that "headlines" what it is we want to do with the presentation. Try developing 3 or 4 statements. Speak them out to a colleague, family member or friend. Better yet, speak about the purpose to the people or organization you know will populate the audience. If your purpose is not clear, then it is like trying to start off on a journey without being clear of your destination. You may entertain, make someone laugh, inform someone, but to what end?

Gordon had worked hard on a presentation he was to make to a global audience, his boss and fellow colleagues. He had thirty to forty superb, highly technical slides ready to show the audience that might impress, bore, or put the audience to sleep. When I asked him, "Gordon, what is the purpose of your presentation?" He sat for a moment with his mouth open, then said, "You know, I don't really know. I was asked to give a presentation, so I put this together, using a template they provided. I am not really sure what it is I want to accomplish." Gordon's experience is not uncommon.

Time and again I have witnessed people who sweat, agonize and nervously await their dreaded fate of speaking to a large or important public gathering. Yet they have not considered that much of their anxiety comes from not having a clarity of purpose that acts as the goal to focus both their planning and preparation, and their measure of how well they have done. With the clear purpose comes confidence that underpins their whole experience. Gordon did come up with a purpose. He then went on to "Wow" his audience of seasoned international experts in his field. As a result, his card was marked for being given additional responsibilities and promotions.

The Second of the Six P's

Who are the People in your audience?

Examine every link the listeners may have with your subject. *Develop a genuine interest in your audience and their needs.* Consider their personality preferences, background, stated and non stated interests, cultured way of making decisions, etc. As we have said before, remembering a person's name is one of the best ways to connect and let the audience know you are interested in them.

Remember Gordon? One of the factors that made his presentation so outstanding was that he frequently involved people in the audience, calling them by name. This really kept their attention and interest, because they never knew whether Gordon may call on them at any moment. Very effective. Here is a table of things to try to get to know about your audience:

- **People's Names**
- **Personality Preferences**
- **Culture**
- **Background**
- **Interests**
- **Decision Making**

Now we have a purpose, and know the people, at least the key influencers in the audience. Now we can go on to the content by asking ourselves:

The Third of the Six P's

What is the Proposition or central theme?

Find a theme, a *central idea – a thread which you and your audience can cling to*. Keep this theme running through your presentation. What message will your listeners carry away with them? Could be an analogy, a metaphor, visual building blocks, comparison with some other product or service, what the competition is doing, etc. From our discussions of the Laws of Learning, perhaps developing a VHF (Visual, Hearing and Feeling) way of outlining the presentation will serve both you and your listeners well. Develop two or three you could use, then practice delivering each, see which one connects.

Some heads of organizations we work with see so many presentations, especially from technical people, that they insist that the presentation begin with the "bottom line." "What is it you are asking of me by making this presentation?" they ask. "Is it a decision you want? Is it more budget? Is it something else? Then state it for us clearly at the beginning of the presentation." This is good advice for all of us. It will undoubtedly relate to your purpose, but is put in terms of the audience, and what it is you want from them, not simply your purpose. Here's an example. Let's suppose your purpose is: "To persuade the audience that they could get even better results and improve team work if they would take the time to build bridges of understanding."

The proposition or central theme then could be the *bridge of understanding*. We could use this visual metaphor of a bridge all the way through. We could introduce the benefits of a bridge to cross boundaries and obstacles. We could discuss those things that make bridges collapse, what foundations we need in place to build the bridge upon. We could also include the construction of the bridge, pressure points, strains and stresses, etc. Get the drift? Now that we have a central theme or proposition that we think might work, we can go on to the detail. They are the points we ask our audience to consider that back up our proposition, but done in a bite-sized way.

The Fourth of the Six P's

What are the Power Points?

Power Points are the *hard facts that give strength and truth to your assertions*. Pick out the powerful convincing ideas or incident details that support your message. Put together a series of Evidence, Action, Benefit case studies, experiences, or scenarios that make your proposition or central theme convincing. A structure I recommend you follow is

Bite-sized Evidence Packages

Remember our previous discussion on **I**ncident **A**ction **B**enefit structure for persuading a listener to take action? An incident or experience is just one form of evidence we can use.

INCIDENT

Deliver in 2 to 3 minutes maximum

ACTION

Take no more than 20 seconds to make your point/request action

BENEFIT

Take a mere 10 seconds or 8 words to state the benefit then go to the next Power Point

A longer talk is a series of evidence packages; not always in the order of Incident, Action, Benefit, but certainly containing all three. This evidence in the Body of the Presentation **DEFEATS** the skeptics, the doubters and unconvinced. Evidence combined with persuasive benefits makes our proposition hard to refute.

So what forms of evidence are there that **DEFEATS** the doubters?

· **Demonstrations**
· **Experiences and incidents**
· **Facts**
· **Exhibits**
· **Analogies and metaphors**
· **Testimonies**
· **Statistics**

Demonstrations

Show how something works.

Some examples:

· Demonstrate a new sales approach to sell a certain product; working with a group member, the leader role-plays with him/her the new sales approach. This is repeated several times so the group understands fully how to carry out the new sales approach. The use of video makes this even more effective.

Evidence Package

Demonstration- action-benefit

"So you have seen how the form is to be completed, simply and accurately. If we all adhere to this way of completing the form we will be able to quickly and accurately pay the expenses you are owed."

Experiences and Incidents

Personal experiences or experiences of others

Some examples:

·   A personal experience of the speaker
·   Manager overlooking the cost of freight transfer in pricing an item
·   Hiring 'mistakes' and the consequences
·   Sales manager's failure to get a sale because of a weakness in customer service
·   Design omissions that caused an expensive cost overrun
·   Quality control problems regretfully ignored
·   Another person in your company whose experience underlies the point you are making:

N.B. Get clearance to use any story and quote the person who had the experience – be sure to check all the facts!

Your organization's experience

An example:

·   Frequently your organization has lived through an experience that emphasizes your points. Again, be sure of your facts.

Experiences of other executives in other organizations

An example:

· Business and professional journals and periodicals are filled with such experiences. Be careful to quote the person and the source of the article.

Other organizations' experience

· Similar to the 3rd example. This information can be found in business and professional journals and periodicals.

Evidence Package

Experiences

Facts

Information that substantiates its truth or trustworthiness by itself, needs no justification

Some Examples:

· When the heart stops for a certain period of time, the brain dies
· A company's marketing function is split into various product/ support areas
· Grass is generally green
· The rain in Spain falls mainly in the plain

Evidence Package

Facts–action-benefit

"We have been behind our budget for three consecutive months. Our face-to-face time with customers and prospects

has shown similar downturn. Let's all make a concerted effort to double our face-to-face time this coming month and see the impact this has on bringing in more business."

Exhibits

A visual, chart, graph, picture, powerpoint slide or other tangible object

Some examples:

- A plan showing a construction site on which the company is about to erect a building. A large copy of the plan was mounted on the front of the wall of the meeting room, with copies distributed to each person in the audience. While explaining how the construction site will be utilized, the speaker used a large pointer to identify the various points in the plan and the members of the audience followed on their own copies.
- An architect's drawing of the completed building would be an excellent exhibit to illustrate the result of the group's efforts. In this case, the drawing was on a slide which was projected onto a large screen in front of the group.
- Large visuals of new products, new advertising or new packaging of a product. In one instance a speaker had examples of television advertising made up in large still photographs on easels in front of the room. As he was making the points about the advertising, he would refer to the photographs, this making it easy for the audience to understand what he was saying.
- Packaging differences which are being considered. In this example, the speaker used both the old and the new packaging to illustrate the impact of the change that was being contemplated. The new packaging was passed round the audience so that they could not only see the difference, but could get the feel of the product, the smoothness of the print and the solidness of the container.

- An enlarged photo of a display to illustrate exactly how a product will be offered to the public. In this case, the speaker had taken a photograph of the shop window display. It showed not only the impact of the company's advertising and packaging, but also its impact in relation to the other competitive material and products in the window. In one photo, the speaker was able to educate the audience as to how the display should look and also indicated how it should be placed away from competitive items.

Evidence Package

Exhibit-Action-Benefit

"This new product design is much more tactile, as you can see and feel. When introducing this to the client, let them touch it themselves, and it is highly likely they will want to buy."

Analogies

Relating a complex idea to something simpler and easily understood by your audience.

Some examples:

- From a presentation on goal setting, 'Pursuing pre-established goals, regardless of the type, is often like driving in rush-hour traffic. Though the process may be slow, the important thing it to stay the course and keep moving ahead.
- From a presentation on how to increase sales in an organization, 'Trying to sell while ignoring our past successes and failures is much like bowling under a curtain hung across the alley – we do not know how well we have done and where to throw the next ball.'
- From a presentation on a new engineering design, 'In view of the frequent changes in policy by local municipalities, it is necessary to design for maximum anti-pollution standards.

Not to do so is like trying to drill an accurate hole through jelly. Once we turn the bit, the shape changes.'

· From a presentation on communication skills, 'Getting someone to listen to you is like being one of many television channels your listener can choose; the other channels probably feature programs of his/her past experiences, present plans and future hopes. Unless we are interesting and highly relevant, our listener has simply to change channels to hear another, more stimulating program.

Evidence Package

Analogy-Action-Benefit

"Getting the golf club into the hitting area on your golf swing needs to feel like you are swinging a tennis racquet to hit the oncoming ball. If you repeat the 'tennis motion and feel' with your golf club, you will develop more power and consistency."

Testimonials

Words written, recorded or given orally by someone the audience would verify that the person has earned the right to offer their opinion, advice and comment

Some examples:

· Statistics from a reputable government agency or department. In one case, it was important for the speaker to convince the audience of the effect of population and demographics on the purchase of a certain product. She was able to do this by using the Department of Environment statistics to indicate the increases and decreases of certain age-groups in the population.
· Engineering data and results from an engineering society which is respected by the group. One speaker, a chem-

ical engineer, quoted the American Institute of Chemical Engineers as the source of some data on changes in pollution design to augment a point he was making about the relative cost of controlling pollution vis-à-vis the entire cost of an expansion to a chemical plant.

In whatever field under discussion, a universally respected leader is quoted as to certain findings of a study. In previous workshops, there have been quotations from leaders in such fields as highway design, laboratory procedures, health care background and several other specific fields of endeavor. The key is to make sure that the leader who is quoted is respected by the audience.

A key company executive's opinions are quoted about a new procedure. Here we are concentrating on the respect that this executive receives from the audience. His/her position, reputation and credibility, demonstrated in the past, will be important in making any quotation of this kind.

Evidence Package

Testimony-Benefit-Action

"Thomas Edison once said, 'Genius is one percent inspiration and ninety-nine percent perspiration.' You can develop the genius inside you by getting struck in and never giving up!"

Statistics

Numbers indicating increases, decreases, % changes, comparisons, trends and summations

Some examples:

- Sales data reflecting year-to-year comparisons by product lines, indicating both gross sales and profit contributed by each line

- Population growth figures, and the demographic changes in each city per year
- Quality control data indicating changes in 'passed' equipment, by year and assembly line, to show the effects of automation of several of the lines
- Comparisons of year-to-year drilling activity, broken down by oil and gas wells, number of completions, and seismic crew activity
- Actuarial statistics to justify increases in insurance rates

Evidence Package

Statistics-Action-Benefit

"Seventy percent of people working in large companies in major cities wish they could change their lifestyle. If we could tap into this group of people with a sure-fire way of helping them make the transition, we would have an excellent business opportunity."

Now let's summarize by using our next 'P' – Profit

The Fifth of the Six P's

What is the Profit or Benefit?

What is the *summary statement* of all of your 'Evidence Packages' that consolidates all the audience will gain by agreeing with your recommended action(s)? This could be something that comes to your mind only after delivering your Evidence Packages.

It is good to have one or two summary thoughts already prepared as backups. For example, suppose we take the proposition discussed earlier that to improve a relationship is like building a bridge of understanding. Let's further suggest that the Evidence Packages gave a personal experience of how I went out of my way to do something for someone, and how that helped build a bridge of understanding.

Then perhaps I could relate some statistics from Harvard Business School that showed how improving one's human skills was much more important than getting a degree when it comes to progressing in the corporate world. Finally, let's say I present an Evidence Package that showed what experts in psychology such as Daniel Goleman has discovered in his study of Emotional Intelligence. Now, it is time to summarize the profit of building bridges of understanding. "So if we want to increase the chances of our success in our modern world, we must learn to adapt, to place a priority on building understanding and make a study of what makes people different to us, just as our experiences and the facts show."

The Sixth P

What is the final Punch or closing statement?

The *impact at the end of the presentation* – known as the 'punch' or closing statement is the sixth P. Make it brief and bold. It must pack a solid punch. Try six different endings. You may then have your favorite and one or two more than you could use. Then, when faced with the moment, go with your "gut feel" as to which one will do it for you.

Using the above building understanding presentation, we could close it like this: "Make this the day you strengthen the foundations of your bridge-building with people – it could just prove to get you across troubled waters at a time when you need it the most!"

So we have looked in detail at what we say when we communicate, and some tips on how to do it better. Yet the real power in communication is how we listen, and what we can do to become an attractive listener. Let's explore this further once you complete your debrief for Chapter Fifteen.

IMPACT Creative Action Debrief Chapter FIFTEEN

Do these before continuing to Chapter Sixteen!

1. Can you recall from memory what forms of evidence **DEFEATS** the skeptic?

- **D**
- **E**
- **F**
- **E**
- **A**
- **T**
- **S**

2. Which of the **Six P's** for a longer presentation are you most interested in developing for your own use?

- **P**
- **P**
- **P**
- **P**
- **P**
- **P**

3. Think of a formal talk or presentation where you could practice using the Six P's, and have a go, then record your reflections.

Sixteen

Attractive Listening

~

Foundational Skills for Communication

If we truly want to make an impact that makes a positive differ-ence, one communication skill that is arguably more important than being able to speak well is your ability to become an attractive listener.

What do we mean by attractive listener? Let's define it by first of all looking at the unattractive listener. We probably all know the unattractive listener – you know the type – she asks you a question, and then rather than listen starts to give her view about what she was asking you about. You can tell the unattractive listeners another way. They don't give us their full attention. Instead, they listen with one ear, and continue to do something else. You can watch their gaze focus on something or someone other than you.

My wife accuses me of this "unattractive listening" when she comes into our lounge while I am watching a sports program on television and starts to tell me something that is important to her. Yet after the first sentence is out of her mouth, I immediately get "dis-tracted" by the television, and stop giving her my fully undivided attention. Result – I have become an unattractive listener. She claims when I am in this mode, she'd rather speak to the wall! Oops.

Level II Listening

Attractive Listening happens when we engage in the other person's ideas, concerns, facts, interests, values, beliefs and emotions. The Coaching Training Institute calls this *Level II Listening*[67], not to be confused by the Communication Level Two area, the Opinion area. I define it as listening with the other person in mind, without prejudicing what we think or feel about what they have said. It is attractive because speakers get listened to so little this way, and when we listen, the speaker is drawn to us, because we really hear them. We can also use our attractive listening skills to help the speaker communicate on the four levels introduced earlier.

How do we decide which Communication Level to employ when we are the listener? One way is by observation of the behavioral style and preferences of the speaker, using our "gut-feel" thinking. What are the desired results of this communication? Is it to build the relationship? Is it to better understand the speaker? Is it to begin to build a bridge of communication so we can work better with the person in the future? Let's look at some different scenarios that lend themselves to listening at Communication Levels One and Two, the fact and opinion levels.

Someone who is an acquaintance or friend and simply
wants to pass the time of day

Here is a good place for listening and asking questions about their day, what they think about the weather, how their best team did at the weekend, etc. This "passing the time" is very attractive at the beginning of the day, when we first meet the person after a period of absence, and as the start of a more in depth conversation. Certain types of behavioral preferences, the introverted feelers and extroverted feelers really appreciate someone listening to them at the beginning of a conversation, rather than jumping straight into the more substantive issues we might be exploring. Remember, as listeners who are asking the questions, we are the ones who guide the conversation.

An IT Specialist at a company we are working with (let's call him Mark) recently described at situation in which he became an attractive listener. "I wanted my boss to agree a small expenditure for an item we needed. My normal approach was to go straight in and argue my point for getting the extra cash. In the past this had taken quite some time and my boss would demand lots of justification and challenge my request. This time, I decided to be an attractive listener. I approached him first of all asking how he was feeling, as he had been away ill for a couple of days. We spent a good 5 to 10 minutes when I just listened to him describe his illness. Then immediately afterward I asked if he would sign the requisition form. Without any hesitation my boss signed it and I went happily on my way – just because I was prepared to listen!"

If you know, for instance, the person has recently moved jobs, bought a new home, had a new child, etc., then ask questions to get the person's facts and opinions about the new or changed situation. Just common sense, and it does help you become a more attractive listener.

Here are some more guidelines to encourage your speaker to disclose what is going on in his or her world. These apply to all levels of communication, and are certainly important for increasing the likelihood for gaining insight into the speaker's world. Give the speaker your undivided attention and focus as we stated earlier during our discussions on Interpersonal Intelligence. I describe this as

"Wherever you are, BE THERE!"

In today's professional coaching circles, the best exercise in the industry that helps coaches remain mentally tough and confident is to "Be Present". To me this means acting with total integrity, being yourself, transparent, open and honest with what's going on inside whilst interacting with this other person. It means we are focused totally on them, applying every ounce of our being to listening, watching, smelling and even breathing in harmony with the other person. It means we will establish a rapport and empathy with the person which conveys, "I'm here, present, just for you, and if I leave for a moment, I'll tell you honestly, and then quickly get back." This practice gets you out of the way, and allows for an almost spiritual connection to help you to serve the other person. You become an instrument of a power much greater than your own to help the person unblock something that needs releasing, or encourage the person to take a necessary risk.

Have only one thought on your mind – fully listening to the speaker, asking relevant questions, and being in the moment. Encourage the speaker to share by using your eye contact, body language, and helpful utterances that say, in effect, "I'm listening, and believe you have something worthwhile to say." If the person lacks confidence or is speaking in a language not their native tongue, your attentive body language and noises may relax the person, and encourage them they are a good communicator, because you are an attractive listener. As we have said earlier, people do not generally care how much you know, but they do respect the fact that you care, and will appreciate you more for it.

Show you understand by saying, "I understand." "So that's the way you see it, is that so?" An even better way is to acknowledge the speaker, "So what you are saying, Jennifer, is in order for you to do your job better, you think more time needs to be devoted to helping Jim, Brian and Mary to learn how to manage their time. Is that right?" If Jennifer says, "Yes", she is also saying, "Wow, you have really listened to what I have said, and I did a good job of communicating how I see things." If you summarize and it is not accurate, the speaker will still acknowledge you have made the effort to understand, and respect your attempts. Of course, this will only work once or twice. After that if you continue to "get it wrong", they'll know you are not a good listener, and your summarizing incorrectly will make a big withdrawal of trust.

We must ensure we don't say, I understand." when we do not understand. It is much more attractive if we just *keep asking questions until we do understand.* It is no disgrace to not fully understand someone whom we are just getting to know, or who is in a role or job or situation new to us. It is much better human relations and listening etiquette to indicate, "You know, Terry, I just cannot grasp exactly what it is you are saying and it is important to me to do so, what could I ask you that might help me to more fully appreciate what it is you are saying?"

Tom Peters, the management consultant guru of the 1980's, said one of the essential skills for someone who wants to search for excellence is to be good at getting close to the customer through naïve listening.[68] He says it helps to listen as if you were brand new to the situation, and knew nothing about what the person was describing or explaining. Then we could be totally engaged in what the speaker was saying, without judgment, and perhaps pick up some fresh thoughts. Besides making us more aware of situations, it also makes us more attractive listeners.

Let's address another scenario when we might wish to use attractive listening. Frequently, those closest to us, whom we care deeply for could really appreciate our attractive listening skills. Our partner arrives home from a hard day at the office. We, too, have had a very challenging day. It would add hugely to our ability to cement or improve the relationship if we could be disciplined to ask our partner:

"How was your day, sweetheart?" and really listen, using those guidelines we have mentioned. Here is one more guideline – *remain non-judgmental*. That means, unbiased listening, refraining from trying to correct her or pass judgment on how she relates the facts and her opinion of things. Just listening, and showing you care and understand. Once she is finished, you will be surprised at how often the favour is returned, and you are asked to share your day as well. It will certainly make for more meaningful dinner conversations, if not warmer atmospheres later on in the evening.

Very often, if you know the person who is speaking quite well, and they continue to stay in the facts and opinions levels, it could be a "smokescreen" for them wanting to communicate at a deeper level, but not knowing how or when to start.

Let's say you come home from work, and greet your spouse or partner, then ask "How was your day today?" If they say "Fine," very often it does not mean "Fine" at all. It's not that the partner is lying to you. But chances are something happened to them at a deeper level and they want to get it off of their chest, yet does not do so. What can we do? I suggest you probe. "So what was the best part of today then, honey? Was there any part of the day that did not go so well?" We might then find out what *really* happened, how they were feeling, etc., and we'll communicate at a deeper level. Besides that, they'll be very grateful you did not accept their initial response!

"What" questions seem to work better for most instances than "Why" questions. 'Why' implies we are judging them, while "What" keeps us more objective. Example: "Why did you wear that red dress?" Implies you must think there is something wrong with it, or the choice she made. Instead, we could ask, "What is there about that red dress that made you choose it today?" If we ask it with a non-judgmental tone of voice, we are most likely to find the information we want, and will be less likely to put the person on the defensive.

Building the Right Environment

How do we build or create the right environment that leads to more open communication? Here are some things to consider.

· First of all, get rid of distractions, like the TV, phones ringing, other people listening in and noisy crowded places. Especially as I get older, I find it almost impossible to listen well when in a noisy pub, bar or when there is loud music playing. Very often when the music begins to play, my wife and I excuse ourselves to a quieter part of the room, or choose to leave. Genuine communication and distractions just do not mix.

· Secondly, give yourself plenty of time to communicate. Don't enforce tight time constraints on the conversation if we want people to be open, honest and trusting. Although it is good practice to get people to practice speaking in short time frames to improve their communication, it is not condu-cive for really exploring at deeper levels, beyond the opinion level.

· Thirdly, if practicable, reduce the physical barriers between you and the speaker. Table or desks are great for working on, however; if we truly want to communicate more effectively, we'd be wise to both get on the same side of the table or desk so we can talk without hindrances. Be careful, though, not to get too close. Some behavioral types or people who do not know us well may choose to keep a respectable space between you. Be aware of this, and watch for body signals that might give you clues as to whether or not you are too close for comfort!

There are times, of course, when we just cannot listen fully – we are deeply entrenched in some other activity, and to stop could lose some important information, train of thought or problem-solving ideas. Perhaps we are engaged in a conversation with someone else, and to break off the conversation to listen to your present speaker just would not be appropriate. How do we handle this? Why not try the truth? Simply apologize to the individual, and explain that as much as you would like to, you just cannot not give your full attention at the moment. Suggest an alternative time or place that would be more convenient. If we are sincere, most people will be more than happy to oblige, without being offended.

Refrain From Giving Advice

What if, in listening to a close, personal friend or companion, she is saying things and *you know* just what she should do to resolve her situation? General rule? DON'T! From painful personal experience, I have paid the price for declaring the "answer" for the person, thinking I'd get all kinds of kudos for helping. *I confused being an attractive listener for being a problem fixer*. It is very rare you can be both, so pick which you want. Believe me, if the relationship is important, and you want to earn the right to have an impact on the person later, stick to listening, and keep your advice to yourself – even if asked for! OK, there may be times when we just have to say, "Look, Tom, if you are afraid of getting run over by those cars and trucks, then perhaps you need to think about not playing in the road." People generally don't need our advice, they need *someone who will listen, and then help them sort out their own thinking*.

How can you use other "signaling devices" to aid your listening? One of the best pieces of information I read on becoming attractive as a listener was in Covey's "Seven Habits" book.[69] He said one of the best ways to "listen", was to *listen with your eyes*. The eye can take in so much more than our ears. As we have mentioned before, the optic nerve is 11 times bigger than our aural nerve, so needless to say, we are being bombarded by sensory perceptions by our eyes. As we have discussed earlier, so much of the message we send and receive is not the words, but the body language. So if we are listening wholeheartedly, we need to be listening with our eyes as well.

What can we do when on the phone, then? I like to use my inner eye; to imagine the person speaking on the phone, whether they are standing or sitting, what they might be communicating with their eyes, their facial expressions, etc. You will be amazed how much more attractive it makes us as a listener. Now let's look at what other skills we can employ when listening to someone who is communicating at the deeper levels.

Advanced Skills for Communication Levels Three and Four

Let's explore some other skills used by counselors, coaches and other people who make a profession from listening skillfully to others. We will do this by first of all describing some common scenarios I have heard through the years listening to people who come to us for help. As an executive coach and trainer for years, quite often these scenarios come to our attention.

- Third Party facilitation – Sam needs to get something off his chest at Communication Levels Three or Four (feelings and values) when you are not party to their conflict or issue. Their beef is with a significant "other" who has upset or disappointed them.
- Person close to you (a) – Clare wishes to "unload" and you are the person whom they see has caused the conflict or issue.

- Person close to you (b) – Susan wishes to clear the air and you and others are the parties whom they see has caused the conflict or issue.

Do these sound familiar to you? How often have you been in the firing line for one or more of these? What a great place to put our attractive listening into practice. Let's explore some useful guidelines and tips, and then come back to each of these.

Asking questions that help the person clarify not only the situation, but the emotions they were feeling or are feeling, how their "rights and beliefs" have been violated, etc., is a valuable way of supporting the speaker. Putting words to the feelings somehow helps the person to dissipate the strong emotion and allows them to think more clearly and speak more lucidly.

In Scenario One, Sam has something he feels strongly about, he is incensed and may need help getting his mind around what he really wants to achieve from the discussion.

With Clare in Scenario Two, since you are the object of her disgust or displeasure, you may need to delay clarifying the purpose until she has had time to vent her feelings. If this is the case, then patiently listen and desperately bite your tongue until she has finished expressing her emotions and feelings.

For Susan in Scenario Three, the same things apply. Her willingness to share her feelings in a group situation indicates the depth of her feelings and the strength of her courage. In both cases you can comment genuinely on this observation. It very likely will take some of the steam out of the encounter.

Accept their communication, without trying to help, defend or give advice –*suspend judgment* until they ask for your opinion. This can be a tough thing to do, especially if we are the ones who the offended one thinks or feels are at fault as with Susan and Clare. It is human to go on the defensive, and yet if we do this at the incorrect time or in an inappropriate way, we suddenly become a most unattractive listener! We immediately risk making a huge withdrawal from the trust bank. So whatever the speaker is saying, accept it as valid, as justified, even if you suspect it is irrational at best.

I recall accepting what Sarah was saying and feeling, as she went on about how appalled she was that Mike had not come home when he said he would, and how she felt like leaving him. My first reaction was to say, "You can't leave Mike, that would be really bad!" But I held my tongue, and just listened. If it was true that is what she felt like doing, then who was I to criticize? It was her feelings, and she had them, so why not express how she really felt! Later on, once she had calmed down and felt she had been heard, we could then discuss things without the emotions unduly getting in the way.

Try to summarize often by paraphrasing what they are saying and ask them to verify.

A superb way of helping the person as they speak at Levels Three and Four is to play back to them what they have just said. When he hears what he had just said, he can then either agree or modify what he has said, yet knowing he had been heard. "So John, you feel you are trying so hard to be accepted, that you are not being yourself, and the pressure is building up so that you don't really know what you should do next, is that right?" If we have truly listened and responded, John will really appreciate being heard. He can then either modify what he has just said, or elaborate even further in an effort to get to the bottom of the situation, and towards resolution. From our point of view, we have done our part of being a skilled and attractive listener.

Cushion and Counter

If you are asked to facilitate during a conflict between two parties or people, your listening is particularly demanding. This can start early such as when we are dealing with our children. Very often the person who is speaking is looking for your agreement, and therefore can ask for your advice, opinion or who you see is "in the right." As you can imagine, the way you respond is critical if you are to keep your facilitative role. Picking sides will take away your ability to help resolve the issue, and maintain impartiality. So how can we approach this situation? A general principle is to *cushion the emo-*

tive question from your speaker, then *counter with a question of your own*. Ask both parties, what other options are there for obtaining possible solutions. Ask if there are precedents, what has happened previously. What external guidelines or criteria might help determine what is fair? This keeps you from being forced to decide, and maintains your equanimity.

Sometimes despite your helping them to think things through the situation is stalled. You intuitively feel the right thing to do is to offer some options or advice. If handled properly, you can help resolve the issue and still be seen as fair and trustworthy. Preface what you are going to say by offering a disclaimer. For instance, you might say, "This may be way off-base, and not at all relevant, so please treat it as such. But as you have asked for my opinion, here is what I think and feel right now. I will not be at all offended if you disagree, so do tell me honestly how you think and feel about what I am going to say." Very often this approach will lower the possible emotions and feelings of vulnerability either party may display, and help them turn into better listeners, more apt to act upon what you will then say. So what, then, do you say? *Just go with your 'gut feel.'*

On the other hand, perhaps you are pressed to give your advice or opinion, and your intuition is saying, "This is beyond my experience. We should defer this to a later time, or even to someone else more qualified." Again, go with your intuition, delay the meeting or refer to someone more qualified. Generally, your role as a facilitator will not have been compromised, and the parties will respect your honesty.

Check Our Own Motives

Whenever there is a great deal of miscommunication at Levels 3 and 4, and we are involved in the breakdown of trust and mutual respect, we have a massive construction project to begin to build new bridges upon which to communicate. Before we engage too much in the content of the dispute, it is good for us to think for a moment, and check our own personal motives and attitudes towards the other person. Are we holding a grudge or resentment? If so, is

258

this helpful to effectively resolving the conflict? Do we need to admit we, too, have harbored attitudes that have contributed to the misunderstanding, and try to make this a fresh start? We might wish to actually admit this to the aggrieved party to see if this helps build a small bridge of trust and respect. Then, start to agree some behaviors that might just help deal with the issues. Such behaviors as:

- Assume what the other person is saying is logical and meaningful, even if you find it difficult to comprehend at the moment.
- Give each other the benefit of the doubt
- Be open to being influenced by what the other person does or says.

Just recently, I was involved in a dispute that meant I had to meet with someone that the rest of the organization had castigated from pillar to post. I was supposed to go "sort the person out." You can imagine what might have been my frame of mind when I approached the meeting with the person in question. I had to consciously choose to allow my first meeting to be unprejudiced by the other things people have said about him, and not only give him the benefit of doubt but to allow his perspective to influence the way I saw the situation. This has helped immensely in the conciliation role, and in the end, produced an outcome which served all parties best.

- Seek fully to understand the "message behind the message" especially in conflict situations
- Ask permission before you interrupt, and only at natural pauses – if the other person feels fully heard, she or he will be in a better frame of mind to hear your view and feelings about the situation
- Help the speaker to draw a conclusion, if it seems appropriate
- If the other person says things that are not true, or are completely different from your perspective, note it down and wait for an appropriate time to confront

·   Summarize each other's points of view and expression of feelings until there is a mutual agreement that each view is fully expressed accurately

When is it appropriate not to listen?

·   When despite repeated efforts to enforce the behaviors, the other party refuses to hear your point of view or show they believe you
·   When the solutions posed are not win-win
·   Either you or the other person has "had enough" to chew on, and needs time to assimilate – particularly useful for "the cool blue behavioral preference people"

What should we do as attractive listeners when the listening is over, and we are going our separate ways?

·   Keep confidences and assume you have been in a "rubber room" for communicating. Everything we have said is in confidence and should stay there, as if we had been in a rubber room where all the sound was absorbed in the walls.
·   Use the "golden rule" before you say anything or allow anyone else to say anything about that person. As a reminder, the Golden Rule states, "Love your neighbor as yourself."
·   Thank the person for their honesty and courage in sharing how they feel and believe

How do you conclude the listening naturally?

·   Agree that the session is over
·   Offer them the chance to summarize the progress or extent of the conversation
·   Agree the next step

What advice do you have when wanting to assert your point of view to stop someone's behavior from causing you problems?

- Observe some good point about the person, or their behavior and state it
- Describe the situation that triggers certain emotions and reactions that you perceive as harmful
- State the emotions this behavior produces in you
- Offer an alternative behavior that you find acceptable
- Ask the person, "What do you think and feel about this?"
- Really listen to what they say, and work towards an acceptable solution
- Reassert you are not prepared to allow them to behave in the way that you see is harmful, and you will remind them if you see the behavior resurfacing

For example, let's say I detect that someone, let's call him Jake, is not always describing to me the situation in the same way with the same facts they might with someone else. This is a manifestation of someone who wants to please everybody, and at all times to keep things in harmony. (I know this scenario well, as it is typical of behavior I am trying to change in myself.) They may describe a situation to Paul, putting Paul in a good light, and then describe the situation completely differently to Mary, putting Mary in a favorable position, and making it seem that Paul was in the wrong. Jake doesn't mean to lie per se, but twists the situation around to avoid any embarrassment or conflict that might land on his side of things, or end up putting someone in the hot seat. I might then start the conversation with Jake like this:

"Jake, thanks for relating the situation with Paul, Mary and yourself. It is an important matter, and if we are going to be the high performance team we want to be, we need to address these issues. Your description of events; however, leave me confused, and doubting you are being totally open here. I have spoken to Paul and Mary, and their views don't tally with yours. I appreciate you don't want to be seen as the cause of the problem, yet we must have total honesty if we are going to resolve these situations. Don't you agree? How do you feel about this?" After I have completely listened to Jake, I can then respond by saying, "Jake, I'm glad you have explained this, and you admit you might not have been completely open in your description. This takes confidence, and I appreciate you exercising some here. Please ensure in the future, regardless of who you think is in error, we focus on the full facts, not leaving anything out. I'll let you know right away if the facts I am getting from others is different from yours."

This is learning to be an attractive listener, some foundational skills and then more advanced skills for listening at a deeper level. We'll use all the IMPACT! tools, principles and techniques from Interpersonal Intelligence to effective Communication as we look at becoming the Transformational Leaders we will need to be, in order to make a positive difference.

IMPACT Creative Action Debrief Chapter SIXTEEN

Do these before continuing to Chapter Seventeen!

1 What are personal barriers you face to attractive listening?

2. Who might benefit if you engaged with them and used more attractive listening?

· How might you benefit?

3. Practice listening when you are with your family, friends, and even people you are meeting for the first time over the next couple of weeks. Observe particularly when they are communicating at Levels One and Two, and record your findings here:

· What went well

· What did not go so well

· What I learned

4. Exercising real impact now – think of someone who could use some coaching and clarifying of some aspect of their lives – write their name here

5. List below some of the questions you could ask that might help the person to communicate with you at Communication Levels Three or Four

6. What might you do to set the appropriate environment around which to hold this "Clarifying Session"?

7. Now do it and record your findings and reflections here:

Seventeen

Lead by Helping Others to Transform Their Lives

⌒

The 'T' in IMPACT! represents Transformational Leadership. As we discussed earlier, if we are to make a positive impact upon our communities, clubs, workplaces and families, then we need to exert leadership. The type of leadership that has proven most effective especially in the highly participative cultures we live in is Transformational Leadership. According to Google, there are over 320,000 entries related to this very popular description of leadership. The theories and concepts were purported to have begun with the writings of Max Weber, Sir MacGregor Burns and the Earl of Bass. All agree the leadership that has a moral foundation and adapts itself to different situations is much more effective long term than a bureaucratic style of leadership that may get things done, but without transforming anything. Very often, transactional leadership, the other end of the spectrum from Transformational Leadership, actually has detrimental effects long term.

Let's take a look at some example scenarios:

A young, bright new employee named Emma has just begun working in your company. How effective would you be as her leader/manager if you were to say to her, "Emma, welcome to the company, what would you like to do today? Attend whatever meetings you want, make whatever decisions you want, we'll back you. We'll be back at the end of the month and you can let us know how the business has done. Good luck, we believe in you and your ability."

What would the Board of Directors think of your leadership in that situation? Not much, would they? As well meaning as your approach was, it was inappropriate for the situation and person.

Here is another one.

A highly competent and long serving project manager has come to your office. He has recently been assigned to report directly to you. He asks you to outline how you might be dealing with him in your capacity as head of the division. What do you think would be the relationship with your new direct report if your response is, "John, I have one way of dealing with my team, and that is to be tough, set out what I want from them, and then demand they report back immediately the results." In other words, being highly directive. Chances are your highly experienced project manager might not perform well with this type of leadership and management.

The obvious point is this - in order for us to get the best from others, we are more likely to achieve these results by employing a highly dynamic and *situational style of leadership* which varies dependent upon the competence, commitment and experience of the other person. Even with one person we might need to vary our approach and style, dependent upon their competence and commitment, when dealing with a certain area of their responsibility which is new or difficult for them.

Transformational Leaders, therefore, use situations to get the job done, but more importantly *use the completion of the task to help transform the performance and the relationship of the people involved*. What is in it for you to be a Transformational Leader? As Max Weber stated, it is "morally acceptable". We are helping ourselves most when we help others. The Bible states it as the Law of Sowing and Reaping. We get back what we give, and even more so than we give.

We gave our grandchildren a special present for Christmas, an outdoor trampoline. They have said how much they enjoy it, but I can assure you, Heidi and I enjoy seeing them using and benefiting hour after hour on the trampoline much more than they do. It is truly more blessed to give than receive.

We stated in the Passion with Purpose chapter that if our dream is big enough, it simply cannot be done without the help, energy and support of others, especially our Creator. Therefore using a style that engenders support from others is obviously much more beneficial than a "help me and I'll pay you" transactional style. What more incentive do you need to become a transformational, "Make-it-Happen" leader? Ken Blanchard, famed author and creator of the Situational Leadership model[70,] and many current day experts in the field of leadership development, all vouch for the situational approach if you want to make a lasting difference when working with others. Let's pause for a moment.

Reflect upon your Impact Journey,

from I to T

What has happened to you? Haven't you been transformed yourself? Aren't you more "attractive"? Since you now know how and have practiced using your Interpersonal Intelligence, aren't you more comfortable with strangers and different people?

Hasn't your confidence, resilience and self- esteem grown as you applied the ideas and thoughts on being *mentally tough*? Aren't you now more purposeful, grounded and resolute and more expressive of your *Passion with Purpose* and energy? As you look around you, don't you now see people respecting you more, as you communicate? Aren't they listening to your ideas and explanations and coming to you more often to have you listen to their issues? You have probably already experienced people expressing how much better they feel about their lives by associating with you, how much lighter they feel and hopeful for the future. What a joyful feeling this must bring!

That feeling in itself must be a great incentive to be a powerful *Transformational Leader*.

Three Qualities of Outstanding Leaders

From my experiences, observations and reading about the most effective leaders, three qualities besides those we have spoken of in other chapters spring to mind. The first is, the *best leaders know how and when to follow*. Let's face it, we cannot always be in the lead.

Like the strongest of geese migrating hundreds if not thousands of miles, the lead goose in the V formation does not always stay out front. He learns that being out front all the time wears us out, leaves us feeling alone, and drains our enthusiasm. For very practical reasons, then, the head gander lets others lead, and he just follows. This increases the distance the gaggle flies by an additional 70%, if not further, according to research.[71]

Further evidence is the number of bright, enthusiastic leaders in many fields such as the police, ministry, the military and government who serve as apprentices in their fields of endeavor, prior to being recognized as capable of having others to follow them.

I can remember soon after I began working with a church community in Norfolk, we on the leadership team would be approached frequently by people who were convinced they had God's answer to our church if not the whole world. They complained, "Why don't we let them speak and preach and be recognized as leaders?" The truth was that indeed, they may have had something to say, but when we would ask them, "Who have you followed over the years? Also, who is following you at the moment?" Their answer was, "No one just yet."

Want to be an effective leader? *Become a great follower* who does whatever is asked of you until someone recognizes that because you have learned to follow, perhaps you can be trusted to lead without destroying the organization or team.

The Law of Sowing and Reaping

What is another sign of excellence in a *Transformational Leader*? Obey The Law Of Sowing and Reaping or "Expected Return". I believe it is best expressed in some of Jesus' words. He said, "From everyone who has been given much, much will be demanded".[72]

This is a universal principle of giving as a corollary of the Law of Sowing and Reaping. If we sow much we will reap much, then Jesus said the opposite is also true. If we have reaped much we are expected to give much. For instance, it is easier to learn to "tithe" – give away 10% of your income – when you are earning a $100 than it is when you are earning $1 million. Therefore, because you have developed the habit of giving when you earned little, you will be more likely to continue the giving when you have much.

The Law of Sowing and Reaping tends to apply with all of your gifts and talents. God expects us to use what we have been given, or we'll lose it. It could easily be argued that singers like Britney Spears have not used their talent and abilities well, and therefore have seen the Law of Expected Return work in reverse. Once they were transformational in their industry and chosen career. Now in many circles they are criticized and ridiculed because they have not used what they had been given, but wasted and squandered it away. OK Magazine claims Britney spent $65 million in one year. Pity. Let's ensure we make the most with what we have, and to apply our gifts, talents, experiences and abilities in all areas of our lives.

Commit Yourself to Balance

Transformational Leaders have a *commitment to balance*. They have put into practice what we discussed in Chapter Three regarding our Wheel of Life. They understand that if "charity begins at home," then providing leadership and investing in their family relationships matters foremost. One of the major qualifications for leadership in the first century church was that leaders had earned the right to lead others by showing leadership in the home.[73] We probably all know of people who in the pursuit of becoming a success in their career, sport, community or business forgot to apply the energies at home first.

Recently, I was helping an entrepreneurial couple sort out how they could make their business more successful, and make it more profitable. They complained that money was tight, and that in their personal life, money seemed to disappear, leaving them without sufficient funds to plan for their financial future. Funny enough, this was echoed in their business. After we discussed the situation more fully by becoming "brutal with the facts"[74] as Jim Collins purports, we discovered neither of them had assumed responsibility for the finances in their home. After some debate, the couple decided to place responsibility for this with the husband. Almost overnight, their finances took on a whole new order. But it spilled over into other areas as well. Their lives have been transformed by applying their leadership at home first.

Let Work Become Fun

Those of us selected or choosing to apply our efforts in employed work have a tremendous opportunity to become transformational, and when we do this well during our working day we can experience amazing fruitfulness in our lives.

In my early years, my brothers and I were taught putting in the hours was simply not enough, whether it was gathering eggs, fixing fences or sweeping the floor. Mother constantly used the familiar adage, "If anything is worth doing, it is worth doing well." Dad reinforced this by ensuring the line of fence posts were the straightest they could be. The haystacks had to be properly formed and made correctly. The result for me, and most of my brothers was that work was fun. Work was worthwhile, and character building.

Work gave us the opportunity to express ourselves, work as a team and build our relationships. Heidi and I have tried to foster this in our own family. As wonderful as it is to get together at holidays, birthdays, etc., our family learns the most about each other when we work together. It could be making cookies, cleaning the yard of rubbish or speaking to people. No matter, so long as it is family working together, much of our leadership work with them is transformational. We have laughter, we have tears, we have times we want to give up. We have had late nights and arguments, but most of all we have learned how to grow up, become dedicated to supporting one another.

Transferring this "work ethic" to work is easy if you have applied it at home. You respect what other people have started and want to accomplish through the organization. You work hard to fully understand your role, to find out how you can add value and what it is you need to learn. You get to know the team members, what their strengths and weaknesses are, and how you fit in. When you spot inconsistencies or things that need improvement, you helpfully suggest options, not simply complaining and pointing out what's wrong. This attitude and way of working will transform the organization, the team and you. You'll become someone worthy of leading others.

Andrew Harrison demonstrates this, in my experience. As a child he moved from the Northwest of England with his parents, and when he left school he went to work for a local abeit international company. The reputation of many people who move to Norfolk or who have grown up there is that they settle into a lifestyle that doesn't necessarily create ambition. There is nothing wrong with this lifestyle, yet for many this means the impact we have on others is minimal. Andy decided to be different. As he says, "I've always believed in myself, but it would be fair to say that I was reserved and reluctant to take a chance." Ian, Andrew's manager at the time, spotted his potential and he was encouraged to enroll on an IMPACT! Program. His boss believed he had the spark to raise his sights and become a valuable contributor of the technical team he was part of. Andy agreed to invest 7 evenings of his life developing his impact skills.

His boss's boss, who wasn't so sure Andy could make the transformation, was amazed at the difference, just a short two months after Andrew finished the program. Andy was contributing more at meetings and even offering fresh ideas as to what could make things better. Again, as Andrew says, "The difference was I took on more challenging things, not following the routine, taking chances – taking-on high profile projects away from my area of expertise. The big change for me was moving away from the safety of being an insular process expert in my Comfort Zone, to operating at a different level – IMPACT was the catalyst that started the process off and helped me un-lock my potential."

He set goals for his life, and began asserting himself. Now, just a few years later, Andy's life is transformed. He is a very happily married family man, serving his company in extraordinary ways. He has released others on his team to make valuable contributions that have saved his organization millions of dollars in revenue and reduced cash flow. He has even persuaded his employers to allow him to work some of the time from home, as he also devotes much of his time to traveling around the world.

Andrew is not through yet. He is a quality leader who inspires others to fulfill their potential. Andy tells me he still wants to develop even more. He wants to gain new skills that will improve his ability to coach his team. We are currently investigating how we might incorporate his development as we help him help his team members to become Transformational Leaders as well. His sights are now set on taking a global role for his organization, impacting an even wider group of people.

Get Involved in the Community

I doubt if any of us live in the perfect community. As communities are full of people, then they are anything but perfect. Most of us understand the power of "working" in our family and in our job or profession. There is still more. The Law of Sowing and Reaping really comes into play when we give ourselves to the community and to projects where there is no way we can receive a return from those in whom we apply our efforts. Companies all over the world now recognize the need to reinvest in the community. This Corporate Social Responsibility ethic works for organizations because when we give ourselves away, we are making a statement that it is a privilege, not a right, to be able to live and work in the community. Think of those places around the world where the amenities and what those of us in the western world would call necessities do not exist. Want to trade living in Dallas and Darlington for Darfour?

We all have a responsibility to behave and act as representatives of our community, showing those outside what our community stands for and values. Communities aren't just the physical structure of those homes and families that live there, of course. The culture and fiber of the people in the community to a large extent permeate through to form the community, so playing our part is vital. Transformational Leaders know this, and take an active part.

Learn to Share with Others

As we read about Andy earlier, Transformational Leaders are eager to share what they have learned with others. One of the most effective ways is finding people with the attitude and way of looking at life that indicates they have the potential to make a positive difference in others. Then look for ways to support, challenge and encourage them. By sharing, we learn twice. In order for us to help others, we really need to know our stuff. If we don't walk the talk, then our credibility is shot, and our ability to transform others is limited. The 'make it happen' message we are sharing with others is reinforced in our own lives every time we help someone else. Our belief systems get re-convinced, and so we go around the Cycle of Experiential Development ourselves once again.

I would just love to read your Mission for Life Plan, and discover what your motives are for "Making a Positive Difference". What drives you, what is at the base? Is it fame, fortune, or something else? How does it connect to your inner being, your Passion? If you can honestly say that your faith and belief in a higher calling, an inner dream that is bigger than you could ever imagine, and in completing it, you'll help a lot of other people get what they need and want in life, then go for it!

Make a small but positive difference every day, and allow the Law of Sowing and Reaping to go to work for you to grow your dream. That's the sure-fire way to be a Transformational Leader.

Feed Your Soul, Exercise Your Body

You will need sustainable energy if you are to complete your journey. As we detailed in the Quality of Life section, we suggest you have as part of your journey a definite plan for how you will get and stay fit, mentally, physically and spiritually. This means, feed your soul. Use music, good books and the association of like minded people to support, encourage and challenge you to be the person God wants you to be. Exercise your body and eat healthily. It is the framework that will allow you to do the walking, talking and living that your dream requires.

Keep mentally stimulated by varying the type of input you feed your mind. Read some character-building books or attend seminars and workshops. Complete higher and further education courses that challenge your views and thinking. Invite people successful in areas you want to excel to a meal or evening in a bar or pub. Then ask them questions and listen! Fight the urge to let these guests of yours know how much you know. Be naïve. Play dumb. Just ask questions, take notes and shut up! We have asked someone instrumental in building one of the most successful retail superstores, who chairs large multinational organizations to lunch, very honestly shared our business, its history, plans and foibles, then listened for an hour or so to how he would go about building our future. 'Priceless,' as a well-known credit card would say.

Finally, get yourself wired right spiritually. Personally, for me this was to find a living faith that made sense to me, then I aligned my value system in light of my beliefs. Next I chose to build a personal relationship with the most influential person in history, Jesus Christ. I only did this once I investigated His claims – what He said about Himself, His aims – what He said He was here for, and His death and resurrection. It all made sense to me, and 50 years on, still does, more than ever!

Your journey will be unique, and spiritually, you may have discovered something that makes sense to you. If, however, you have not, then rather than live without knowing, I encourage you to explore the Christian faith, and see why so many successful people who have made a positive difference have chosen this route to spiritual fulfillment.

Practice, Practice, Practice

Hone your IMPACT! skills. We all know of people who wish to avoid their minds growing dull play Sudoku, do crosswords and play bridge. This is admirable and really seems to work. Likewise, if you wish to keep sharp as a speaker and influencer of people, practice. Psychologist David Kolb calls this *active experimentation*.[75] Volunteer to speak to groups. Tell your story, what your dreams are and how you think things could get better. Join clubs and organizations where your skills as a communicator and team member will continue to be honed and refined.

Rehearse and rehearse your own "commercial" – develop a 10 second, 30 second, 2 minute and 10 minute version. Then after you have met someone and asked him or her, "What is it you do?", listened to their answer and encouraged them, you can have a well structured, inspirational answer when they ask you, "What is it you do?" One just never knows when that person may know someone who knows someone who can help make your *Passion and Vision* come a little closer to reality.

How to Handle Change

What do you do about changes to your plans, circumstances, working relationships, which will inevitably happen? If appropriate and possible, be the first to lead the change. If we anticipate the changes and help shape them, we are going to be much more positive and flexible to adapt to the change and take advantage of it. Let's face it, wouldn't we be better off helping to form the shape of the change than be surprised and unprepared for it?

Another way of dealing with change is to first of all scrutinize what the change is attempting to accomplish. If it genuinely is aligned with your own beliefs and values, and in some way will help you get even closer to where you are going, developing necessary skills, and giving you the opportunity to learn to be a Transformation Leader, then find a way to help manage the change.

If you are not able to lead the change or help manage it, then you need to decide to what extent you can embrace it. To go with the flow, even with imposed change, can be a great learning experience. However, there are changes that do not sit well with our value systems. Our response then may very well be to resist the change, ask why the change is being imposed, and help explore options that would help us keep our integrity. Before we resist too vigorously, check it out with a friend or someone who knows you well. It might be the reason we are resisting is our pride rather than our belief systems, or our belief systems have some faults needing correction.

Some Final Thoughts

If I were to try to summarize how to become and lead a life of impact as a Transformational Leader, I believe it would be put this way:

·   Work hard
·   Don't be lazy, and particularly work hard to develop a positive attitude
·   Rather than concentrate on what you can get out of life, focus most of your energy on what you can give, and give and give!
·   Define your Life Purpose, then live it every day. And don't ever outlive your dream.

Your reading of this book has helped me reach another dream. Now make this portion of my dream really live by sharing what you have learned with others. I'd love to hear from you about your plans, and what this book has meant to you.

God's very best to you and your impact on making a positive difference. The whole world is waiting for you to make it happen. Become a Transformational Leader who makes a positive IMPACT!

IMPACT CREATIVE ACTION DEBRIEF CHAPTER SEVENTEEN

BEFORE YOU PUT THIS BOOK AWAY – MOMENTARILY!

1. What "cause" outside of work really captures your interest and imagination?

2. Who could you speak with that might give you some guidance about whether or not to get more involved?

3. How would the community or group benefit from your involvement?

(Consider making this one of your goals and objectives as part of your Mission for Life Plan)

4. Who would benefit from reading this book and embracing these principles, ideas and techniques? What would you tell them to encourage them in their IMPACT! Journey?

Endnotes

1 Stephen R. Covey, Seven Habits of Highly Effective People, page 28, ISBN 0-671-71117-2
2 James Allen, As a Man Thinketh, ISBN 0-875-16000-X
3 W. Clement Stone, The Success System That Never Fails, ISBN 0-138-59363-9
4 Skip Ross Cassette Tape Series on Dynamic Living, and book entitled, Say Yes to Your Potential ISBN 0-849-90309-2
5 http://history1900s.about.com/od/famouscrimesscandals/a/columbine.htm
6 http://www.guardian.co.uk/uk/1993/nov/02/bulger.tomsharratt
7 Samuel Smiles, Self Help, pp 2&3, ISBN 1432618296
8 Personal Interview with Simon Wilsher, August 2009
9 www.adrian-snell.com
10 Stephen R. Covey, Seven Habits of Highly Effective People, pp 81-88, ISBN 0-671-71117-2
11 Christopher Reeve Paralysis Foundation, 500 Morris Avenue, Springfield, N.J. 07081
Telephone: 1-800-225-0292 or 1-888-711-HOPE
12 Christopher Reeve Paralysis Foundation, 500 Morris Avenue, Springfield, N.J. 07081 Telephone: 1-800-225-0292 or 1-888-711-HOPE
13 Zig Ziglar, See You at The Top Tape series, www.zigziglar.com
14 William James Quote, www.brainyquote.com
15 http://learn.genetics.utah.edu/content/tech/cloning/whatiscloning
16 Zig Ziglar, See You at The Top, page 35, ISBN 088289-126-X

17 Stephen R. Covey, Seven Habits of Highly Effective People, page 99, ISBN 0-671-71117-2
18 Daniel Goleman, Emotional Intelligence, pp 111 – 126, ISBN 0-7475-2830-6
19 Ian Dowey, manager of Crystal Palace when asked by the press how the football team would cope with maintaining their position in the Premier Division having just been promoted and facing the shock of the "big boys".
20 Bob Gass, Word for Today 10 Mar. 05 "Developing Strong Roots"
21 Jim Collins, Good to Great, page 168, ISBN 0-06-662099-6
22 Laura Berman Fortgang, Take Yourself To The Top, page 38, ISBN 0-7225-3771-9
23 Dale Carnegie, How to Win Friends and Influence People, ISBN 0-671-42517-X
24 For more information about the history of this concept, read Behaviors of Normal People ISBN 978-1-4437-2072-4 by William Marston, and Spirit Controlled Temperament ISBN-10: 0842362207 by Timothy LaHaye.
25 Anthony Stevens, Jung, A Very Short Introduction, pp 85-101, ISBN 0-19-285458-5
26 The Bible, Matthew 22 verse 39
27 Stephen R Covey, Seven Habits of Highly Effective People, page 185 ISBN 0-671-71117-2
28 Karen Pryor, Don't Shoot The Dog, ISBN 0-553-25388-3
29 Skip Ross, Dynamic Living Cassette Tape Series and Book, Say Yes to Your Potential, ISBN 0-849-90309-2
30 Stephen R Covey, Seven Habits of Highly Successful People, page 51, ISBN 0-671-71117-2
31 Skip Ross, Dynamic Living Cassette Tape Series and Book, Say Yes to Your Potential, ISBN 0-849-90309-2
32 The Bible, Gen 1:26 and John 15:16
33 Rudyard Kipling, IF
34 Roger Connors, Tom Smith, Craig Hickman, The Oz Principle, page 11, ISBN 1-59184-024-4
35 John Roger, Peter Williams, You Can't Afford The Luxury of a Negative Thought, page 143, ISBN 0-00-710756-0,

36 Tim Humphreys, Jesus Ministry Conference, copyright © Clover Creek Bible Fellowship, Revised May 2008

37 Robert H. Schuller, www.crystalcatheral.org

38 Susan Jeffers, Feel The Fear and Do It Anyway, ISBN 0-7126-7105-6

39 Dale Carnegie, How to Stop Worrying and Start Living, ISBN 0-671-50619-6

40 Patrick Lencioni, The Five Dysfunctions of a Team, ISBN 0-7879-6075-6

41 Min Basadur Simplex© Method – The Power of Innovation, page 71, ISBN 0-273-61362-6

42 Napoleon Hill, Think and Grow Rich, ISBN 0-8015-7554-0 page 35

43 BBC News Tuesday, 5 February, 2002

44 Viktor E. Frankl, Man's Search for Meaning, pp 122,127, ISBN 0-671-02337-3

45 Zig Ziglar, See You at The Top, page 229, ISBN 088289-126-X

46 Viktor E. Frankl, Man's Search for Meaning, page 157, ISBN 0-671-02337-3,

47 Paul Chutknow, Visa The Power of an Idea, ISBN 0-159-00479-9

48 Robert H. Schuller, Move Ahead with Possibility Thinking, page 79, ISBN 0-515-08984-2

49 Zig Ziglar, See You at the Top tape series

50 Skip Ross, Dynamic Living ISBN 0-849-90309-2

51 Skip Ross, Dynamic Living ISBN 0-849-90309-2

52 The Pygmalion Effect, http://en.wikipedia.org/wiki/ Pygmalion Effect

53 The Bible, Ephesians 6:10 – 18, The Living Bible Translation,

54 Stephen R. Covey, Putting First Things First, Section 1 pp 15+, ISBN 0-671-71283-7

55 Albert Einstein, "We can't solve problems by using the same kind of thinking we used when we created them.", http://rescomp.stanford.edu/~cheshire/EinsteinQuotes.html

56 Edward de Bono, http://www.edwdebono.com/

57 Stephen R. Covey, Seven Habits of Highly Effective People, pp 81-85, ISBN 0-671-71117-2

58 Laura Whitworth, Henry-Kimsey House and Phil Sandahl, Co-Active Coaching, page 87, ISBN 0-89106-123-1,

59 The Bible, Philippians 4:8, The Message ©1995

60 The Bible, 1 Thessalonians 5:18, New American Standard Version ©1995

61 Daniel Goleman, Emotional Intelligence, page 194, ISBN 0-7475-2830-6

62 Daniel Goleman, Emotional Intelligence, page 195, ISBN 0-7475-2830-6

63 Stephen R. Covey, Seven Habits of Highly Effective People, pp 235-260, ISBN 0-671-71117-2

64 Steve Manning, "How to Write a Book on Anything in 14 days", Chapter 6, ISBN 0-0692613-1-4

65 http://www.grc.nasa.gov/WWW/K-12/airplane/newton.html

66 Dale Carnegie, How to Win Friends and Influence People, page 258, ISBN 0-671-42517-X

67 Laura Whitworth, Henry-Kimsey House and Phil Sandahl, Co-Active Coaching, page 35, ISBN 0-89106-123-1

68 Tom Peters, Thriving on Chaos, page 149, ISBN 0-133-45427-8

69 Stephen R. Covey, Seven Habits of Highly Effective People, pp 81-85, ISBN 0-671-71117-2

70 Ken Blanchard, Situational Leadership II, www.kenblanchard.com

71 Ask Yahoo, 22 February 2002, "Why do geese fly in a V formation?"

72 The Bible, Luke 12 v 48

73 The Bible 1 Timothy 3: 1-7

74 Jim Collins. Good to Great ISBN 0-06-662099

75 Google Kolb Learning Styles for dozens of explanations

INDEX

V

values   46, 50, 58-9, 69-70, 76, 79-80,
    113, 147, 155, 182-3, 203, 205-8,
    249, 255, 270-1, 274
van Andel, Jay   131
Victoria, Queen   66
Vision   64-5, 84-5, 87, 95, 97, 123,
    137, 143, 155, 157-9, 162, 165,
    173, 179, 184, 274
VSOMA Planning Tool   84

W

Weber, Max   264
Wesley, John   131
Wheel of Life   72-3, 168
Whitworth, Laura   196, 280
Wilsher, Simon   vii-viii, x, 45, 49, 78-
    80, 109, 185, 210, 277
Wilsher Group   x, 45, 49, 149, 208
wisdom   ix, 20, 23-4, 142
word picture   26-7, 112, 220
words   17-18, 20, 25-6, 57, 66-7, 93,
    111-12, 118, 122-3, 129-32, 195,
    210-11, 219-20, 226, 229, 231
Work Become Fun   269
work life balance   37
www.wilsher-group.com   108

Z

Ziglar, Zig   60, 163, 221, 233, 277, 279
Zoos, banham   165

CPSIA information can be obtained
at www.ICGtesting.com
Printed in the USA
FFHW021946210119
50261231-55259FF